The Origins of Europeans

The Origins of Europeans

and Their Pre-Historic Inventiveness from 6 Million to 10,000 BCE

by Neil Harrison

Algora Publishing
New York

Library of Congress Cataloging in Publication Control Number: 2019010978

Names: Harrison, Neil, 1961- author.
Title: The origins of Europeans and their pre-historic Inventiveness: from 6 million to 10,000 BCE / Neil Harrison.
Description: New York: Algora Publishing, [2019] | Includes bibliographical references and index.
Identifiers: LCCN 2019010978 (print) | LCCN 2019015965 (ebook) | ISBN 9781628943795 (pdf) | ISBN 9781628943788 (soft cover: alk. paper)
Subjects: LCSH: Prehistoric peoples—Europe. | Anthropology, Prehistoric—Europe. | Antiquities, Prehistoric—Europe. | Technology and civilization.
Classification: LCC GN803 (ebook) | LCC GN803 .H373 2019 (print) | DDC 936/.01—dc23
LC record available at https://lccn.loc.gov/2019010978

Printed in the United States

There is . . . no doubt that the various races, when carefully compared and measured, differ much from each other,—as in the texture of the hair, the relative proportions of all parts of the body, the capacity of the lungs, the form and capacity of the skull, and even in the convolutions of the brain. But it would be an endless task to specify the numerous points of structural difference. The races differ also in constitution, in acclimatization, and in liability to certain diseases. Their mental characteristics are likewise very distinct; chiefly as it would appear in their emotional, but partly in their intellectual faculties. Everyone who has had the opportunity of comparison must have been struck with the contrast between the taciturn, even morose, aborigines of S. America and the light-hearted, talkative Negroes. There is a nearly similar contrast between the Malays and the Papuans, who live under the same physical conditions, and are separated from each other only by a narrow space of sea.

— Darwin, C. (*The Descent of Man*. 216)

Owing to this struggle for life, any variation, however slight and from whatever cause proceeding, if it be in any degree profitable to an individual of any species, in its infinitely complex relations to other organic beings and to external nature, will tend to the preservation of that individual, and will generally be inherited by its offspring. The offspring, also, will thus have a better chance of surviving, for, of the many individuals of any species which are periodically born, but a small number can survive. I have called this principle, by which each slight variation, if useful, is preserved, by the term of Natural Selection, in order to mark its relation to man's power of selection.

— Darwin, C. (*On the Origin of Species*. 62)

Ideas that require people to reorganize their picture of the world provoke hostility.

— Gleick, J. (305)

By the same author

High Horizons
High Horizons in Switzerland

Table of Contents

Foreword

The preparation of this book started way back in the 1990s when the prevailing, even overwhelming view on Neanderthals was that they were a primitive humanoid and an evolutionary dead-end. There was a wide range of conflicting, often contradictory reasons given for their mass extinction. For reasons that will become clear in this book, this view didn't pass what the industry in which I worked at the time called a 'sanity test'.

In short, the theories didn't match the observable realities. At the time, very few voices were suggesting that the DNA evidence for Neanderthals leading to a dead-end was unreliable — and even plain wrong. But at that time, the prevailing view was that the Out of Africa II Theory was factually correct.

The Out of Africa II hypothesis proved to be the catalyst that launched me into 20 years of studying the origins of humanity. Initially, it seemed barely believable that a hypothesis which was promoted with such widespread assurance could prove to be ungrounded and ultimately false. But as I looked into the subject, it became clear that science had been subjugated by both religious and political imperitives. The story of human origins is a very sensitive subject. It wasn't that long ago that the majority of people believed that that story began in the Garden of Eden. Post-World War II guilt has also played a role in establishing an acceptable narative that steers clear of tricky issues. A host of such factors have contributed together to muddy the waters, compounding the mistakes.

This book puts to one side such influences and concerns and focuses on the science. But to do this with clarity we need to look back, not to some small group of migrating Africans 70,000 years ago, but way back to the very origins of our species, back 6 million years ago, when we still lived in the trees in tropical Africa. That is truly where our story can be said to begin.

Les Agettes, Switzerland
March 2019

Introduction

Of all the histories written, none could be more important for humanity than the history of human evolution over the last 6 million years. That's only a brief moment in time compared to the 4,600 million year lifetime of the planet, but around 6 million years ago a small tree-living ape descended from the trees in equatorial Africa and set out on a path that ended in him becoming the most powerful creature by far on the whole planet, influencing the survival or extinction of many other species, even the climate and managing to project some members of his own species and others into outer space and on to other bodies in the solar system.

If only writing had been invented 50,000 years or so ago, we wouldn't have been so ignorant about our relatively recent history. The very late arrival of writing in our history has rendered the study of our more distant past very problematic. On the one hand there is the Creationist view from Genesis, on the other a wide range of Evolutionist views. The one thing that Genesis tells us today is that fascination with our very origins goes way, way back in time. We are no less fascinated today than the writers of the Old Testament. A whole host of new dating techniques have appeared over the last 20 years or so, which have enabled us to plant some firm sticks in the sand. But squaring newly established facts with previous ill-founded assumptions has led to a confusing melee of uncertain truths and hard evidence, sometimes difficult to distinguish. Sorting the chaff from the wheat was necessary, which involved starting again from first principles, from established facts based on scientific evidence and putting aside the old assumptions. This is what I have attempted to do in this totally new look at our pre-history, with a particular focus on the Europeans. The results are fascinating.

This book examines how this amazing sequence of events took place. In the past, it has frequently been asserted that Europeans were a support cast for the main actors, the Africans. Certainly, the story begins in Africa and it is already a significant achievement that these ancient Africans left their continent, their warm climate and struck out into a strange and dangerous new world, one for which they were ill prepared. But once that has been done, the spotlight shifts to Europe. It's mostly in Europe that the major developments occur.

This book highlights the crucial role in human evolution that European ancestors played through the millions of years of our history, while shedding a lot of new light on the key stages of human progress, technological and social. For the last half a million years, and particularly the last 50,000 years, Europeans pioneered far-reaching changes in the way peoples around the world lived their lives, which even affected their physical appearance. Europeans in particular had a hard time surviving, but it was overcoming these great challenges that set them apart.

It has become a popular political mantra to pretend that all the peoples of the world are identical. Not only scientifically is this untrue but it is patently obvious to even the most casual observer that different races are indeed different. These differences take many different forms from resistance to diseases, to eye and hair color to general size.

The world of paleoanthropology is one in which there are very many disagreements of the profoundest nature. This is partly because it is a young subject of study whose foundations were laid before Charles Darwin wrote the Origins of Species, partly also because of deep-rooted prejudice some of it religious in nature. Without sound scientific groundings in fact, the subject has gathered layers of half facts and assumptions to become a tangled mix of fact and fiction.

In order to put together this book I have relied on the empirical evidence of thousands of archaeologists and anthropologists who have conscientiously uncovered our past from deep under the ground, without whom we would have no clue whatsoever about our origins and to whom I extend my profound thanks.

Photographic images, drawings and diagrams not otherwise credited are the work and property of the author.

The Human Family Tree

For all our differences every person on the planet today belongs to the species *Homo sapiens sapiens*. The first part of that binomial 'Homo' is the genus to which our species belongs and which includes our ancestors reaching back to the earliest in the genus, *H. habilis*. Homo is Latin for man, and the genus in general is humankind or humans in the largest sense of the word.

But the human story didn't start with *H. habilis*, indeed there's no fixed date to which we can point and say 'This is the beginning', but it is interesting digging way back into our history to a point when the latest common ancestor of both ourselves and our closest living relative around today (the chimpanzee) was alive. From this point onwards in our evolutionary line there have been many species and sub-species, some of which were dead ends, but the only living descendant is ourselves. *Homo sapiens sapiens*. This book is about how that evolutionary line produced the Europeans.

The human family tree below shows the four major genera, still living, and how they relate to the last common ancestor to our closest living relatives the chimpanzee/bonobo species. That ancestor is now believed to be *Sahelanthropus tchadensis*, who lived between 7 and 6 million years ago.

Below is the Hominidae family tree which includes orangutans (*Pongo*), gorillas, and our closest surviving relatives in the animal kingdom, the *Pan* genus, which includes chimpanzees and bonobos. It is considered that we split from the *Pan* genus around 7 or 8 million years ago, about the time that *Sahelanthropus tchadensis* occupied northern central Africa. Fossil remains of our ancestors from this period are very thin on the ground and there is no DNA from *Sahelanthropus*, so there is still plenty of debate about exactly who was our latest common ancestor; but *Sahelanthropus* is certainly one of the most likely candidates as the last common ancestor of the chimpanzee and human lines.

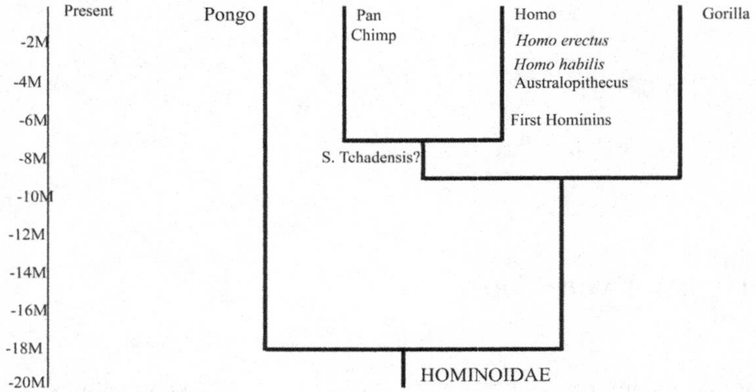

Illustration 1. Hominidae family tree

Sahelanthropus tchadensis

This prehistory of the Homo genus begins around the time when *Sahelanthropus tchadensis* occupied the trees and seemingly started to live part of his life on the ground. Details of S. *tchadensis* are sketchy in the extreme, with just one unique fossil skull including some teeth and part of the mandible (lower jaw), dating to very roughly 7 million years ago. To date there are no other specimens, and hardly any ancestral fossils of chimpanzees or gorillas of comparable age, so there is considerable uncertainty of exactly where *tchadensis* fits into the human or indeed pan family tree. It was found in loose sand in the Chad desert. Some researchers believe that it had been reburied possibly twice before making the dating of the fossil uncertain.

The little that is known of S. *tchadensis* comes from a description of the remains, which have been considerably distorted during the fossilization process. The brain volume is estimated to be between 320 and 380cc, similar to a modern chimpanzee's. S. *tchadensis* has a very pronounced brow ridge with quite small canine teeth and an anterior foramen magnum. The latter is a hole at the base of the skull, allowing the main nerve bundles to exit the brain and enter the spinal column. For quadrupeds where the skull projects forwards from the body, the foramen magnum is located at the back of the skull, where it articulates with the spine. For fully bipedal humans, the skull balances on top of the spine, so the foramen magnum is located closer to the base of the skull in a more central location. This tell-tale location of the foramen magnum in *S. tchadensis* already indicates a degree of bipedal ability. There is considerable debate over the interpretation of the fossil remains of *tchadensis*, but to date it is the closest that we've come to a latest common ancestor with the chimpanzee.

Orrorin

Orrorin is potentially an early human ancestor, living roughly 8.1 to 5.7 million years ago. We don't have a complete fossil skeleton, so there is once again considerable conjecture about the exact link between *Orrorin* and the human family tree. But *Orrorin* does show some quite human traits particularly in the teeth, possessing microdont dentition compared to characteristic ape macrodonts, curiously smaller than the much later *Ardipithecus*, who we'll meet shortly. If *Orrorin* is indeed as old as estimated, then it shows advances towards human characteristics which throw some doubt on whether the later *Ardipithecus* with its more ape-like teeth is a human ancestor at all. Of course, even if *Orrorin* is as old as estimated, it may have led to an evolutionary cul-de-sac, and the main branch of human evolution developed smaller teeth at a later date, as a result of changing diet.

Below is the generally accepted family tree showing the early hominids and what is usually believed to be the relationships between them. The paranthropus group on the left is a recently extinct branch of the hominids with no living descendants and we will meet some of these interesting paranthropus in later chapters.

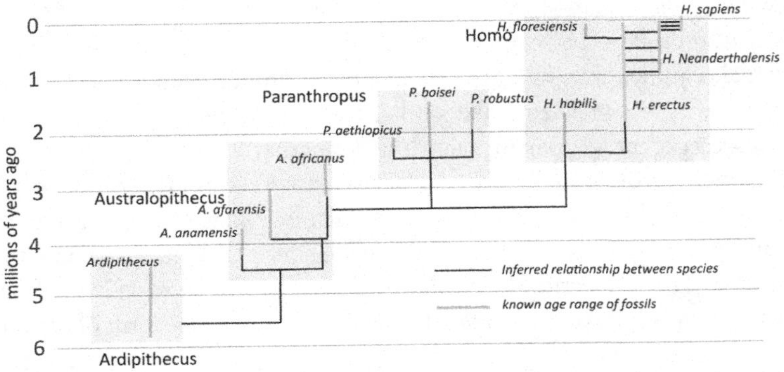

Illustration 2. Early hominids

Ardipithecus

Ardipithecus may well be the earliest of our direct ancestors, after they diverged from the great apes, but there are so few fossil specimens that there is still considerable debate about where exactly to place *Ardipithecus* in the family tree, and whether in fact *Ardipithecus* should be included in the Homo genus. Part of the confusion comes from the slightly vague definition of the term genus. As we shall see later, efforts at shoe-horning individuals of slightly differing physical characteristics into one genus or another, or one species or another has led to some far-reaching misunderstanding in the study of paleoanthropology.

Ardipithecus lived in the African forests around the period of 5.6 to 4.4 million years ago. He was small with a small brain of around 330-350cc, which is slightly smaller than a female chimpanzee, to which he was closely related. Including other closely related cousins, his finds have been mainly in the rift valley from Northern Kenya to Egypt, but also extending into what is now the Sahara, which at times in the past was well watered with trees.

It would seem from the opposed and grasping big toe (abductable hallix) that *Ardipithecus* still spent a lot of time living in the trees, but he was also capable of bipedal movement, but not for extended periods. It is generally considered that *Ardipithecus* inherited tree dwelling characteristics from his pan ancestors but was beginning to spend more time on the ground. So that the big toe is less abductable than that of a chimpanzee, and that the pelvis configuration was beginning to change to allow more efficient bipedal movement. We can picture *Ardipithecus* as similar to a chimpanzee, possibly a bit larger, but with more of an aptitude for walking than chimps.

Ardipithecus teeth lack the specialization of other mainly vegetarian great apes which tells us that he was an omnivore eating fruit and meat, and not so dependent on leaves. The canines are smaller than chimpanzees and particularly male canines are similar in size to female canines, which is suggestive that there was less male-to-male conflict than in chimpanzees where large canines are a potent weapon in male-to-male combat. This may imply greater cooperation in groups such as occurs in bonobos today. Further interpretation of the lack of sexual dimorphism in the canines suggests that *Ardipithecus* was developing long standing male-female bonds and increased parental investment. The suggestion being that *Ardipithecus* was moving away from the Alpha male chimpanzee dominating a group of females, form of organization. To achieve this domination, alpha males must fend off other males, so males need longer canines for fighting other males. Whereas with *Ardipithecus* whose male and female canines are of a similar size, the belief is that most adult males and females maintained at least semi-permanent bonds, which in turn allows for a greater genetic diversity. One of the problems of an alpha male possessing all the females in a colony is that he is likely to become father, grandfather and great grandfather of the younger members, and end up mating with his female children and grandchildren. Such is the conundrum facing the management of brown bears in the Pyrenees where a large alpha male, Pyros, is so dominant the he has just about all the female Pyrenean bears in his harem, which is posing a threat to the survival of the whole colony due to the lack of genetic diversity and the risk of homozygosity, which reduces the biological fitness of a population.

The clue of the teeth together with an aptitude for bipedal movement may be the key reasons why *Ardipithecus* was more successful and adapted to new environments over his close cousin the chimpanzee who has remained relatively unchanged over the same time period that *Ardipithecus* evolved into modern humans.

The lack of fossil evidence means that there are still many question marks hanging over who *Ardipithecus* actually was and what his life was really like.

Australopithecus

Australopithecus is the next stage in human development following on from *Ardipithecus*. The earliest remains of *Australopithecus* date from around 4 million years ago and the youngest fossils date from around two million years ago, so *Australopithecus* bridges the large gap between the earliest of our ancestors who descended from the trees to the earliest member of our genus, *H. habilis*. Over this vast period of time various subspecies of *Australopithecus* evolved: *A africanus*, *A deyiremeda*, *A garhi* and *A sediba* with varying degrees of robustness. In general *Australopithecus* was a diminutive character, between 1.2 and 1.4m tall. Footprints preserved in petrified mud dating back to 3.6 million years ago and which are assumed to belong to *Australopithecus* much resemble modern human footprints, suggesting that *Australopithecus* was fully adapted to bipedal movement, *Ardipithecus*' grasping toe for life in the trees was now gone.

Crucially it seems *Australopithecus* was the first hominid to possess the SRGAP2B gene which is a variation on the SRGAP2 gene present in all mammals. This gene is responsible for encoding the way in which neurons work. But it has been changed three times in human development. Two of those occasions were during the development of *Australopithecus*, the first (SRGAP2B) around 3.4 million years ago and the second (SRGAP2C) around 2.4 million years ago. The latter is one that all humans alive possess today.

This new version of the gene allows for a faster migration of neurons within the brain, slows down their maturation, and crucially allows for a greater density of synapses within the cerebral cortex. So, at two points during the evolution of *Australopithecus* his brain became increasingly more powerful, and evolved in a new direction from that of the rest of the mammalian world.

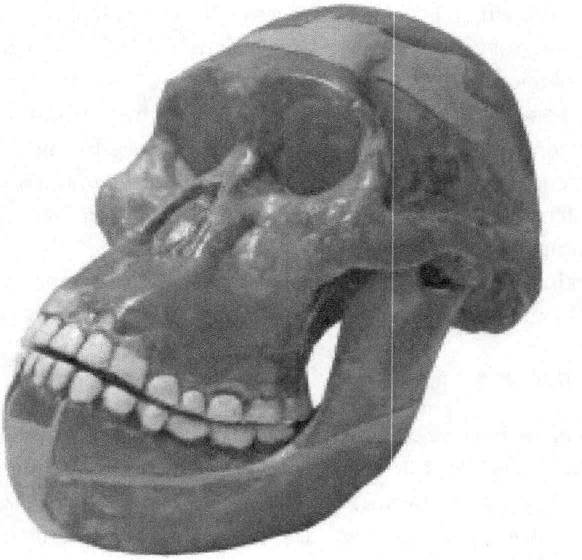

Illustration 3. Australopithecus with his massive jaw

Not only was the brain more powerful but it was becoming bigger, reaching about 500cc, about a third the size of our own, but a significant development compared to *Ardipithecus*. With an average weight of around 35Kg his brain to body mass ratio was around 1.4% compared to *Ardipithecus* with a brain to body mass ratio was only about 1%, a very significant increase and surprisingly close to our own brain to body mass ratio of around 1.6%. We shall look more closely at relative brain sizes and how they affect our behavior in later chapters.

One of the main areas of focus on the behavior of *Australopithecus* of which we can have a degree of confidence is bipedalism. The proof is found not only in fossilized footprints, but also the geometry of the hips and feet, and also the length ratio of the limbs.

The intermembral index is a method of assessing bipedal motion from the fossil record by comparing the relative length of the arms and legs; it is calculated by dividing the forelimb (arm) length by the hind limb length (leg) and expressed as a percentage. In humans the intermembral index is between 68 and 70. This relatively low index shows that humans rely on their legs for locomotion. Chimpanzees have an intermembral index of 106, meaning that their arms are longer than their legs, and that all four are used for propulsion. So, what about *Australopithecus*? The ratio for *Australopithecus* is around 88 almost half way between chimpanzee's quadrupedal movement and human's bipedal movement. Looking at the individual bones, *Australopithecus* has a noticeably shortened humerus (from shoulder to elbow), whereas the leg bones are not much longer than *Ardipithecus*. This lengthening of the leg appears later in human evolution, particularly with *Homo erectus*.

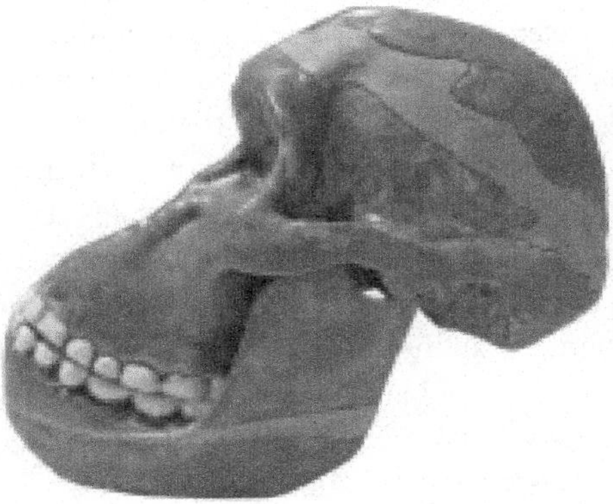

Illustration 4. Australopithecus skull side view

So, *Australopithecus*' skeleton was adapting to life on two legs, but why change? Chimpanzees have flourished in their niche habitat in central Africa for the last 6 million years, and have changed very little over that time period. Whereas the majority of fossil finds of *Australopithecus* are located in the East of Africa, covering a much wider range of environments. Some of *Australopithecus* remains have been associated with open woodland, and some have been associated with open savannah. This diversity of environments suggests that *Australopithecus* was becoming more flexible in terms of his living space, and far less dependent on dense forest. He still had arms long enough to allow climbing trees, when living in woodland, but ease of bipedal movement opened up the possibility of living in open countryside.

Other living species have evolved bipedalism and have been the subject of considerable study. Some lizards employ temporary bipedalism, mainly to allow themselves to escape predators because they can move faster than on four legs. Amongst mammals bipedalism is rare and as a permanent means of locomotion virtually unknown. bears rear up on their hind legs to reach food that they wouldn't be able to reach otherwise and also to see further from a higher vantage point and also to attack their prey, liberating their powerful front legs and claws as weapons, but they prefer to move around on four legs. No other primate is exclusively bipedal, although some like chimpanzees adopt bipedalism for brief periods. Gibbons and indriids become exclusively bipedal when they leave the trees where they spend most of their lives.

Despite it being rare amongst mammals, bipedalism does offer certain competitive advantages over quadrupedalism in certain circumstances such as raising the head for a clearer vision of the surrounding environment either to search for prey or for hazards. Similarly, bipedalism is an advantage when wading through rivers as it keeps the head well above the water, a skill which baboons have acquired. Crucially, though, bipedalism liberates the fore limbs or arms for many other purposes than just locomotion. Also, although quadrupeds like leopards, cheetahs and horses etcetera can outrun humans, it would seem that over large distances humans have the advantage which is explained by the Endurance Running Hypothesis. In short, this hypothesis states that the mechanisms of walking and running are entirely different in humans. Walking involves a pendulum movement with the body's center of gravity swinging over the forward extended leg. With running, however, there is a mass spring mechanism, where energy is stored in the elastic tissues of muscles and tendons. This energy is released during the extension of the muscles and the faster the run, the more efficient this mechanism becomes. This efficiency is not achieved during walking.

However, in order to run, humans have to stabilize the head which otherwise would flop around, hindering balance and vision. This stabilization is achieved partly thanks to the nuchal ligament which is attached to the skull posterially. The attachment of the ligaments leaves a ridge (where the bone is pulled), and small tell-tale pits where the ligament fibers root into the bone. Whereas these features are clearly visible from *H. habilis* onwards, they have not yet evolved with *Australopithecus*, implying that he was not a good runner, and at this point in evolution may not yet have learnt that particular skill, even though we take it for granted.

So, interestingly, changing to two-legged motion was not about moving faster. *Australopithecus* seems to have evolved this skill in order to free up his hands and to better observe his environment for hunting and for security.

In the previous century, it was widely considered that *Australopithecus* first evolved a larger brain and then later developed bipedalism, but with the discovery of human-like footprints early in the *Australopithecus* story, this now seems unlikely. Quite the opposite seems true, it would appear that bipedalism which was present in the earliest of *Australopithecus* fossils 4 million years ago, opened up a world of new opportunities for *Australopithecus* which were not available when he was confined to life in the trees. We know from his teeth that he was no longer a specialized leaf eater as were his predecessors, he became an omnivore, capable of adding meat to his diet. We can see from the wide geographical range in which his fossils have been found, that he was adapting to varying environments, and we can see that he was becoming increasingly more intelligent, two facts which are inextricably linked.

Expanding his niche from the forests to the open woodland, where he could still find safety in the branches above the ground, he then expanded his range again to open savannah, a totally new environment for our ancestors. This move away from the specialization of life in the trees to life on the savannahs required *Australopithecus* to learn a whole new way of life, with new foods, and new methods of protection from predators.

Speculation on how *Australopithecus* abandoned his specialized habitat is helped to a degree by the recent discovery of tools which he made and used. In the previous century it was considered that *H. habilis* was the earliest of our ancestors to use tools, we now know that he inherited that skill from *Australopithecus*. In 2010, fossilized bones with traces of butchery marks on them were found in Ethiopia in conjunction with *Australopithecus* fossils. These have been dated to 3.4 million years ago and to date these are the oldest traces of butchery discovered.

In 2011 a group of archaeologists from Stony Brook University discovered a hitherto unknown culture of tool making, the oldest known to be produced by humanity. The site known as Lomekwi, near to Lake Turkana in Kenya, gave its name to this newly discovered technology. Subsequent examination confirmed that these stones had been deliberately knapped and that the large stone core had been rotated as the knapping process continued. On site, some flakes were fitted to their cores, suggesting that the tool had not been successfully made and subsequently discarded at the site where it was being knapped. The date given to these artifacts is 3.3 million years ago.

The consequences of these discoveries on our understanding of our human ancestors are considerable. It means that *Australopithecus* was now manufacturing tools to help him process meat. Rather than being dependent on a vegetal diet of leaves and fruit, he had now extended his diet to include the meat of other animals, but because he hadn't evolved the natural attributes on his own body to properly deal with this meat (i.e., sharp claws and large canines), his resourcefulness had led him to making those tools artificially. The great evolutionary step to purposeful tool making had begun. This is a significant departure from the rest of the animal kingdom. Some species of primate are capable of using tools, as either weapons or for smashing nuts, but they don't have the intellectual capacity or willingness to deliberately modify these stones to make specific tools out of them. From the little evidence that we have of these tools, they seemed to be specifically used for preparing meat. *Australopithecus* had developed thought processes unique in the history of evolution.

The use of deliberately manufactured tools was considered to be the defining characteristic of the Homo genus. But we now find that over a million years earlier than *H. habilis* (handy man) his distant ancestor was already doing it. In the light of this discovery, *Australopithecus*, often considered to be little more than a ground dwelling chimpanzee or bonobo, deserves to be reclassified as belonging to the Homo genus.

At Bouri in Ethiopia more signs of tools used by *Australopithecus* have been discovered. In layers contemporary with *Australopithecus* remains and dated to 2.5 million years ago, bovine bones have been found with cut marks on them, which when examined under a microscope were consistent with stone tool cuts, there were also signs of having been smashed by hammer stones. Nearby, but not in the same context, Olduwan tools were found.

As *Australopithecus*' diet changed from herbivore to omnivore and meat began to play an increasingly important role in his daily needs, and as so often necessity is the mother of invention, another great change occurred. Introducing meat into a diet brings great advantages, such as high concentrations of proteins and energy in fat. In most cases carnivorous mammals have specific adaptations, sharp teeth and claws for killing and disarticulating prey, a shorter digestive system that isn't required to break down tough cellulose and forward facing eyes to make the perception of distance possible and enhance the ability to trap prey. Herbivores almost always have sideways facing eyes to achieve a greater all round field of view for detecting predators.

Australopithecus and *Ardipithecus* both had forward facing eyes, but not the teeth and claws that purely carnivorous mammals need. *Ardipithecus* and early *Australopithecus* only had their teeth as a means of skinning the animals that they needed to eat, and then to tear the meat off the bone. This was a potentially dangerous business. An *Australopithecus* who broke his teeth on animal bones would soon starve. Ill equipped to eat meat, but nevertheless needing meat to survive was a gamble for early *Australopithecus*. But he found a solution, unique to carnivorous animals, which was to give him a crucial advantage, and which be the single most important stage in his development. He conceptualized creating objects to prepare his meat, which would speed up the process of feeding, and make tearing meat off the bone a far less dangerous business. He started to make stone tools with his hands which had become freed-up since becoming bipedal.

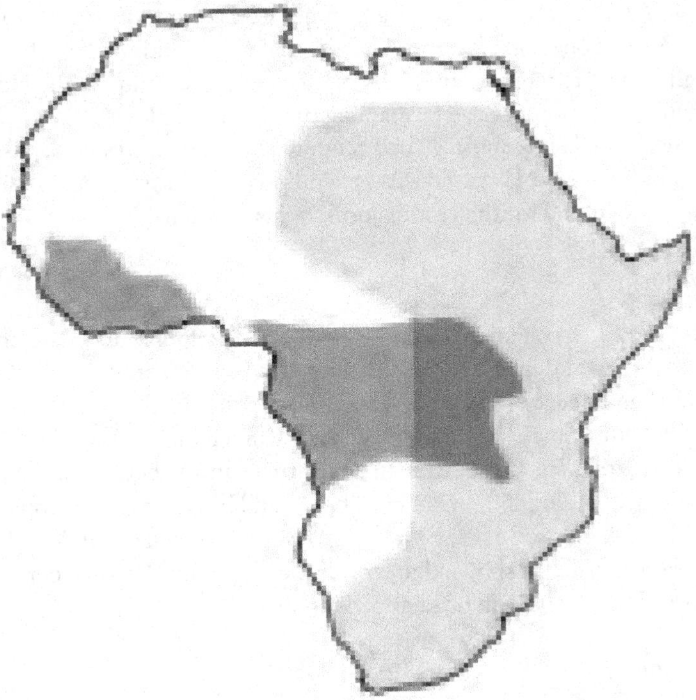

Illustration 5. Chimpanzee, Bonobo and Australopithecus ranges

Map showing the current range of chimpanzees and bonobos West and Central Africa (dark gray) and the range of *Australopithecus* based on fossil finds East Africa (pale gray)

It may well be the change in diet with a higher intake of proteins than before, in conjunction with the complex task of hunting in groups that stimulated the unique evolution in the brain's chemistry that occurred around this time, which allowed *Australopithecus* a greater concentration of synapses with more processing power in his brain. *Australopithecus* became the smartest hunter in Africa.

Orangutans and chimpanzees also use tools such as sticks that they poke into ant's nests. But these aren't worked like the earliest stone tools were. The earliest worked stone tools have been given the name of Lomekwian and have been discovered on the West Bank of Lake Turkana in Kenya in 2011. The Lomekwi tool kit consists of anvils, flakes and cores.

As its name suggests the anvil is used as a working surface on which the core is placed. The core is struck by a hammer stone onto a core in an oblique fashion. When done correctly, this causes a flake to be chipped off the core. If enough flakes are removed in the correct fashion, a technique called knapping, then a blade or point can be manufactured. This blade can then be used for cutting animal skin, muscles and tendons. In short *Australopithecus* had created a butcher's tool kit, and this general process of knapping would accompany humankind for the vast majority of his existence.

Lomekwi

These are oldest manufactured stone tools ever found and date to 3.3 million years ago and invented by *Australopithecus*. There are two key differences between Lomekwi stone tools and the later, more advanced technique called Oldowan. Lomekwi stones are generally much bigger. Lomekwi tools were made by putting the core on an anvil stone, and either knapping it on the anvil, or by holding the core in both hands and bringing it down onto the anvil. Oldowan tools are made by holding the core in one hand and the hammer stone in another, and by judging both the angle and the force correctly, a correctly shaped flake can be knapped off the core.

Olduwan

The earliest Oldowan tools, also invented by *Australopithecus*, found so far date to around 2.6 million years ago, and were found in the region of Afar, Ethiopia. These tools were to accompany human ancestors as late as *H. erectus* over most of the old world from South Africa to China and were in use in Europe as recently as 500,000 years ago.

The Oldowan tool kit became quite varied, as needs became more diverse. Basic choppers are formed by knapping the edge of a round pebble core to form a single edge. This can further be improved by knapping the other side of the core, which produces a bi-facial chopper. Hammer stones are stones made from a harder material used to break the core. Discoid tools are made from creating an edge in a circular fashion all around the circumference of the pebble. The by-product of the finished core tool, the flake was also used as a tool. This thin shard of stone could be used as a slim blade or if pointed, as an awl. Thick chisels were made; the term used in archaeology for the chisel is burin, from the French for cold chisel. Also, scrapers with straighter edges were used for preparing skins, by stripping away the flesh from the skin to be used as clothing.

Both *Ardipithecus* and *Australopithecus* lived in the Pliocene Geological Epoch (5.3–2.6 million years ago), which was generally characterized by average temperatures 2–3 degrees warmer than today and with less global ice, global sea levels were about 25m higher than those today. Continental drift played a major role in the world's climate, with continental plates travelling as far as 180km during the epoch. South America drifted into North America and the Isthmus of Panama was formed, cutting off the Pacific and Atlantic Oceans. There were two important consequences of this joining of the continents. Equatorial currents circulating warm water from one side of the planet to the other were cut off causing a drop in global temperatures, and the animals of North and South America were brought into contact with one another resulting in the complete extinction of South America's marsupial fauna, including a marsupial equivalent of the Euro-Asian saber toothed tiger.

As a result of the creation of the Isthmus of Panama global cooling gathered pace, ice started to cover the Arctic and glaciers began to form in mid latitudes, trapping fresh water, and lowering sea levels. This cooling of the climate towards the end of the Pliocene is considered to have caused the onset of widespread savannah biotopes and the shrinking of forest cover.

In the previous century it was frequently considered that the spreading of savannahs at the expense of forests in Africa was the reason why *Ardipithecus* descended from the trees in the first place. But more precise dating of the disappearance of forests towards 3 million years ago post-dates bipedalism by a large margin.

But climate does seem to have played a role. Focusing on Africa again, throughout the Pliocene bovine fossils are abundant and varied, typically constituting a major part of the fossil record. Some of these species being particularly reliant on environmental conditions reveal clues to the habitat in which they lived. Three aspects have been analyzed:

- Shifts in the species, and rates of extinction
- Shifts in the abundances of these species
- Changes in morphology of these species, specifically considering the limb bones

Curiously, throughout the epoch in Africa there were three groupings of first and last appearances of certain bovids, i.e., new species were identified in the fossil record and subsequently disappeared. The first of these groupings was between 2.7 and 2.5 million years ago with the particular bovids only surviving for a mere 200,000 years. Other groupings of first and last appearances occurred at 1.8 million years ago and then finally at 0.7 million years ago. This suggests to us that the environment was in a state of flux. New environmental conditions arose causing new bovid species to appear, but then the conditions changed again, and those conditions disappeared causing these new species to disappear again.

This rapid change in the environment during the Pliocene has given rise to the Turnover Pulse Theory of Evolution which we will meet again later during the story of human evolution. This theory suggests that species evolve and become extinct during phases of rapid environmental change, causing ecosystems to periodically experience significant disruptions; these in turn result in mass extinctions and speciation. This would imply, if the Turnover Pulse Theory is accurate, that climate change has an effect on all groups, from bacteria to hominids.

Modern studies of individual populations have shown large cyclical shifts in phenotype/genotype that correlate with climatic variations. These studies, in turn, enable scientists to create a better turnover model.

Extinctions often impact on specialists more than generalists, wherein the generalists will thrive within the environment by exploiting new environmental opportunities, or by moving elsewhere in diasporas to take advantage of other environments. The specialists will experience more extinctions, and a "pulse" of positive and random speciation within their groups.

These two events lead to specialists being concentrated in isolated areas whereas the generalists will become more ubiquitous. This geographic isolation is a common thread in evolution. It is a key factor in the evolution of species on a grander scale.

Changes in the climate not only caused changes in the bovids but also changes in the appearance of the landscape. Not only did the Pliocene epoch show a marked decrease in forest cover but it showed a change in the type of woodland, from dense tropical forest to more open woodland. Changes in fossil remains discovered in Ethiopia demonstrate a marked decrease in forest species such as pigs and monkeys during the period from 3.6 to 2.4 million years ago in favor of species more suited to mixed, open woodland.

By 3.6 million years ago *Australopithecus* had been around already for 400,000 years, but the environment around him was changing. Species that he may have relied on for food such as monkeys and pigs were disappearing and larger grassland browsers were taking over. *Australopithecus* had to adapt to his new world or die out like many of the bovids. To cope with the fast changes in climate and fauna he needed to be flexible and innovative. The tendency of his ancestors to occupy a specialized niche in his environment during times of rapid change would have been a handicap. However, he had already adopted a varied diet as shown from the non-specialized nature of his teeth. For his size, he had a large brain, and despite the challenging circumstances during the Pliocene, he did indeed survive.

The 'variability selection' hypothesis emphasizes the importance of secular changes in climatic variability (amplitudes and durations of departures from the mean climatic state) on faunal adaptation, selection, and evolution. In contrast to habitat-specific hypotheses, variability selection calls upon environmental instability (such as changes in the amplitudes and durations of orbital-scale wet–dry cycle amplitudes) as agents for introducing genetic variance, natural selection, and faunal innovation. Variability selection argues that the largest faunal speciation and innovation pressures should occur during those periods when the amplitudes of climate variability change markedly. This hypothesis proposes that African hominids and other fauna would have occupied increasingly diverse habitats following increases in climatic variability. Many of the largest African faunal evolution events occurred when there were increases in the amplitudes of climatic variability.

These environmental changes caused *Australopithecus* to adapt to the prevailing local conditions and so the fossil record reveals a variety of variants which have been classed as sub-species. Out of one of these sub-species or possibly even from several a new Genus evolved, that of Homo. *H. habilis* had arrived. But *Australopithecus* didn't simply bow out when *H. habilis* appeared and disappear entirely. He stayed around for at least another 100,000 years if not longer. But before we leave the world of our non-Homo ancestors for good, let's take a close look at a close relative of them, still living today, who could teach us a lot about our ancestors at the time. He has a surprising amount to teach us.

Our Closest Living Relation

Old bones and stones can only teach us so much about our earliest ancestors. We are left to imagine what his life was like, and just how much he resembled us today. When did speech appear? When did we learn to make tools? When did we begin to think beyond the immediate imperatives of survival? How did *Ardipithecus* live? Was he solitary or gregarious? These and many more questions would seem intractable ones which would have to remain unanswered.

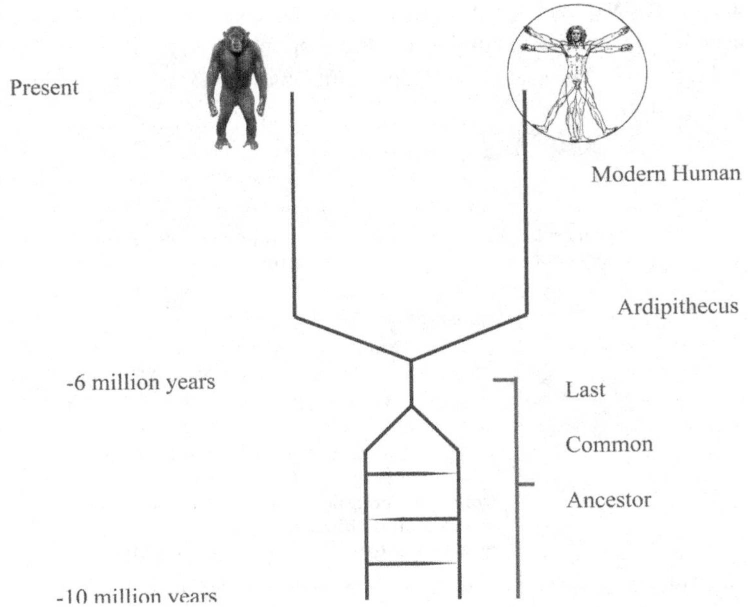

Illustration 6. Last common ancestor

At least, that would be true if a very close relative to our earliest ancestors weren't around today. Like us, chimpanzees (*Pan troglodytes*) and bonobos (*Pan paniscus*), the two surviving species of the pan genus, from Central and Western Africa, belong to the Hominidae family or great apes.

How closely related we are to chimpanzees is much debated, but it would seem that our ancestors and chimpanzee ancestors interbred and produced hybrids from as early as 13 million years ago to as late as *Ardipithecus*, possibly even just 4 million years ago. When we look at chimpanzees and bonobos, we recognize facial expressions and inherently feel a vague sensation of kinship. There is something human about them.

Advances in genetic studies over recent years suggest that the last split between pan and hominids occurred as early as 7 million years ago. It would seem that human ancestor and chimp hybrids were being spun off for a vast period of time over 6 million years and for possibly as many as 9 million years, creating a plethora of different hybrids. These hybrids may well have given rise to some of the differing species or sub-species that we have seen in the chapter on *Ardipithecus*. Unfortunately, very few fossil remains of these hybrids exist, so what we can learn from them is very restricted. Given the vast number of potential hybrids of pan and hominids, many of which may have contributed together over great periods of time to produce an early *Ardipithecus*-like hominid, it would seem futile to try and identify a single creature and say 'that is our latest common ancestor with the great apes'. In terms of DNA we are very similar to our chimpanzee relatives, sharing about 99% of our DNA. The story of human evolution is therefore a story of just 1% of our total DNA.

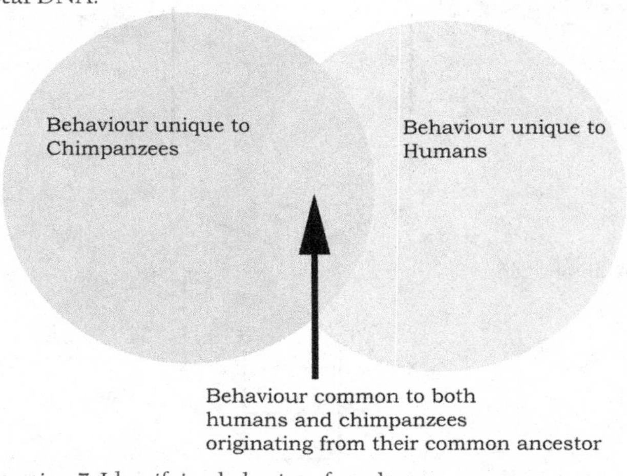

Illustration 7. Identifying behavior of our last common ancestor

By identifying common behaviors in humans and chimpanzees or bonobos we can infer that our common ancestor also possessed that behavior. This can be demonstrated with this simple Venn diagram.

Using the same method, comparing such common behaviors with other great apes such as gorillas or orangutans, we can see just how far back such behaviors are rooted in our distant evolutionary tree and which are more specific to chimpanzees and our earliest ancestors. The more common the behavior across the range of great apes, the more ancient the behavior, as a general rule.

The relative lack of evolution by the chimpanzee provides us with a rough idea of the appearance of our latest common ancestor. As we have seen from the Venn diagram above, any human-like features which chimps display today were very probably also present in those common ancestors, and allowing us a clear baseline of early human characteristics.

There has been a considerable amount of energy expended on studying the behavior of chimpanzees and bononos, which has thrown up some revealing information which we can probably associate with our earliest ancestors.

Chimpanzee Bipedalism

Chimpanzees have bodies which are designed for life in the trees. Their arms are far longer than their legs, indeed when fully extended their arms are longer than their entire body. Despite being most at ease in the trees, chimpanzees readily knuckle walk, using the knuckles of their hands as front feet, indeed they can achieve considerable speed in quadrupedal motion. In addition, chimpanzees can also walk on their hind legs alone, which they tend to do when their hands are occupied with carrying items. So, it is highly likely that ancestors before *Ardipithecus* could also walk bipedally when necessary allowing them considerable advantages over purely quadrupedal animals.

Chimpanzee Tools

Depending on the definition of the term 'tool', many animals use tools. Birds use tools; some use bright objects that they gather to attract mates, and the New Caledonian crow uses twigs for foraging in holes. Even insects use objects in their environment to make their lives easier. But the great apes are unique in their use of tools made from both wood and stone.

Forest living chimpanzees find wood more readily available than stones; nevertheless they do use stone tools, and systematically teach their young to use them, too. Mainly chimpanzees use stones as hammers to crack open hard nuts. Surprisingly, perhaps, most of these stones are in the range of between 1Kg and 9Kg, whereas human stone tools from pre-history weigh less than 1Kg. It is worth noting that on average chimps arms are about twice as powerful as human arms.

Humans and chimps are not unique amongst primates in using stone tools. Bearded Capuchin monkeys (*Sapajus libidinosus*) from Brazil also use stone tools to crack nuts, and long tailed macaques in Thailand (*Macaca fascicularis aurea*) use stone hammers to crack open crustaceans that they forage for on the sea shore. These two species along with chimpanzees and bonobos have entered the Stone Age.

So stone tools are not unique to direct human ancestors, and we can safely assume that even before *Ardipithecus* stone tools of a basic form were already widely used, and that *Ardipithecus* inherited this knowledge from his own ancestors. This concurs with the strong suggestion that he was capable of limited bipedal motion with the ability to carry stones while walking.

But not only do chimpanzees use stones for cracking nuts, they also use them as weapons. What's more, not only do they use rocks as weapons, they also fashion spears for hunting. The spears tend to be about 60cm long and about 1cm in diameter. Although sometimes used for prodding in holes to skewer bush babies or other small animals, they are used mostly as bludgeons for delivering a powerful blow to their prey. These weapons are used when chimpanzees hunt colobus monkeys. There is a deliberate process in the manufacture of these weapons. Chimpanzees select straight sticks and, using their teeth and fingers, they strip off the bark and side branches and fashion a point with their teeth.

Lead researcher Jill D. Pruetz of Iowa State University recalled such an incident, saying, "It was really alarming how forceful it was," adding that it reminded her of the murderous shower scene in the Alfred Hitchcock movie *Psycho*. "It was kind of scary." Also, chimpanzees have been known to throw their rocks at prey to injure or kill them.

As if the use of purpose-made weapons isn't surprising enough in the animal kingdom, chimpanzees take the use of weapons one stage further and actually wage deliberate, coordinated war. One of these wars, the Gombe chimpanzee war, has been well documented. This war, also known as the 4-year war, took place between two communities of chimpanzees in the Gombe Stream National Park in Tanzania.

The two groups, the Kasakela and Kahama belonged, initially to a single group but split and occupied areas in the north and south of the park respectively. Hostilities seem to have started when 6 male members of the Kasakala group attacked and killed a young Kahama male who was feeding in a tree. Systematically over the next four years, all 6 male members of the Kahama group were assassinated by the Kasakela group. Of the Kahama female chimps, one was killed, two went missing and three were beaten and kidnapped by the males from Kasakela. The Kasakela then took over the Kahama territory, thus ending the war with outright victory for the Kasakela.

Chimpanzees and Warfare

This simple conflict in the chimpanzee world could so easily have been a story of small scale conflict between human communities. Male warriors, responsible for the defense of a community are systematically killed off until the community is defenseless at which point the women and land are taken by the conquering side.

Warfare between rival communities of human ancestors was probably a feature from the very earliest times, prior to *Ardipithecus*, with spears, bludgeons and stones being the standard weapons.

Not only do chimpanzees wage war on each other, but in a real life version of the film *Planet of the Apes*, they also waged war on humans, deliberately killing 10 people and injuring 17 more in the Virunga National Park in the Democratic Republic of Congo in 2012.

The source of the conflict appears to be human incursion into the chimpanzee territory. Defense of territory is common throughout the animal kingdom, including sharks, lions and insects etcetera. Once again, we see the causes for chimpanzee wars mirroring modern human wars and confirming that this behavior has been part of human behavior from the very earliest of our ancestors, and in all likelihood where competition over territory and resources became acute from *Ardipithecus* onwards warfare was engaged between our ancestors, even when different sub-species were involved.

Land Ownership

Chimpanzees are highly territorial and go to great lengths to protect the resources on their land from competitors. As part of normal chimpanzee behavior, every couple of weeks or so, the males in a group will gather together and head out in single file, silently, towards the borders of their territory. This method of travelling is unique to what has been called 'border patrolling behavior'. Normally chimpanzees make considerable noise when travelling in groups. If the border patrol encounters a solitary chimp from a neighboring group, they will attack it and try to kill it. If the solitary chimp is lucky, it will escape with its life. If the border patrol meets a larger, more powerful group, it will flee. If the border patrol encounters an infant with its mother from a neighboring group, they will attempt to snatch the infant and eat it. If one group manages to break the defenses of a neighboring group, they will annex the neighbor's land, gaining more resources, which in turn enables them to expand as a group. As the size of the group grows, so does its force of militant males making them even more of a threat to their neighbors. This long-term strategy is a feature of all chimpanzee communities.

In this way communities develop, associated with particular areas with more or less fixed borders and ownership of the resources on that land. This has led to three separate subspecies of chimpanzee developing in Africa: Western, Central, and Eastern, known as *Pan troglodytes*, versus *Pan troglodytes troglodytes* and *Pan troglodytes schweinfurthii* respectively. This conclusion is the result of research done in 2007 which involved DNA analysis of chimp and bonobo populations across Africa, and refuted earlier claims that there were no differences between the *Pan troglodytes* species. It was further confirmed that there is virtually no genetic exchange between these three groups, ensured in part at least by the rigorous patrolling of the borders by the males.

Altruism

The Max Planck Institute performed experiments on chimpanzees which demonstrated that chimps show altruism to unrelated and unfamiliar chimps. These chimps performed services or acts of kindness with no expectation of a reward in exchange even when considerable effort was required to perform that service or act of kindness. Chimpanzees have also been known to extend such kindness to unfamiliar humans, analogous to human charity.

Sex For Pleasure

Bonobos use sex for more than just procreation, and they perform it frequently, which has led to the phrase 'Make Love not War' being associated with bonobos. Whereas chimpanzees engage in violent conflicts, which can result in serious injury or death, this rarely occurs with bonobos. They prefer to resolve their differences by having sex.

They are the only animals other than humans to engage in face to face sex. They are also particularly promiscuous. Same gender sex is frequent, partners are not fixed, and sex with infants is regularly practiced. Frans de Waal, an ethnologist who has studied bonobos, was commented, "A lot of the things we see [today, in human society], like pedophilia and homosexuality, may be leftovers that some now consider unacceptable in our particular society."

The inventive and amorous bonobos have been recorded performing the following: kissing with tongues, GG rubbing, penis fencing, tribadism, pedophilia and fellatio. All this sexual activity makes special demands on the bonobo genitalia. Chimpanzee and bonobo testicles weigh about 110gms a piece, about three times the weight of a human testicle, and given that chimpanzees have smaller body masses, they are truly impressive, being relatively about five times the size of human testicles. Bonobo clitorises are very large too, so much so that they waggle visibly when they walk.

Deception

Chimpanzees regularly practice deception as a strategy as well as making careful plans for future eventualities.

This following is an account of a dominant male called Santino, at Furuvik Zoo in Sweden, who made stashes of projectiles in his enclosure by pulling up pieces of concrete, which he later used to throw at human visitors.

> Santino not only hid projectiles behind logs and rocks, he also manufactured ones from hay. All projectiles were placed near the visitors' area, and helped lull visitors into a false sense of security, allowing him the chance to fling his missiles at crowds before they had time to back away.
>
> The chimpanzee made his first hay hiding-place after zoo guides had repeatedly backed visitors away from him after noticing a projectile in his hands. At one point, after a projectile-throwing attempt by Santino, a tour guide left the chimp alone for hours without visitors. When the guide and a visitor group came back, Santino acted nonchalantly while holding projectiles and walking toward the group.
>
> "To the guide, his appearance did not suggest intentions of throwing. The chimpanzee even stopped and picked up an apple floating in the water, from which he took a bite as he continued approaching the visitors,"
>
> "Just within range, he made a sudden throw at the group."
>
> After several attempts at deceiving visitors, Santino created this concealment when the people he intended to fool were out of his sight,

meaning he was capable of planning even without having any targets immediately available as aids to his plans.

"The results indicate that he can anticipate behaviors of others who are not present in the situation where he makes his preparations." (Choi)

Researcher Brian Hare performed an experiment to demonstrate chimpanzee deception: chimpanzees sometimes attempt to actively conceal things from others. Specifically, when competing with a human in three novel tests, eight chimpanzees, from their first trials, chose to approach a contested food item via a route hidden from the human's view (sometimes using a circuitous path to do so). These findings not only corroborate previous work showing that chimpanzees know what others can and cannot see, but also suggest that when competing for food chimpanzees are skillful at manipulating, to their own advantage, whether others can or cannot see them.

Katja Karg, at the Max Planck Institute again, performed another experiment to test chimps' forward planning, and deception.

She presented the chimps with plastic boxes containing several trays, some of which held slices of banana. The boxes were partly covered, so by moving the trays around, the chimps could either hide or reveal the bananas.

With some of the chimps, Karg approached the box and took out all the visible bananas, put them in a bucket and carried them away. Afterwards, the chimp could eat any hidden bananas uninterrupted.

With the other chimps, she took out all the visible bananas and fed them to the chimpanzee. The hidden ones were then taken away.

In the second case, the chimps quickly learned to reveal lots of bananas so that Karg would hand them over. But the other chimps, which were never given bananas, learned not to move the trays — ensuring that they got more bananas in the end.

The chimps were less good at actively hiding bananas by moving them under cover; something human children can do by around 2.5 years. This more active approach to deception "might be a cognitive challenge for them", says Karg.

It seems the chimps could infer what Karg was going to do, based on previous experience, and then adjust their strategies accordingly.

"Chimpanzees understand others' intentions, and they can adjust their behavior to these intentions by flexibly manipulating what they make visible to others," says Karg.

This helps individual chimps prosper in their social groups. For instance, junior males may do well to conceal their attempts to mate from the dominant males, who would punish them.

In his book *Chimpanzee Politics*, primatologist Frans De Waal writes of Orr, an adolescent female at Arnheim, who would scream while she was having sex. During sneaked copulations with younger males, however, her screams sometimes caught the attention of the alpha, who would do his mighty best to interrupt the couple. Eventually, Orr learned to suppress her vocalizations when mating with lower-ranking males, while she continued the habit of screaming whenever she mated with the alpha.

> Competition often motivates individuals to deceive in order to get what they want, whether it's sex, power, or food. Once at Arnheim, the chimpanzees all observed the arrival of a box of grapefruit. While they were locked in their sleeping quarters, however, primatologist de Waal brought the box out into the public area and buried the grapefruit in sand. He left a small portion of each grapefruit still uncovered by the sand, just enough for a very observant chimpanzee to notice. After the fruit had been buried, the researcher walked past the chimps with the empty box, and so—understanding what that meant—when they were released from their night cages, they raced off in search of the fruit. Several rushed and scrambled right past the place where the special treats had been buried in sand, but none paused to examine that area carefully. Later on that day, however, as the chimps were relaxing during their regular afternoon siesta, a young male who had been among the group that earlier rushed past the buried grapefruit, now quietly raised himself from his relaxed sprawl, casually strolled over to where the grapefruit had been hidden—away from the gaze of his relaxing fellows—and dug out the fruit and consumed it at his leisure. (Waal Frans de 62)

Finally, an amusing anecdote from Jane Goodall's primate research station.

> Like several prominent primatologists of his generation, Plooij was first trained in field research at Jane Goodall's research site in Tanzania, where he studied the group of chimpanzees already made famous by Goodall's early work. As Plooij recalls, at Gombe all researchers were forbidden from interacting in any way with the chimps. The reasons for that rule were obvious. Interaction could affect the research results, so it was bad science. Interaction could also endanger the chimps, who are capable of contracting virtually every infectious human disease. Finally, it could endanger the people, both through disease transmission and also through plain physical damage, should the

chimps ever appreciate how remarkably weak people are. When the chimpanzees made any attempt to interact with researchers, therefore, they were instructed, in Plooij's words, "to act like pillars of salt."

Plooij had spent more than a year studying the behavior of the chimpanzee Passion and her two offspring, Prof an infant and his elder sister Pom. The chimps were normally disinterested in the humans around them and the researchers were instructed to try and become part of the background so as not to influence the chimp's behavior. One day however, Pom started grooming Plooij, which although gratifying was also disturbing as he was instructed to not interact with the chimpanzees. So, he remained immobile showing no signs of outward pleasure. Despite this lack of encouragement, Pom continued the grooming.

Then, remembering a curious incident that he had previously observed with other chimpanzees when one of them had managed to get rid of a pesky individual without causing offence, Plooij attempted the same strategy. He turned and stared intently into the distance at an imagined curiosity for some time as if something fascinating was happening over there, moving his head from side to side as if to obtain a clearer view.

'He pretended that he had suddenly discovered some astonishing event in the distance. He looked up, gazed intently, and even moved his head a little from side to side as if focusing his sight acutely. And it worked! Soon Pom had stopped trying to groom Plooij and was looking in the same direction he was. Pom then walked tentatively a short distance toward the imagined point of interest, looked back at Plooij, who continued gazing. Finally, the young chimp decisively moved off and out of sight, headed into the forest in the direction of that imaginary event--and so the researcher was at last able to return, unimpeded, to his observations of Passion and Prof.

A short while later, though, Pom came back, marched directly up to Plooij, and slapped him sharply on the head. Then, for the remainder of the day, she pointedly avoided him.

Laughter

Chimpanzees, gorillas, bonobos and orangutans show laughter-like vocalizations in response to play chasing and tickling. Although chimpanzee laughter isn't similar to human laughter and not easily recognized by the non-expert, it takes the form of a sort of rapid inhalation and exhalation. One study reported very similar sonographic patterns between human babies and bonobos when tickled, although the bonobos' laughter was pitched higher. Chimpanzees and humans share the same ticklish zones of the body, under the arms, soles of feet and the belly.

One of the conclusions thrown up by studying laughter amongst the great apes is that gorillas and bonobos laughter tends to last three times the length of the breathing cycle which suggests that both species have control over their breathing, an essential component to speech.

The fact that all great Apes share laughter shows that laughter developed early with primates long before humans and chimpanzees evolved separately.

Language

The origins of language in humans have been the subject of heated debate. Until recently it was widely accepted that language was only mastered in the last few moments of human evolution, figuratively speaking, and that even Neanderthals were incapable of speech. While we will return to take a closer look at language later on in the book, it is interesting to note how much communication our last common ancestors were capable of?

A lot of research has been done studying the linguistic capabilities of the great apes. Orangutans and chimpanzees have been taught to communicate with humans in sign language. Perhaps the most impressive example is Washoe, a chimpanzee who was born in 1965 and captured for use by the US Air Force to take part in research for the Space Program. She was taught American Sign Language. Washoe was given her own trailer to live in with refrigerator, drawers, kitchen, clothes, grooming equipment, bed and sheets etcetera. The intention being to raise her in a human environment, she ate at a table with her trainers. Previous attempts to teach chimps language had failed. It was later realized the reason being that they weren't capable of the variety of controls of tongue and voice box which humans utilize to make the complex sounds needed for speech. Washoe was therefore taught sign language. After the first couple of years of learning sign language she started to pick up new words intuitively as her teachers signed new words between themselves. Washoe observed, learnt and later reproduced the signs in an appropriate context. Washoe's language extended to 350 different sign language words. In addition, Washoe created combinations of words to form phrases from her own initiative.

One of Washoe's caretakers was pregnant and missed work for many weeks after she miscarried. Roger Fouts recounts the following situation:

> People who should be there for her and aren't, are often given the cold shoulder—her way of informing them that she's miffed at them. Washoe greeted Kat [the caretaker] in just this way when she finally returned to work with the chimps. Kat made her apologies to Washoe, then decided to tell her the truth, signing "MY BABY DIED". Washoe stared at her, then looked down. She finally peered into Kat's eyes again and carefully signed "CRY", touching her cheek and drawing her finger down the path a tear would make on a human (chimpanzees don't shed tears). Kat later remarked that one sign told her more about Washoe and her mental capabilities than all her longer, grammatically perfect sentences. (Fouts)

So much for chimpanzees learning to communicate with humans, but what about amongst themselves? Researchers at the University of St Andrews believe that they have translated 36 signs which chimpanzees in the wild in Uganda use to communicate with one another. For example, if chimps wanted to play, they would stamp both feet, or if they wanted sex they would clip leaves. This form of communication falls into the category of non- vocal communication, but are chimpanzees, like whales, capable of vocal communication, and what is it like?

The answer is that chimpanzees can communicate vocally. It has been observed that on finding food they utter grunts, a noise which they only make in relation to food and in no other circumstance. It was further observed that the rate of grunting and the pitch of the grunt also varied upon circumstance. Experiments by Slocombe and Zuberbuehler revealed that the pitch of the grunt varied upon the desirability of the food, the higher the pitch the more desirable the food.

The building blocks of language are differentiated between single noises or calls which signify a single meaning. For example, vervet monkeys (*Cercopithecus aethiops*) produce three different calls depending on their three main predators: leopard, snake or eagles. But in human speech a highly complex arrangement of pitches and tones combine together to form speech sounds which in turn combine to form syllables which are further combined to form words, the result being an almost infinite variety of words and corresponding meanings which vary from single objects to conceptual meanings such as for example the word 'variability'. Linguistic experts refer to this more sophisticated use of language as functionally referential. The question of whether chimpanzees have truly mastered functionally referential language has yet to be fully resolved. This does not mean that chimpanzees are not capable of abstract thought though, but it does mean that we are unsure as to whether they are capable of communicating abstract thought verbally.

Gorillas also understand sign language. Koko, a lowland gorilla, learnt around 1,000 American Sign Language signs as well as understanding 2,000 spoken words in English. But there was no indication that Koko could produce semantic communication with these signs, and she never progressed beyond the cognitive level of a human 2- to 3-year-old.

In the book *Kanzi's Primal Language* (by Segerdahl, P., Fields, W., Savage-Rumbaugh, S. [Palgrave Macmillan]), Sue Savage-Rumbaugh describes the amazing linguistic abilities of the bonobo Kanzi.

Kanzi apparently learned by eavesdropping on the keyboard lessons researcher Sue Savage-Rumbaugh was giving to his adoptive mother. Kanzi learned to communicate with a Lexigram board, pushing symbols that stand for words. The board is wired to a computer, so the word is then vocalized out loud by the computer. This helps Kanzi develop his vocabulary and enables him to communicate with researchers.

One day, Rumbaugh used the computer to say to Kanzi, "Can you make the dog bite the snake?" It is believed Kanzi had never heard this sentence before. In answering the question, Kanzi searched among the objects present until he found a toy dog and a toy snake, put the snake in the dog's mouth, and used his thumb and finger to close the dog's mouth over the snake. (Segerdahl Paer et al 139)

In 2001, Alexander Fiske-Harrison, writing in the *Financial Times*, observed that Kanzi was "asked by an invisible interrogator through headphones (to avoid cueing) to identify 35 different items in 180 trials. His success rate was 93 per cent." In further testing, beginning when he was 7 ½ years old, Kanzi was asked 416 complex questions, responding correctly over 74% of the time. Kanzi has been observed verbalizing a meaningful noun to his sister.

Questioning appears to be a defining separation between animals and humans. Despite the advanced ability to answer questions, all the above apes never seemed able to formulate questions of their own volition. This lack of verbal inquisitiveness is in stark contrast to human children who are capable of asking endless questions. Formulation of questions and listening to answers is a key element in the learning process. A being that doesn't formulate those questions and has no active teacher is going to learn less information, and learn more slowly. Although great ape parents are conscientious teachers, it would seem that it is a one-way process.

Study of chimpanzee vocalizations has led researchers to realize that their vocabulary varies according to their group. As we have seen, the grunt for food has been translated, but comparing recordings of that grunt across different groups has shown that it differs according to the group but remains the same within the group. The same is also true of the sign language used by chimps. For example, in just one group studied, chimps will hold hands with one hand above their heads while grooming each other. Chimpanzee family groups consist of strong social bonds in fixed geographical areas. These groups are protected by border patrols so that mixing of groups is limited, and so three different sub-species have evolved within quite close geographical distances. Even so, some gestures are common to all chimpanzees and indeed some are common to humans, such as extending an open hand meaning requesting food, as used across the planet by beggars.

Cultural differences have developed within the chimpanzee species, where each culture is defined by its own dialect and geographical location, and in some cases these cultural groups have remained fixed for so long that different sub-species have developed. Chimpanzees demonstrate in a primitive form, via the process of learning in isolated or semi-isolated groups, the birth of cultures and nations which dominate human life today.

Chimpanzees are effective communicators. Their level of communication is sufficient for managing a complex social life. However, they are limited in their ability to communicate their thoughts vocally. Here we find a very clear differentiation between chimpanzees and ourselves, and we can conclude that this ability to talk and listen as humans do today is something that is unique to humans. Of all the characteristics that we have looked at, this is the one single most defining difference between ourselves and our nearest living relatives. The origins of complex speech and language must therefore have occurred at some point in our evolutionary story from *Ardipithecus* onwards.

To better understand when this happened, geneticists have studied the development of the FOXP2 gene which scientists believe is employed in the creation of language, and although it is a gene shared by most mammals, there are changes in it which are unique to humans, offering a clue to our unique control of language.

Human and Chimpanzee Brains

Comparisons of human and chimpanzee brains by using immunohisto-florescence and live imaging have revealed that despite the significant size difference (by a ratio of 3 to 1) the cytoarchitecture, cell type and neurogenic expressions of the two brains are remarkably similar. The differences lie in the following areas:

The cerebral cortex, which plays a role in memory, awareness, attention and thought, contains twice as many cells in humans as in chimpanzees. Also, networks of cells in the cerebral cortex behave differently across the two species.

A particularly curious aspect of human brains is that they are asymmetrical with different halves having different functions. The left side is typically associated with language and the right side more associated with spatial reasoning. Typically, although not necessarily, the left side is larger than the right side, giving the brain a somewhat lop-sided appearance. This brain asymmetry is common to a degree with other great apes. In humans the frontal and parietal lobes are significantly larger than in chimpanzees. The comparison of the two brains carried out by Aida Gomez-Robles of the George Washington University concluded that the asymmetry of human brains arises from its plasticity and ability to reconfigure readily depending upon needs. This plasticity, she concludes, was crucial to the evolution of human cognitive development.

The differences between the language related parts of the brains of humans and chimpanzees is an ongoing area of research which has attracted a lot of interest, and as yet we do not possess a complete picture. We do though currently have a fairly complete picture of the areas of the brain involved in language processing, but it is the study of primates' brains which is currently lagging behind. Completed studies have compared the speech related areas of the brains of humans and other primates to see what part of the human brain is uniquely adapted to language, and which are the common areas in humans and other primates used for general vocalizations. Using both PET scans and MRI scans, the results of the research show that humans, macaques and chimpanzees use the upper temporal lobe bilaterally in recognition of familiar voices. This contradicts an earlier widely held view that speech was mainly performed by the left hemisphere of the brain. In particular the recognition of a voice is performed in humans and primates by both the anterior and posterior sections of the temporal lobe. However, in humans there is a significant difference with other primates, the position of the voice recognition within the temporal lobe is lower than in other primates. Chimpanzees also have voice recognition areas lower in the temporal lobe than in macaques, where it is in the upper areas of the lobe. What this suggests to us is that primates and therefore our last common ancestor were capable of distinguishing other individuals in the group simply by hearing their voices. This is both helpful in a thickly forested area where visibility is limited and in a highly social environment where recognizing individuals is crucial in ensuring that one behaves appropriately towards that individual. This in turn tells us that our earliest common ancestor was in all likelihood well adapted to a structured social environment with a well-developed social hierarchy, such as chimpanzee society and lived-in close-knit communities, rather than as solitary hunters.

Wernicke's Area

Wernicke's Area is a part of the superior temporal gyrus which encircles the auditory cortex on the border of the temporal and parietal lobes. It is one of the two areas of the brain which is specifically linked to speech. The other area is Broca's Area, which is used in the formation of language.

Lobes of the human brain

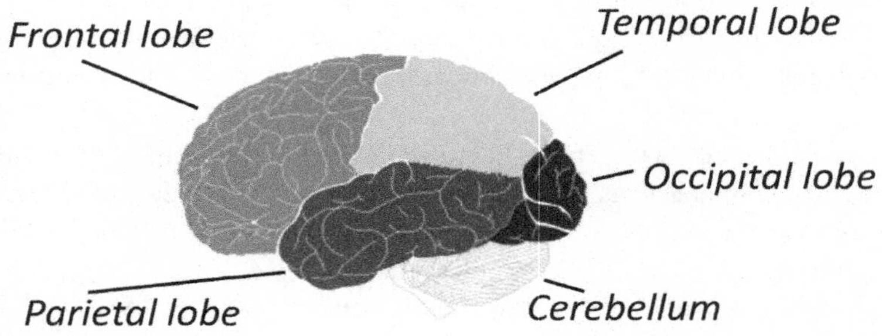

Illustration 8. Lobes of the human brain

These two crucial regions of the brain involved in speech although being well separated, are linked by an information highway constructed from bundles of axons, and is called the Arcuate Fasciculus (which itself is divided into two separate pathways, one deep and one shallow). Damage to specific parts of the Arcuate Fasciculus results in various speech defects including stuttering and different forms of Aphasia.

The diagram below compares the Arcuate Fasciculus in humans, chimpanzees and macaques. Not only is the arcuate fasciculus broader and capable of transporting more information in humans, but it reaches far deeper into different parts of the temporal lobe than with chimpanzees. In macaques it hardly reaches the temporal lobe at all.

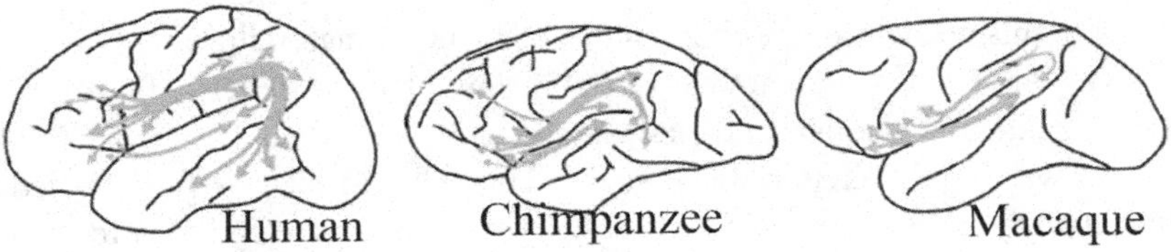

Illustration 9 Extent of the arcuate fasciculus

Credit: Glasser, M., & Rilling, J. (2008). DTI Tractography of the human Brain's Language Pathways, *Cerebral Cortex, 18* (11), 2471-2482 DOI: 10.1093/cercor/bhn011

Macaques diverged from the chimpanzee and human lines of evolution about 25 million years ago, compared to the split between chimpanzees and humans occurring somewhere between 10 and 6 million years ago. Macaques have less evolved communications than chimpanzees, and although they have a repertoire of body language, facial expressions and vocalizations, they have so far not been taught sign language, unlike chimpanzees.

Chimpanzee's brains have the basic building blocks for language, the Wernicke's area, the Broca's Area and the Arcuate Fasciculus, but they are far less developed than in humans, in particular the Arcuate Fasciculus. So, our last common ancestor certainly had the ability for basic communication between other members of his group, but not the capacity for something we would recognize as language. However, crucially he had all the elements and the highly flexible brain to be able to develop verbal communication, and since our divergence with chimpanzees, that is exactly what he needed to do, and what he did.

With all these inferred details about our Last Common Ancestor, we have a lot clearer idea of one of his descendants, *Ardipithecus*, who inherited a number of these characteristics and who starts the long journey to humanity.

So, to summarize, referring back to the fossil record, we know that *Ardipithecus* was capable of both bipedal and quadrupedal movement, with a preference for bipedalism for his new life, on the forest floor, out of the trees. His brain was slightly larger than modern chimpanzees although he was barely taller than modern chimps.

We know that he used tools with his hands, both stone tools for crushing nuts and cracking open bones. He also fashioned spears which as with stones he used as weapons. Although he probably threw stones as projectiles we don't know whether he threw spears. The prevailing opinion today is that he didn't. But it seems more than likely that if he threw rocks to maim his targets he would most likely have thrown spears for the same purpose. Proof of this one way or another will probably never materialize.

We know that he already displayed various characteristics of humanity such as laughter, altruism and deception.

He was highly territorial and social. The males in his groups defended his territory and did not hesitate to resort to violence to defend the precious resources in his territory as well as other members of his group. There was a strict social hierarchy in his group, with a chief or apex male/female who maintained total authority over the group and the territory. Every member of the group held a specific social status depending on age and affiliations to senior members of the group and also dependent on personal strength. Communication through vocalizations, gestures and facial expressions played a major role in his daily life. Communication helped to coordinate group activities such as hunting, border patrol, foraging and discipline with the group. Communication was a vital part of the learning process between mothers, elders within the group and youngsters. As life, use and manufacture of tools and social complexity assumed a greater role in daily life so the need for communicating increased, and slowly over a great period of time, simple vocalizations evolved into a primitive language.

As groups became better coordinated and better organized their chances of survival increased. Better chances of survival would have increased the population, putting increased pressure on the resources available within the group's territory. So, inevitably large groups would split apart with small groups of individuals heading off to try and form communities where resources were more readily available. In this way, better social organization and communication led to increases in population and a general spread of *Ardipithecus* throughout wide swathes of Africa. His bipedalism, growing intelligence and cooperation within the group allowed him to better defend himself against other large predators and so to spread into their areas, and away from the confines of the treetop environment where his ancestors found security. In this he differed significantly from chimpanzees who have never evolved beyond their own environmental niche.

Of all the advantages that *Ardipithecus* had inherited from his ancestor the Last Common Ancestor, by far the greatest was his flexible brain, which allowed him to improve his communications, his tools and weapons. Better communication leads to better teaching and better survival skills in a challenging world.

We will return to the hugely important question of speech and language later in this book, as we reach the last 100,000 years of human evolution.

Homo habilis

> Whether primeval man, when he possessed very few arts of the rudest kind, and when his power of language was extremely imperfect, would have deserved to be called man, must depend on the definition which we employ. In a series of forms graduating insensibly from some ape-like creature to man as he now exists it would be impossible to fix on any definite point when the term 'man' ought to be used. (Darwin, Charles : *The Descent of Man* 235)

Exactly! As Charles Darwin says, you've got to draw the line somewhere, and for all the imperfections of the choice it was drawn here at the start of *H. habilis* over a century ago. Recognizable human ancestors existed well before *H. habilis*, but they miss out on the recognition of being part of the earth's most dominant genus. We use a very imperfect system of classification and have little choice but to live with it. Let's take a look at those classifications within the Homo genus. That is all types of creature or hominid, that have been identified on our planet. The original designation of Homo was based on those species which at the time were considered to have used tools. As we've already seen, *Australopithecus* mastered stone tools without a shadow of a doubt. Currently four distinct species have been identified within the Homo genus. In chronological order *H. habilis*, *H. erectus*, *H. neanderthalis*, *Homo sapiens*, although plenty of others have been named in the past such as *Homo Denisovan*, *Homo soloensis* and *Homo javanensis* and *Homo heidelbergensis* but most of these have been reallocated into one of the four categories just mentioned. His geographical range was limited to just East and South Africa. He was surprisingly small, weighing an average of 32Kg and with a height of 100-135cm, but with a relatively large brain, of around 600cc, representing about 1.7% of his body weight which is a significant increase on *Australopithecus*. His cranium was low and he had large projecting jaws giving him a prognathic face, but less so than *Australopithecus*. Like his ancestor *Australopithecus*, the foramen magnum, the opening in the base of the skull to allow the spinal cord to exit the brain was located centrally, so that as with humans today the skull was balanced vertically on the spine, indicating that he was already fully adapted to walking upright on his legs, rather than on four legs. In quadrupedal mammals the foramen magnum is located right at the back of the skull, facing the tail. In apes it is actually under the skull but located towards the back.

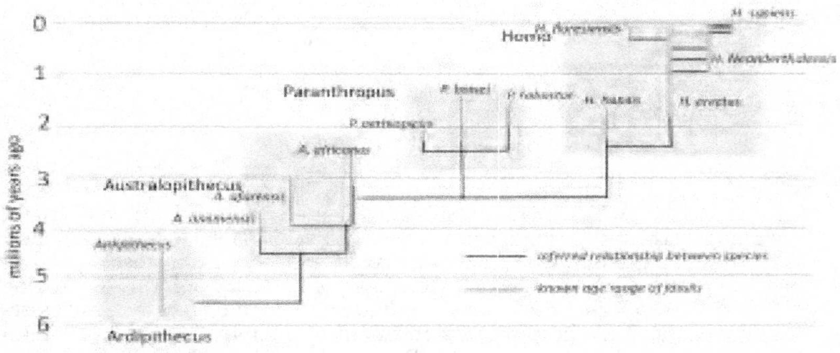

Illustration 10. Homo family tree

He had the relatively long arms compared to his body size, a trait that today we associate with chimpanzees, who are both bipedal and quadrupedal. It is possible that like chimpanzees, *H. habilis*' long arms allowed him, when necessary to sprint on the ground like chimpanzees with the aid of his arms allowing an extra turn of speed when fleeing predators or attacking prey, but equally when using his tools or carrying things he could walk erect. The ability to stand upright on his legs also allowed him to peer above the grasses in the African savannah. The choice of bipedal or quadrupedal behavior allowed *H. habilis* far greater versatility of behavior, and variety of environment for living. He may have been equally at home in the trees as on the open savannah. He inherited *Ardipithecus*' social hierarchical and communication skills, living in close knit communities of related individuals. Usage of large Olduwan stone tools prepared by knapping was now standard behavior, indeed essential for the preparation of meat, and possibly also for sharpening wooden spears.

Social organization and communication allowed *H. habilis* to hunt in a coordinated fashion and although he was a diminutive individual as a member of an organized group he was becoming a fearsome predator in Africa.

Better armed, better organized and therefore a better survivor *H. habilis*' population started to increase and with his adaptable behavior so did his footprint on Africa way outside the range of *Australopithecus*. Human ancestors were on the move.

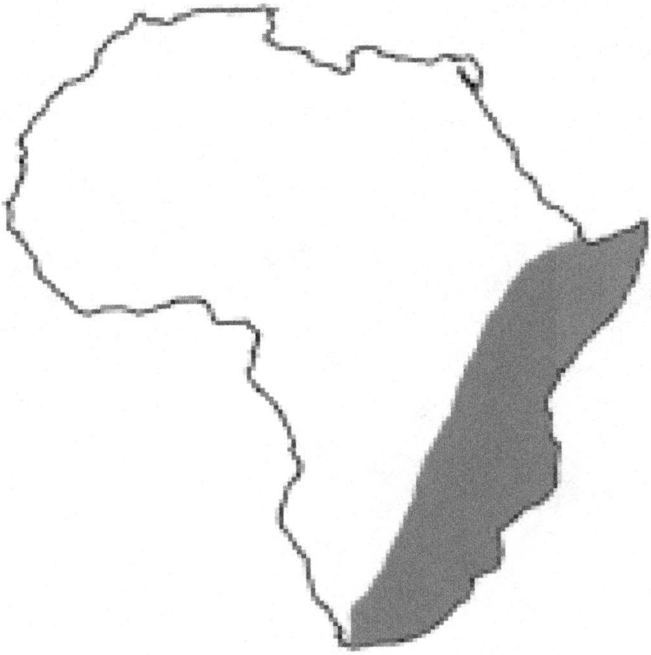

Illustration 11. Homo habilis territory

Technologically, *H. habilis* inherited the Olduwan stone technology from *Australopithecus*, which reaches back to around 2.6 million years ago in the Afar Triangle in East Africa. As with later technologies, the tools fall broadly into scrapers, awls and burins. From the tools, it has been surmised that *H. habilis* scraped hides, which he then used for clothing and wrapping.

For all his versatility, *H. habilis* was an African hominid evolved and adapted to life in Africa, which meant life in a warm climate. Over time, improving language skill, improved diet and a lively intelligence, *H. habilis* evolved into *H. erectus*, who was the first early man to colonize the entire old world, from Africa to South East Asia. Man was about to become a global phenomenon.

Homo rudolfensis

Homo H. rudolfensis is probably more of an enigma than the other early Homo species. There is considerable disagreement about whether *H. rudolfensis* is actually a separate species at all or just a slightly different race of *H. habilis*. In addition to date there are very few *H. rudolfensis* fossil remains, and no complete skeleton. It is considered that *H. rudolfensis* existed in East Africa between 2 and 1.5 million years ago concurrently with *H. habilis* and *H. erectus*. His remains have been found at that highly productive Kenyan site of Koobi Fora by Richard and Meave Leakey, who are the chief advocates of the idea of H. *rudolfensis* being a separate species.

Those who defend the designation of *H. rudolfensis* say that his jaw does not fall inside the limits defined for *H. habilis*, particularly earlier *H. habilis* fossils. In general, it is considered that *H. rudolfensis* has a larger brain, more massive incisor teeth and a less prognathic face than *H. habilis*, especially with regard to much older *H. habilis* fossils.

Detractors of *H. rudolfensis* as a separate species consider that the original definitions of *H. habilis* were too narrow, and that the similarities between *H. habilis* and *H. rudolfensis* by far outweigh their differences. The two sides of the argument have not as yet reached agreement on this heated question, where several high-profile reputations in the world of palaeoarcheology are at stake.

In terms of taxonomy, both *H. habilis* and *H. rudolfensis* belong to the genus of Homo. According to the Encyclopedia Britannica, the definition of genus is "biological classification ranking between family and species, consisting of structurally or phylogenetically related species," in other words a class of things which have common characteristics but which can be subdivided into subordinate kinds. From the same source, the definition of species is: "a classification comprising of related organisms that share common characteristics and are capable of interbreeding."

So, from a purely scientific point of view, nothing short of the recovery of DNA from both *H. habilis* and *H. rudolfensis*, and the cloning of each followed by attempts at breeding from the two, to ascertain whether they are the same species or not. Lacking this hard evidence, it is pure guesswork as to whether they are the same species or not. They clearly have many common features which justify their classification in the genus 'Homo', but further than that we are never likely to know for sure.

Again, from a purely scientific point of view, it would probably be more prudent to talk with allowance for some wriggle room, as we do of *H. erectus*, as *H. habilis* sensu latu, and *H. habilis* sensu strictu, the former including H. *rudolfensis*.

As a general point, when thinking about our remote ancestors, especially the early ones who had emerged from a very specific environmental niche, but who were evolving to adapt in many different environmental niches, it is not surprising to see a number of varying adaptations each with their own diet and adaptation to climate etcetera. As the climate changed and these people moved around, the various groups would have mingled creating a rainbow of features which renders the paleoanthropologists' attempts at strict classification a complex and sometimes meaningless task. We see this same problem reoccur time and again during this pre-history.

More caution should be given to the description of *H. habilis* in terms of narrow physical characteristics, because *H. habilis* evolved over a long period of his existence. He didn't appear out of nowhere a fully formed *H. habilis*, but evolved slowly and possibly in a stuttering nature from earlier Australopithecines, and probably evolved into *H. erectus*. This evolution didn't come about overnight in a sort of Genesis moment, but as a result of slow changes in his environment and ability to adapt over probably 10s of thousands of years, with all sorts of evolutionary dead ends along the way, any of which might be picked up as a fossil and described as a separate species. The reality of this debate about classification is far more complex than a simple pigeon hole of *H. habilis* or *H. rudolfensis*. We can refer to some of these intermediate fossils showing common features of both ancestors and descendants as 'transitional'. But when looking at evolution over hundreds of thousands of years, all these fossils are transitional to a degree.

So, to simplify the debate from here on I'll refer to *H. rudolfensis* as *H. habilis* in the sensu latu form.

Homo erectus

The earliest remains of any human ancestor outside of Africa are to be found at the site of Dminisi in Southern Georgia, close to the border with Armenia, and not far from the Turkish border. These remains belong to the most long lived of human ancestors, *H. erectus*, and date back to an astonishing 1.8 million years ago.

These Georgian *H. erectus* remains mark a very significant landmark in human evolution. Not only are they located a very long way from the traditional *H. habilis/Australopithecus* range in tropical Africa (meaning that *H. erectus* could travel) but he managed to adapt to a very different climate in a very different region. The flexibility that *Australopithecus* started to display was now bearing fruit.

The most likely theory regarding the origins of *H. erectus* is that he evolved from *H. habilis*, *Homo ergaster* or a close cousin of *H. habilis* in Africa and at some point prior to 1.8 million years ago ancestors of these Georgians migrated out of Africa, most probably taking a route through the Levant and Turkey. This leaves open the possibility of even older fossil Homo remains to be found in Turkey and the Levant. It would seem likely that *H. erectus* evolved in Africa from *H. habilis* and migrated up the Rift Valley and into Eurasia. As *Homo ergaster* originated in Eastern and Southern Africa and is now considered to be an early variant of *H. erectus*, it is probably safe to conclude that *H. erectus* originated in Africa probably around 2 million years ago.

But there is still some doubt clouding the issue. The earliest *H. erectus* remains that have come to light, to date, are those from Georgia, meaning that it is possible that *H. erectus* evolved in Europe. If this is the case, then we don't know who *H. erectus*' direct ancestor was. Some of the Georgian *H. erectus* brains are of a comparable size to *H. habilis*'s brain, which suggests a close link to *H. habilis* within Europe, which in turn is tantalizingly suggestive of *H. habilis* having left Africa first. Although this isn't a likely scenario, it does however remain within the realms of possibility. If this unlikely case is borne out by future fossil finds, then it opens the door to a retro-colonization of Africa by *H. erectus* migrating from Europe. Or indeed that variations of *H. erectus* were simply a logical step forwards from any *H. habilis*, i.e., that *H. habilis* populations in Europe and Africa both evolved into *H. erectus*. We just don't know the answer to this puzzle at the moment.

Because *H. erectus* was so successful in colonizing the Old World and occupied his territories for such a long time there are considerable variations in his appearance, which has given rise to considerable debate in the palaeoarcheological community about classifications. A welter of different subspecies of Homo have been named, such as *H. ergaster*, *H. erectus*, *H. georgicus*, *H. javanensis*, *H. heidelbergensis*, *Peking man*, *H. rudolfensis*, etcetera, based upon different appearances of skeletal remains from different geographical locations. A compromise has been reached where a typical *H. erectus* has been defined (*Homo erectus* senso strictu), and variations have been associated with it (*Homo erectus* sensu latu), bringing all these disparate *H. erectus* types into the same family or sub-species of Homo. So, we have a compromise arrangement prevailing *H. erectus* in the strict sense and *H. erectus* in the broad sense. Once again, the rigid world of classifications is attempting to adapt to a changing rainbow situation.

Generally speaking *H. erectus* walked upright and possessed distinctly modern features. His crania or brain size ranges from about 850cc to 1100cc which overlaps with modern human brain sizes, so he was clearly intelligent, considerably more so than *H. habilis* who had a much smaller cranium size ranging from 500cc to 690cc, roughly half that of modern humans. As with modern humans he was sexually dimorphic, with males averaging about 1m79 roughly 25% taller than female *H. erectus*, and of a similar height to modern humans. *H. erectus* had a slender appearance with long arms and legs. His head on the other hand had a robust appearance with pronounced brow arches inherited although less pronounced from *H. habilis* and earlier ancestors. The face was more prognathic than modern humans (meaning the center of the face protruded in a pronounced fashion).

The combination of these features gave *H. erectus* what we would probably consider to be a somewhat primitive appearance. Several facial reconstructions have been made based on skull remains and the final result is a distinctly human, albeit robust, face. The general impression would be of a somewhat thuggish looking human, who one wouldn't particularly want to meet alone in a darkened alley. *H. erectus* (upright man) represents a significant stage of development towards modern man. He was tall, having abandoned forever a life on four legs.

The latest *H. erectus* fossils are surprisingly recent, just 70,000 years old (although not entirely accepted by the scientific community, it is thought that the species lived on in some south east Asian islands until as late as 50,000 BP), giving *H. erectus* an unrivalled and mind-boggling span of 2 million years on the planet.

As a species, having survived for nearly 2 million years, *H. erectus* was perfectly adapted to his surroundings wherever he found himself. His large and versatile brain finding solutions for adaptation to local challenges. *H. erectus* exemplifies the change from a niche adapted species such as *Ardipithecus* confined to living in tropical forests, to a human capable of adapting to very many different environments. This body also adapted to different environments, very different indeed from his original African homeland. For example, in the Northern latitudes in Europe where he received less sunlight on his skin, it became lighter so that he could process more essential vitamin D. Shortly, we'll take a look at various different incarnations of *H. erectus*.

So far there have been five *H. erectus* skulls found at Dmanisi in Georgia, Dmanisi 5, with the smallest brain size of 550cc, barely larger than *Australopithecus*, the other four having larger ones ranging up to 730cc, markedly smaller than typical *H. erectus* brain capacities, and more in line with *H. habilis*. However, the skeletons measured between 150 and 166cm making him taller than *H. habilis*, although not as tall as most other *H. erectus* specimens. So, these earliest Europeans don't fit conveniently into either the *H. habilis* or the *H. erectus* categories. These five skeletal remains found at Dmanisi date to the same distant period of 1.8 million years ago.

Once out of Africa, *H. erectus* then spread both East and West, with the earliest finds in China dating to around 1.6 million year BP, and to Spain around 1.2 million BP. It was in China around 1.2 million BP that we find possibly the first controlled use of fire, a *H. erectus* innovation, although it doesn't appear widespread in the fossil record until about 400–300,000BP.

Fire allowed humans to increase the variety of food that they could consume and by killing or deactivating harmful organisms such as viruses and bacteria in the food would help to keep the family group in a good state of health.

As *H. erectus* spread around the Eurasian continent he took with him his Olduwan tool kit, which has been found in Western Europe and as far East as China, as well of course as in Africa. By 1.76million years ago *H. erectus* improved this technology and invented the hand axe, initially in Kenya, where he still continued to thrive. By 1.5 million years ago these hand axes were being manufactured in South Asia and in Western Europe by 900,000 years BP. Because of his vast geographical range and over the 1.5 million years or so of exploitation of this stone working technology many regional variations evolved which have been classed according to various modes. Acheulean technology overlapped with the preceding Olduwan technology, with both technologies being found in the same time horizons at various sites, and also overlapped at the later end of the Acheulean period with the succeeding Mousterian technology, which started to appear more or less at the same time as Neanderthals. The principal feature of Acheulean hand axes and cleavers was that both sides of the tool were worked symmetrically, producing two worked faces and therefore a better edge. In virtually all cases, the tools were made and used close to the source of stone, suggesting that the knowledge for use and manufacture was shared throughout the *H. erectus* population in Africa, Europe and Asia.

During the nearly 2 million years that *H. erectus* thrived on the planet he adapted to local conditions giving rise to many different features. It takes little imagination to imagine that from *H. erectus*'s first arrival in Europe from Africa he started to adapt to the new environment. For example, the manufacture of essential vitamin D in Europe may have caused him to develop paler skin to better absorb the sun's rays weaker than in the tropics. In addition, there was the challenge of adapting to cold winters, requiring more and better clothing, an item which was less of a priority in tropical Africa.

Homo Erectus In Africa

In Africa different forms of *H. erectus* have been discovered, which originally were given their own classifications, but are now generally considered to belong to the *H. erectus* family sensu latu. The earliest to appear had been called Homo ergaster, with skeletal remains dating back to around 2 million years in Eastern Africa and seemingly survived there for roughly half a million years. Ergaster's cranial capacity ranges from 700-1100cc, and he has generally thinner skull bones than other *H. erectus* fossils. There don't appear to be any occurrences of *H. ergaster* more recent than 1.4 million years ago, and paleoanthropologists aren't sure why he disappears from the fossil record. It wouldn't be difficult to imagine that he naturally evolved into a conventional form of *H. erectus* and any slight differentiating traits disappeared from the fossil record.

One of the oldest sites for *H. erectus* in Africa is at the extensive and well-known archaeological site of Koobi Fora near to Lake Turkana in Kenya within the Great Rift Valley. Human ancestors have inhabited this site more or less continuously for around 4 million years. The *H. erectus* remains here go back to about 1.8 million years. Also found here are fossilized footprints dated to about 1.4 million years probably also of *H. erectus*, which demonstrate (because of the pronounced imprint of the ball and heel) that his feet were already arched giving the added propulsion necessary for a spring-like gait which today we all take for granted, but which was absent in our earlier ancestors who were still adapting to bipedal locomotion. One of the earliest complete skeletons from this area is the famous Turkana Boy skeleton of a *H. erectus* who appears to have died around 10 years old. Even at that early age he had attained the impressive height of 160cm tall and weighed a hefty 69Kg. It is estimated that if he had reached maturity he would have attained 185cm. His brain size had already reached 880cc and might have reached 1000cc in adulthood. He possessed a modern projecting nose, rather than a flatter nose of earlier human ancestors. Various forensic constructions and artist's impressions exist of Turkana Boy, some of which give the impression of a modern human, although he still retained archaic features such as receding chin, prominent and continuous brow arches and sloping forehead.

Somewhat troublesome to the generally accepted version of human evolution are the contemporaneous fossil remains of *H. habilis* which apparently coexisted on the Koobi Fora site with *H. erectus* for around 200,000 years. Given that *H. erectus* supposedly evolved from *H. habilis*, this coexistence poses some tricky questions. Normally when species evolve they do so because they evolve with a competitive advantage over their ancestors, and are better adapted to the prevailing conditions. But their coexistence for such a long period of time suggests that the situation was not all that simple. Did *H. habilis* and *H. erectus* live together, did they breed together, or did they alternately replace one another? If they replaced one another periodically, was it by peaceful means or was violence involved? There isn't enough evidence available to answer these questions at the moment. There don't appear to be any signs of weapon inflicted injury on the fossil remains, but that doesn't exclude some form of violence. Could it be that the both *H. habilis* and *H. erectus* interbred and weren't in reality as different as we consider them to be today by just looking at their bones? Could they have been migratory, and simply occupied the site for limited periods, alternating between travelling groups of *H. habilis* and *H. erectus*?

Recent archaeological findings in the Afar region in conjunction with fresh analysis of previously found fossils seem to have thrown a whole new light on the earliest appearances of *H. erectus*, his relationship with *H. habilis* and his heritage. In the previous paragraph I wrote that the earliest *H. erectus* fossils dated from 2 million years ago. This is not the generally accepted figure, or at least hasn't been until now. Most sources quote the earliest *H. erectus* remains as originating from Koobi Fora and date to 1.8 million years. However, recent *H. erectus* like fossil jaw bones have been found close to the Awash river in the famous fossil hunting ground of the Afar region in neighboring Ethiopia and have been dated to 2 million years old. In addition, another jawbone known as AL 666-1 has been found which possesses *H. erectus* teeth (slim molars and a characteristic *H. erectus* cusp on the teeth) but with a more archaic chin which dates to 2.3 million years ago.

Illustration 12. Turkana boy

The type fossil of *H. habilis* found by Louis and Mary Leakey in the 1960s contains a heavily distorted jawbone, many pieces of crania and some hand bones which are over half a million years younger than AL666-1 (1.8 million years old). The Max Planck Institute has re-examined these bones using computer tomography scans (CT), and 3D modeling techniques. Their view on these bones is different from the initial conclusions. Firstly, they believe that the jaw was very narrow with parallel lines of teeth, very similar to Australopithecine and ancestors going back to around 4 million years ago. Also, they have recalculated the brain size of this *H. habilis* specimen based on the curves of the cranial fragments and consider that the brain was around 800cc which is comparable with *H. erectus* specimens of the same age.

Given these new findings, Fred Spoor of UCL and the Max Planck Institute believe that our ancestral Homo line must include the jaw type of AL666-1 dated to 2.3 million years ago and that the 1.8 million year old *H. habilis* jaw is more primitive and must therefore be an offshoot and probably evolutionary dead end. They believe that the large brain size of *H. habilis* and *H. erectus* of 800cc must have a common ancestor, who in turn must have been large brained, and that this ancestor predates 2.3 million years ago.

Below is their family tree of *H. habilis* and *H. erectus*.

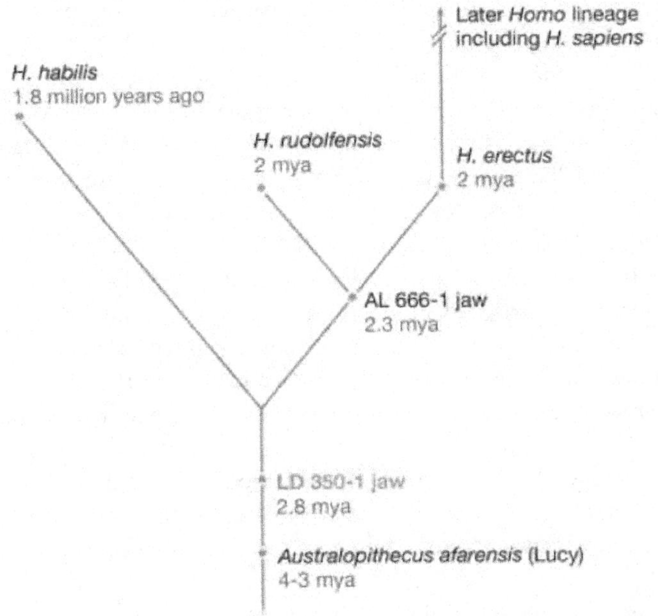

Illustration 13. Family tree of Homo habilis and Homo erectus

Credit: Jamie Shreeve, National Geographic. Mar 05 2015. http://news.nationalgeographic.com/news/2015/03/150304-homo-habilis-evolution-fossil-jaw-ethiopiaolduvaigorge.html

Their logic is not entirely watertight, and it relies on the reconstruction of the Mary Leakey jaw being accurate. They conclude that a hitherto ghost line or as yet unknown common ancestor must exist around what they consider to be the split of *H. habilis* and *H. erectus* at some point prior to 2.3 million years ago based on the interpreted archaic nature of the *H. habilis* jaw, and that the two must have had a common ancestor with a large 800cc brain. But it is entirely possible that the brain size of this ghost line was smaller and that both *H. habilis* and *H. erectus* evolved larger brains for the same reasons.

Another external factor has been detected which may well have played a key role in the development of both *H. habilis* and *H. erectus* in this period between 2.3 and 1.8 million years ago and that is there are signs of climate change in the Afar from a Serengeti type open savannah to a much more arid landscape accompanied by a change in the animals living there (and hence the food sources for both *H. habilis* and *H. erectus*). We shall see later in this book just how crucial changes in climate have been to shape our more recent development as a species.

But here we may find a clue as to the relationship between *H. habilis* and *H. erectus*. Both had tools and weapons, but according to the Max Planck Institute *H. habilis* jaws were more archaic when earlier species had a more vegetarian diet, lived in the trees and relied more on their teeth as tools for cutting and tearing food. *H. erectus* was an accomplished hunter and his jaw became less robust as he relied more and more on tools to cut and prepare his food. It could be that variations in climate favored alternately *H. habilis* and his more vegetarian adapted jaws and then with other swings favored *H. erectus*. Whenever in Ethiopia and Kenya the climate changed locally, *H. habilis* would migrate to where he was better adapted or *H. erectus* would. So that whatever the climatic circumstances at the time there was a Homo who was more suited to fill the niche.

This varying climatic pattern in the period of 2–1.4 million years ago, which is backed up by the fossil record in East Africa neatly explains the apparent co-existence of two different species *H. habilis* and *H. erectus*.

The fossil record pertaining to *H. erectus*' ancestors is very incomplete prior to 2.3 million years ago. Famously, it has been said that Homo remains at this time could be fit into a shoe box with plenty of room left for the shoes. This leaves a cloud of mystery over when *H. erectus* first appeared prior to

2 million years ago, but hopefully this will be cleared up with future fossil finds either in Kenya or Ethiopia.

Further complexity is added to an already perplexing vision of human evolution in Africa by another close relative of the African *H. erectus*; *H. naledi* who lived in the period 335,000BP to 235,000BP in South Africa. There is still open debate as to whether *H. naledi* is a separate sub-species or yet another variation of *H. erectus* sensu latu. *H. naledi* was considerably smaller than most *H. erectus*, with a male height of around 1m50 and weight of roughly 45Kg, the females being smaller still. The dating of *H. naledi* is fraught with uncertainty partly because he doesn't fit conveniently into the picture of an ever evolving human species. His relatively small brain size suggests a much earlier date (although that could be partially explained by his small body mass), and initial datings based on the geological context in which the bones were found put *H. naledi* around 2 million years old. *H. naledi* challenges existing theories on human evolution, his fingers, hands, teeth and arms display a curious combination of very primitive and modern features.

H. naledi is a recent discovery dating only from 2014, we only know about him because his remains were found deep in a cave, only accessible by a 12m chimney which tightens in places to just 20cm, a place inaccessible to large carnivores. The floor of the cave is littered with thousands of *H. naledi* bones at various depths of strata with only a small part of the floor having as yet been excavated. It is conjectured that over a very wide period of time *H. naledi* dead were thrown down the chimney either as part of a religious rite, or to protect the remains from carnivorous predation, representing possibly a form of deliberate burial.

In Asia

There is plenty of evidence of *H. erectus* colonizing Asia and South East Asia. Java man is an example. At the time of the discovery of Java man in 1890 in the very early days of paleoanthropology, his remains were the oldest human species discovered, giving the impression at the time that humans had evolved in Asia. This is a hypothesis which some still believe to this date. The dating of the various remains of Java man suggest a period of between 1.4 million and 400,000 years old. Further study of the existing fossils as well as the discovery of other fossils in the region could well extend these dates out in both directions, but certainly *H. erectus* inhabited Java for over 1 million years.

Estimates consider Java man to have a typical *H. erectus* height of around 170cm, but with a typical sturdy femur, thicker than modern humans. He possessed a brain size of roughly 900cc perfectly placed in the middle of the *H. erectus* brain size range. He had the typical pronounced brow ridge, massive jaw, receding forehead and lack of chin of *H. erectus*.

Another form of *H. erectus* found in Java is *meganthropus*, variously classified as *Homo javanicus* or *H. erectus javanicus*. Skeletal remains suggest that *meganthropus* was significantly more massive than the rest of the *H. erectus* family and modern man. It is estimated that he reached 2.4m in height and weighed in between 180 and 270Kg. Only partial skeletal remains have been found, so these are only approximations, based partly on comparison with gorilla skeletons. *Meganthropus* used stone tools and appears to date from roughly 1.5 million years ago to 900,000 years ago. Concurrent with this giant in Java is another even more impressive being whose remains have been found in China, India and Vietnam dating from 9 million years ago and becoming extinct less than 100,000 years ago. This creature stood up to 4m tall and weighed up to 600Kg. No longer considered to be a close relative of man, this largest of all primates is considered to have been a relative of the orangutan.

While we're on the subject of giant prehistoric human ancestors, some human bones have been found in Southern France; Castelnau and Montpelier which apparently belonged to human ancestors estimated to date possibly as late as the Neolithic, although possibly earlier and belonged to people measuring, it is estimated, between 3.5 and 4 meters tall.

A very well publicized version of *H. erectus* is Peking man, or *H. erectus pekinensis*. The main fossils were discovered between 1923 and 1937 at Zhoukoudian near to Beijing. These include skull caps giving brain sizes of around 900 to 1225cc. The date range for the full collection of these skeletal remains starts at around 800,000 up until about 300,000 BP. In the early years classification of these remains treated them as a new species *Pithecanthropus*, but they are generally considered now to fit comfortably into the *H. erectus* family.

Considerable interest was focused on the remains found up until the Second World War. In order to protect them from the Japanese, the remains were crated and loaded onto a US marine vehicle; and they were never seen again. Various rewards have been offered to recover them, but to date without success. Four teeth only remain from this initial collection; they were sent for analysis to Uppsala University in Sweden. Before disappearing, they were carefully described.

Their importance has been amplified by the Chinese palaeological establishment considering them to be direct ancestors of modern Chinese. This theory flatly contradicts the Out of Africa Theory II. The Peking man remains predate by a clear 100,000 years the putative exodus of Africa which is considered to have been the origin of all modern humans. We shall be looking at this conflict in more detail later in this book.

The oldest *H. erectus* remains in Asia belong to Gongwangling man which date back to as far as 1.63 million years before present, 100,000 years or so younger than the Dmanisi *H. erectus* remains. More *H. erectus* remains in the same region of Lantian County near to Xi'an in China are somewhat more recent, with the oldest at around 1 million years BP with the most recent dating to about 530,000BP. The brain size of these is about 780cc, similar to the contemporary Java Man.

Another site in Asia which has revealed very early *H. erectus* fossils is Yuanmou in China's Yunnan province, where the remains have been dated to about 1.7 million years BP, but there is some disagreement over the dating, with conflicting dates given of just 1 million years BP. A date of 1.7 million years is not improbable, allowing the descendants of Dmanisi and the Levant 100,000 years to cover the 6,500km between the two making an average speed of just 13km/year.

Despite the relative paucity of *H. erectus* remains in Asia, a clear picture emerges of the general *H. erectus* story in Asia. Having arrived in Eastern Europe some *H. erectus* migrated eastwards. This group took no longer than 100,000 years to reach China, where they lived for 1.4 million years, slowly evolving, and spreading out further to more distant regions such as Indonesia. During this period the general *H. erectus* evolution of increasing brain size which occurred elsewhere, is mirrored. The older specimens, and earliest of the Asian *H. erectus* remains display brain sizes at the lower end of the *H. erectus* range of less than 800cc. During over 700,000 years of evolution the brain size increases by over 50% to over 1200cc (within modern brain size range) reaching the upper end of the *H. erectus* range.

So, if *H. erectus* colonized China for over 1.4 million years and arrived from Africa, how did he get there? Currently there are two significant barriers between Eastern Europe and China, the waterless deserts to the North of the Himalayas, and the Himalaya range themselves. One of the most widely accepted theories explaining expansion of humans to China is the southern route via India, which keeps to the South of the Himalayas and avoids the Northern deserts completely. If the Southern route was indeed the main migration route then it would also help to explain the very early dating of *H. erectus* fossils in Java. By comparison, to date there are very few human fossil finds in Central Asia older than 1 million years old. As China invests more time and money into paleoanthropology, perhaps more light will be shed on this question, and it could well be that given how widespread *H.*

erectus had become his migration routes were both to the North and South of the Himalayas.

Passage via India is certainly one possibility. At Attirampakkam on the Kortallayar River, stone tools dating back to 1.5 million years have been found (dated from the context). Curiously, as yet no Homo species bones older than 1 million years have yet been found. On the Soan River in Pakistan, stone tools have been found and dated back to around 2 million years ago, a date which predates the earliest *H. erectus* remains, but frustratingly, remains of the makers of these stone tools are yet to be discovered.

These conclusions for Asia are entirely consistent with the overall picture of *H. erectus* of a resilient, adaptable extremely successful human ancestor who becomes considerably more intelligent and resourceful over his period of existence.

Homo Erectus In The Levant

There is plenty of evidence of early human occupation of the Levant, contemporary almost with the Dmanisi *H. erectus* remains, for example at Ubeidiya to the South of the Sea of Galilee where many thousands of stone tools have been found dating to the period of 1.6 to 1.4 million years ago.

Homo Erectus In Europe

H. erectus emerges as the first human ancestor to extensively populate the old world. He was intelligent and adaptable, thriving equally in the tropical jungles and the great Chinese plains. He was no longer a small mammal prey to the megafauna and terrible carnivores that previously had dominated his world (we will learn more about these terrible creatures in a later chapter); he was an apex predator in his own right, and thrived on the planet for at least 1.4 million years.

We know that even as late as the Roman period, major rivers were still the most important routes across land, such as along the Rhine, the Rhone and the Danube. Large river valleys are usually bordered by wide flat flood plains which make for easy walking; there is always drinking water available both for humans and animals, and resourceful humans can use rivers for transport by sitting on logs heading downstream. They are in effect pre-historic highways, providing the necessities of life: food, drink and also facilitating movement.

From the banks of Lake Turkana, which at various times in its history has been linked to the Nile (seismic movements in the Rift Valley over time have changed the configuration of the upper watershed of the Nile), there is an uninterrupted downhill route following the Nile to the Mediterranean, at which point land travelers can either turn West into the Great Western Desert, or more readily follow the fertile shoreline of the Levant, arriving eventually in Turkey. To the North of Turkey is Dmanisi, and draining to the South East is the Euphrates a corridor of over 3,000km traversing modern day Syria and Iraq and leading to the Persian Gulf, Iran, and eventually India. On the eastern side of India is the Brahmaputra River which gives access to China.

We can join the dots of the earliest *H. erectus* remains, in what may well turn out to be the likely first radiation of *H. erectus* from the Rift Valley. From Lake Turkana, he follows the Nile to the Mediterranean, round the shore, eastwards for 300km or to the Levant, where early *H. erectus* remains have been found. Expansion directly to the East from the Levant would have been limited by the Syrian and Iraqi deserts, so further migration would have likely been channeled to Turkey by following the coast.

Early *H. erectus* remains uncovered to date in Turkey date to as early as 1.5 million years ago. From central Turkey he would easily have migrated down the Euphrates to Iraq and further East to Pakistan where stone tools dating to 1.5 million years ago have been found, with the possibility of even more ancient tools dating back to 2 million years ago. Then, from the Indian subcontinent up the Brahmaputra River to China itself, where the earliest *H. erectus* remains as we have seen date to around 1.7 million years ago

If this model of *H. erectus* colonization is roughly accurate, then we may well expect at some time in the future to find *H. erectus* remains dating back to 1.8 million years ago in Turkey, with similar aged discoveries down the Nile, Euphrates and Tigris Rivers, and *H. erectus* remains along the Brahmaputra valley dating back to 1.7 million years ago, thus confirming this putative migration route.

If this was the case, it was only the start of the great *H. erectus* colonization, starting around 2 million years ago and within 200,000 years reaching China, meanwhile spreading over the African and Eurasian landmasses, covering from South Africa in the south to the English Coast (700,000BP) in the north and from Spain in the west to the shores of the Pacific in the east.

Two important questions regarding *H. erectus* are 'when did he finally disappear?', and 'why did he disappear?' Of all the Homo sub-species, *H. erectus* was the longest lived by far, and he was the first to leave his narrow ecological niche in East Africa and spread throughout the old world, adapting readily and evolving according to the local needs. For a human to be so versatile and so resilient, something spectacular must have brought about his demise — that is, if we are to accept that there even was a demise.

Given the very incomplete nature of the archaeological record, we may yet discover very recent fossil remains of *H. erectus*, but amongst the youngest, *H. erectus* are from Algeria around 700,000BP, from China around 230,000 BP and even dates as recent as 140,000 have been suggested. But even more surprising are the dates established by Carl Swisher, following his research on the island of Java. He has dated the strata from which numerous *H. erectus* fossils have been recovered to a period of between 53 and 27,000 BP. These findings have thrown the long-established narrative of *H. erectus* into turmoil, and have caused experts around the globe to resoundingly reject the findings. These dates were obtained by measuring the radioactive decay of uranium in the fossils from when the uranium was absorbed in the living tissue, the science is solid, and so long as the *H. erectus* fossils died within the same horizon as the dated material, then the evidence would seem to be as reliable as any in the palaeoarcheological world.

So, what is so exceptional about Java that allowed *H. erectus* to survive there for at least 200,000 years longer than anywhere else? The geography of Indonesia may reveal some clues. Java, Sumatra and Indonesia as a whole were part of a land mass attached to South East Asia, known as Sundaland from about 2.6 million years ago. The current land area of Sundaland is about half of its maximum size when the sea levels were at their lowest. This would have allowed *H. erectus* to walk there without crossing any large bodies of water when he reached South East Asia around 1.6 million years ago. As with the rest of the old world he continued to thrive and slowly evolve there for the next 1.5 million years. Even at the greatest extent of Sundaland, it was never connected to the Australian land mass, due to the deep water channels between Java and New Guinea known as the Wallace Line. New Guinea itself was at times connected to Australia forming a continent known as Sahul.

As global sea levels rose and fell over the last 2 million years, mainly as a result of glaciations (huge quantities of sea water being trapped on land in the form of ice caps), so the coastline of Sundaland changed. During the last glacial maximum just 20,000 years ago global sea levels were as much as 200 meters lower than today. But a drop of just 40 meters in sea level is enough to expose a land bridge linking the Malay Peninsula to Java, Sumatra and Borneo. This indeed was the case for much of the last 800,000 years. Thus, it was only following the retreat of the glaciers starting around 18,000 years ago that Java, Sumatra and Borneo became isolated from the Asian mainland and from each other, and remained that way until today.

How does this help to explain *H. erectus* surviving until such recent prehistory on Java? It would be convenient for Out of Africa exponents if Java had been isolated around 100,000 years ago, thus allowing the Javanese *H.*

erectus to be protected by sea from waves of migrant *H. sapiens* radiating out from Africa. That however didn't happen. But a brief glance at a world map does show Java to be out on a limb from the rest of the Old World, even when the Sundaland land bridges were exposed.

At this point it is worthwhile introducing another small player in the human story. Meet *Homo florensis* or Flores man. He is a 3-foot-high midget, sometimes now known as the hobbit, and thrived from 700,000 BP to just 30,000 years ago on the Island of Flores. He is considered to be one of the variants of *H. erectus* who evolved into a smaller person by the well-established natural process known as island dwarfism, which has seen island living woolly mammoths shrink to the size of small horses. Flores is a narrow island about 300km long towards the eastern end of the Indonesian archipelago, and towards the southern and eastern extremities of the old Sundaland.

Here, right at the uttermost extremity of Sundaland where *H. erectus* made his last stand a dwarf *H. erectus* evolved and thrived for nearly 700,000 years. Both, *H. erectus* and his dwarf cousin disappear from the archaeological record about the same time, not long after modern Sapiens started to colonize Indonesia from 45,000BP onwards.

It would seem clear that *H. erectus* in Sundaland was replaced by modern humans during a period of transition between 45,000 BP to 30,000 BP.

But traditions live on of midget humans surviving in the Indonesian Jungle. Tribes in Sumatra insist that their forest is inhabited by a rare small human they refer to as orang pendek, and there are very many firsthand accounts of encounters with orang pendek, not only by Indonesians but also by Europeans. However, there are no reliable photographs and no recent skeletal remains to validate the claims. Orang pendek is not recognized by science. In the early 20th century Dutch colonists also record similar descriptions of orang pendek. Debbie Martyr spent 15 years in Sumatra searching for orang pendek and despite not being able to provide the world with incontrovertible evidence, she states that she has seen the creature on several occasions.

Orang pendek is described as being about 1m tall (the same as *Homo florensis*) being covered in thick gray-brown hair, with a distinctly human looking face. Interestingly his head is described as sloping back to a crest, similar in form to a gorilla's (known as a sagittal crest), and he has a prominent brow arch as does *H. erectus*. The mouth is described as small and neat with oddly broad incisors and long canine teeth. He has broad shoulders, a deep chest, and powerful arms. His feet appeared to be splayed to an angle of about 45 degrees.

The description of orang pendek is more than a little suggestive of a close relation to *Homo florensis*, and given how recent the remains of *H. florensis* are in evolutionary terms, it is not in the least surprising that some close relatives still survive in very remote environments where modern humans are not numerous.

The description of the brow ridge and the sagittal crest are also interesting. The brow ridge is a characteristic of the *H. erectus* skull, whereas the sagittal crest is found in orangutans, and also in some chimpanzees and other more recent human ancestors such as the australopithecines. The sagittal crest running along from front to back on the top of the skull following the sagittal suture has a functional role, that is to anchor very strong jaw muscles from the mandible, and is also present amongst some of the powerful jawed dinosaurs for the same reason. The sagittal crest is consistent with the descriptions of large strong teeth in orang pendek.

If ever we do get to identify and study an orang pendek, he may well be able to help us fill in some of the open questions on the appearance of *H. erectus*.

Out of Africa protagonists use the late presence and partial isolation of *H. erectus* on Java as proof of their theory. Their reasoning being that modern humans arriving from Africa out competed *H. erectus* in the same evolutionary niche, and within just 15,000 years from their arrival had caused the total extinction of *H. erectus*. Alternative explanations are just as plausible. Java is close to the equator, with a tropical climate similar in many ways to equatorial Africa where *H. erectus* evolved and thrived for well over a million years. The lack of freezing winters and steady annual temperatures reduced his need for clothing. Food was readily available throughout the year, with prey being sedentary and plentiful in the forest. The need to evolve which caused so many changes in temperate zones was not present in Java. Thanks to the relative isolation of Java, and its stable climate, *H. erectus* was able to exist well beyond the date of his close relatives on the Asian mainland and in Africa. Only the late arrival of modern humans, wherever they may have originated from with their more sophisticated means of communication, tools and way of life, filling the same ecological niche, left little room for *H. erectus*.

The disappearance of *H. erectus* on Java may well be the blue print for the disappearance of *H. erectus* elsewhere, or it may not. The crucial difference between Java and elsewhere is that *H. erectus* did not need to evolve on Java before the arrival of modern humans, he was perfectly adapted to the conditions which being tropical, remained more or less stable. This was not the case further to the North, and that is where things become very interesting.

The existence of so many different forms of *H. erectus* (Java man, Peking man, *Homo ergaster*, *Homo gautengensis* (from South Africa), *Homo rudolfensis* (Kenya) and *Homo georgicus* and the need for the term *H. erectus* sensu latu, is testament to the way a previously tropical adapted species had evolved to fit into different environments around the world over an immense span of time. In addition, his brain capacity had evolved from barely 600cc in the early days to twice that size in some later cases showing that *H. erectus* mental capacity had increased immensely over that same period.

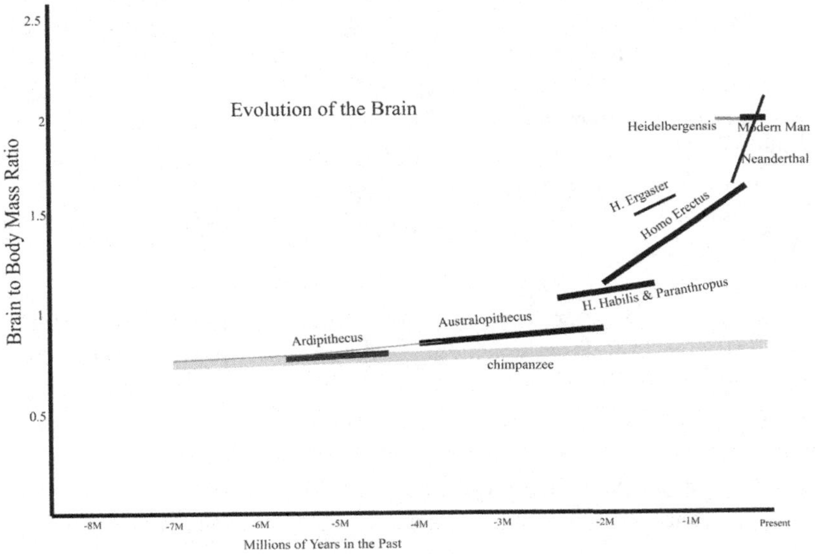

Illustration 14. Evolution of the brain

The graph above shows just how *H. erectus* mental capacity increased dramatically, at a far faster rate than had ever previously occurred in human evolution.

So did *H. erectus* die out like the dinosaurs, after having spread out over Africa, Europe and Asia for well over 1 million years? Understanding the answer to that question is crucial for resolving what was to occur later in human evolution and remains a hotly debated and acrimonious subject.

As *H. erectus* adapted to different environments around the world he changed over vast periods of time, as we have seen, to the extent that some experts debate whether some of the *H. erectus* variants are indeed *H. erectus* at all.

These changes were particularly apparent the further away from his tropical homeland that *H. erectus* migrated to. Surviving in a colder climate, hunting different species require a whole new skill set. Keeping warm was no longer a matter of shivering around the camp fire, it was a matter of life and death, which required careful planning, changes in lifestyle and new measures. We will look at these in greater detail later on.

Species living in colder climates adapt their morphology, their pilosity (hairiness), the amount of body fat that they need for insulation. In order to survive in a cold climate, he needed to make big changes and those changes were reflected in his skeletal remains. *H. erectus* evolved so much that he was no longer *H. erectus* any more, he became, in cold Europe, *H. neanderthalis*.

At this point it's worth reminding ourselves of the nomenclature used to attach labels to species. In the case of *H. erectus*; Homo refers to the genus, which is considered to have started with *H. habilis* but which we now know should also include others such as *Ardipicanthus*.

H. erectus is the name of the species, the definition from the encyclopedia Britannica being: "a classification comprising related organisms that share common characteristics and are capable of interbreeding."

Taxonomic labels are well suited for static situations, but have their limitations in relatively fast changing (in evolutionary terms) situations. Would a *H. erectus* with a brain of 600cc have been able to breed with one of 1200cc? Would a *H. erectus* from 2 million years ago be able to breed successfully with one of just 50,000 years ago? Maybe, or maybe not. The implication of the *H. erectus* species label is that an *H. erectus* would not have been able to breed with *H. Neanderthalensis*, but as Neanderthal evolved out of *H. erectus* that is clearly not the case. Over thousands of years by small steps changes occurred, probably imperceptibly to the people at the time. But looking from a distance of thousands of years we can perceive those differences in the fossil record. Men with more Neanderthal like features would have had children with women displaying more *H. erectus*-like features and vice versa.

This gradual process of change occurred around the world for all the *H. erectus* populations in all their regional diversity.

In Europe, that process of change was accelerated by the cold climate which *H. erectus* a species evolved in the warm winter-free climate of the tropics was ill-adapted for. The result of that change in Europe was Neanderthal.

But how did that disappearance of *H. erectus* occur? Was it simply a species that couldn't compete with Neanderthal in these challenging conditions? Or was it that the two merged? We can see that the traits of Neanderthal become finer over the ages. Neanderthal didn't just appear out of thin air. We know that *H. erectus* evolved into Neanderthal. So, *H. erectus* was indeed changing, adapting to the conditions. In Europe and around the advancing glaciers, Neanderthal was simply an adaptation of *H. erectus* to the Ice Age conditions.

If this is indeed so, why didn't it happen, in China and South East Asia? The answer is simple, they didn't have the same extreme climate to adapt to, although undoubtedly in South East Asia *H. erectus* was adapting to local conditions. Conditions which were probably less extreme, and far less cold.

So, for the first time, in broad terms, around 500,000 BP we see a divergence in DNA between Homo species in Eastern Asia and Europe. In both regions, he's still basically an *H. erectus*, but his DNA is diverging, and his evolution has changed so fast in Europe and the Near East we've given him a new name Neanderthal.

In Central Asia, these two 'species' will have mixed yet again, causing a blurring of the DNA edges.

If we're looking for differences between say a man from China and a man from Scandinavia, we already have the roots of those differences firmly established.

THE EVOLUTION OF THE HUMAN BRAIN

One of the gauges together with stone tool technology which allows us to measure humanity's divergence from the animal kingdom is the volume of human ancestors' crania and therefore brain size and from that general intellectual capacity. The graph below demonstrates that progress with time along the horizontal axis and brain to body mass on the vertical scale. The brain to body mass ratio is a way of assessing the power of a brain taking into account the size of the body that it has to control.

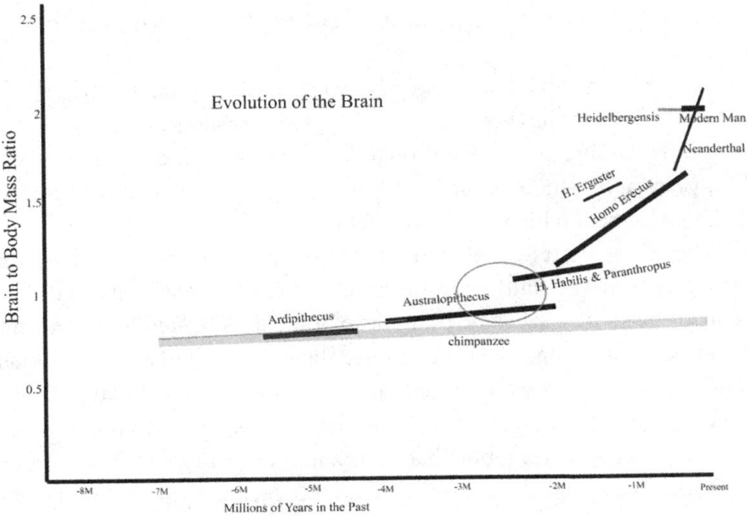

Illustration 15 Evolution of the brain in human ancestors

Because the brain processes information from the nervous system throughout the body, the larger the body the greater the size of the brain required. This ratio is considered to be particularly inaccurate when comparing different species with their different morphologies. For example, field mice appear disproportionately brainy, because of their small size. If, as many do, we were simply to plot the size of the brain over the millennia, it would produce a very misleading story, as the size of our ancestors' bodies increased considerably, which in itself gave rise to an increase in brain size without necessarily reflecting an increase in general intelligence. However, if we use brain size as a ratio of overall body size then we obtain a measure of change in intellectual capacity. As we move up the vertical scale of the graph, we are looking at increasingly intelligent beings. It is a reasonable method of comparing brain size and thus intelligence within a genus, but it also tells us a lot more about the evolution of our species as we shall see in following chapters.

The graph shows with surprising clarity how *Ardipithecus* who had only recently diverged from the common ancestor with the chimpanzee had about the same general degree of intelligence as the latter. Whereas the chimpanzee's brain evolved only slightly over the last 7 million years we see a considerable differentiation beginning to appear by the time *Australopithecus* arrives on the scene. It looks like there is almost a smooth progression between *Ardipithecus* and the later *Australopithecus*, which tells us that there are no important missing links in the fossil record between the two despite a time lapse of several hundred thousand years in the currently available fossil record.

Next, we see a considerable step between *Australopithecus* and *H. habilis* despite the fact that the two overlap in history. This suggests that something important is missing in our evolutionary record around the time period of 2.5 million years ago, which ties in with the theory put forward by Fred Spoor regarding AL-666-1 which we looked at earlier.

Either some better developed *Australopithecus* remain to be discovered or some primitive *H. habilis* are yet to be discovered. *Paranthropus* tells us little more as he shares the same brain development as *H. habilis* over a similar time period, which suggests that despite the various dietary adaptations in teeth and jaws that *paranthropus* was probably quite closely related to *H. habilis*. We can also see that *H. habilis*'s intelligence continues to improve at the same rate as his ancestors, but that he is a markedly more intelligent being. The obvious reason for this as we have already seen is the mental challenges required in using his newly freed up hands to manufacture tools and plan ahead. Far more bodily coordination was required for tool manufacture and we can also imagine that his communicative skills were also improving being the lexicon of grunts employed by the last common ancestor.

Then, *H. erectus* breaks onto the scene, and brain development increases at a faster rate than ever before and over a longer period (by human evolutionary standards). The graph is suggestive of *H. erectus* evolving from *H. habilis*, half the way through *H. habilis*' existence. This in turn suggests that there was a significant evolutionary split around 2 million years ago, with *H. erectus* suddenly branching out from a subset of his *H. habilis* ancestors and becoming very quickly more developed and intelligent, while at the same time leaving a group of *H. habilis* behind to continue on their slow and steady growth (probably remaining in a stable habitat), before disappearing from the fossil record about 1.4 million years ago. One reasonable explanation for *H. habilis*' final disappearance is that while *H. erectus* was spreading around the old world and throughout Asia, he was also spreading into *H. habilis* heartland, but after nearly a quarter of a million years of separate evolution he was easily equipped to out compete *H. habilis* in *H. habilis*' own back yard. The final disappearance of *H. habilis* may also have been, like in so many other cases of human evolution, one of general absorption into the *H. erectus* population by interbreeding.

Then the graph shows another significant gap around 600,000 years ago, as *H. erectus* begins to disappear and Neanderthal and *heidelbergensis* appear on the scene. Both of whom appear with a very powerful brain. *H. ergaster* does nothing to help explain this gap, indeed *H. ergaster* appears out on a limb, and to be a locally adapted intelligent cousin of *H. erectus* (yet another member of the *H. erectus* sensu latu family), which is probably exactly what he is.

Heidelbergensis and *Neanderthalensis*, however, appear to be almost identical in brain development, which must raise the question, how different are they really? This point raised by the brain development graph has also and independently caused some experts to refer to *heidelbergensis* as the muddle in the middle.

Then, finally we see that modern humans appear with a very slight brain underdevelopment compared to Neanderthal. The difference is fractional, and probably of very little practical difference, other than possibly related to reduced visual cortex processing in modern humans. As we shall see in a later chapter the graph is telling us that there are some serious questions to ask about the long-established view on Neanderthal. Indeed, the graph shows just how the long-held belief of Neanderthal as being a stupid ape, is so far from the truth.

Homo heidelbergensis

Otherwise known disparagingly as the 'muddle in the middle', *H. heidelbergensis* is a relative newcomer to be discovered with most of the fossils dating to the last 30 years or so. His fossils date to as far back as 600,000BP, possibly even 100,000 years earlier and disappear from the fossil record around 200,000BP. His very existence as a species remains debatable. It is generally agreed that he evolved out of *H. erectus*.

Skeletal remains labeled as *Homo heidelbergensis* have been found in Africa (South Africa, Ethiopia and Namibia) and Europe (Spain, Italy, France, England Hungary and Greece) and Asia even as far distant as China, with the earliest ones being found in Africa. One of the earliest skulls attributed to *heidelbergensis* possibly is the Bodo Cranium found in the Awash River Valley in Ethiopia and dated to around 600,000BP. The brain size being typical for *heidelbergensis* at 1250cc. Interestingly, it would seem from cut marks, that the skull was scalped very soon after death. But there is still doubt about the official attribution of this specimen as *H. erectus* or *heidelbergensis*.

At Boxgrove in England two pieces of hominin tibia and some teeth together with hundreds of Acheullean flint hand axes were found and dated to around 500,000 BP. These remains are known as Boxgrove Man, although there is some doubt that it was a man at all. But it is considered that the individual was heavily built, weighing around 90Kg, aged around 40 and measuring roughly 1m85. This specimen is attributed to *H. heidelbergensis* purely on dating alone and not to any differentiating characteristics from Neanderthal.

Most skeletal remains, (indeed over 90%) originally attributed to *heidelbergensis* are found in a cave in Northern Spain called Sima de los Huesos. Here, over 5,000 bones from over 32 individuals dating to around 350,000 BP have been found together with an Acheulean hand axe, bear bones and other carnivore bones. In 2016, nuclear DNA analysis attributed these remains to Neanderthal which significantly weakens the presence of *heidelbergensis* in the record.

A physical description of *heidelbergensis* is tricky to nail down. Some researchers consider that he was a human giant with a height of over 2m. Others consider that his average height was under 1m75, with females under 1m60. There is general acceptance that his brain size was 1,250cc, right at the top end of *H. erectus* brain sizes. *H. heidelbergensis* teeth appear to be markedly smaller than *H. erectus* teeth and the canines less pronounced, showing a significant step towards modern human teeth. The original species name was given to a mandible found in 1908 by Otto Shoetensack near Heidelberg in Germany, at a time when clearer details of human ancestors of the period were still little understood.

Some paleoanthropologists remain convinced that *H. heidelbergensis* evolved in Africa and migrated into Europe and Asia, as one of the Out of Africa hypotheses, but there is no hard evidence to support this.

H. heidelbergensis, the muddle in the middle, is a very clear example of the confusion caused when one clearly identifiable species evolves into another. Naturally during a phase of transition, the features tell a mixed picture, some archaic features and some modern features. Indeed, many researchers believe that the very term *heidelbergensis* is purely arbitrary and that point of view seems to hold the most merit.

In reality *heidelbergensis* is the final phase of development or transition of *H. erectus* in his 2 million year long period of evolution in both Africa and Europe. By 600,000 BP *H. erectus* in Europe was evolving into Neanderthal and the Sima de Los Huesos typify that transition. But if *heidelbergensis* has caused some warm debate among paleoanthropologists and archaeologists, then it is only the opening act for the full-blown spats which erupt when dealing with Neanderthal, as we shall see.

Neanderthals

It is unclear when exactly Neanderthals first appeared. Some suggest 600,000 BP some use a date of 200,000 BP, the vagueness being dependent on how one classifies a Neanderthal. *H. Neanderthalensis* evolved out of *H. erectus* either directly or via a transitional form known as *Homo heidelbergensis*.

We can be fairly certain that the species we call *H. erectus* co-existed with the species that we call Neanderthals over some of the latter's geographical domain for over 200,000 years. The current theory is that *H. erectus* evolved into *H. Neanderthalensis*. If we look at what was happening on the ground at any given place in Eurasia between, say 150,000BP and 100,000BP, we have substantial numbers of *H. Neanderthalensis* and *H. erectus* competing for the same food, water sources and shelter. These species were so close that *H. erectus* is considered to have evolved into *Neanderthalensis*.

It is inevitable that these closely related species sharing the same space for almost unimaginably long periods of time interbred, creating hybrids, which if not sterile would again have interbred. So, we have a gradual merging of species over a great period of time, with the surviving traits being those best adapted to the local environment.

But although *H. erectus* was present at some point in time throughout the entirety of the Neanderthals' domains, *H. Neanderthalensis* never spread as far as *H. erectus*. So, during the period of time from the appearance of *H. Neanderthalensis*, say 500,000 BP to the disappearance of *H. erectus* from Eurasia around 70,000BP, we have a range of variations from pure *H. erectus* in East and South East Asia to various combinations of *H. Neanderthalensis* and *H. erectus* in Europe and western Asia. Here we have a split in species types. In China and South East Asia we have a continuation of the pure *H. erectus* line continuing to evolve on its own for at least 1.5 million years.

By contrast, in Europe and Western Asia we have a changing population in a fast-changing climate, with more mixing of different genes and faster adaption to conditions as a result. And changes there certainly were in Europe and Western Asia during this period of the mixing of the genes and adaptation.

The Riss Ice Age started in 300,000 BP and lasted until 130,000BP. Then again, the Wurm (otherwise known as Weichselian) Ice Age started somewhere around 115,000BP and lasted until roughly 11,000 BP. The Riss covered most of northern Europe, half of Britain, and an area covering the Alps. An area of permafrost extended beyond these boundaries. Thus, for 170,000 years or so the mixing populations of *H. erectus* and *H. Neanderthalensis* were challenged by extreme cold, reduction in the amount of available food, and had to adapt to these extremely harsh conditions to survive. The Wurm Ice Age covered a similar geographical territory to the Riss.

No wonder that in the midst of these Ice Ages, we find the invention of the sewing needle to attach pieces of skin to one another to form clothing and protection from the cold. The body louse, which specifically lives in clothing rather than on the skin, seems to have evolved from the head louse around 107,000BP.

From the onset of the Ice Age 130,000 BP we have *H. erectus* and *H. Neanderthalensis* present in extremely challenging conditions in Europe and parts of Asia. Extremely cold temperatures, spreading ice sheets, permafrost, competition for shelter in the caves from animals easily capable of killing man. We have seen that the cold caused genetic changes to woolly mammoths, as it must have done for *H. erectus* and *H. Neanderthalensis*. Conservation of energy favored the Neanderthal type of body, more compact and more efficient energy-wise. And so, we have by 70,000BP after 50,000 years of extremely cold weather the elimination of *H. erectus* in Europe; from then on the Neanderthal reigned.

The name is evocative, it conjures up an image of a brutal caveman covered in matted hair, missing a few teeth, carrying a heavy club and issuing deep grunts like a gorilla. An image created by an accretion of over a century of prejudice. But what do we really know about Neanderthals?

H. erectus had been living in Europe and Asia for over 1 million years by the time the earliest fossil finds attributed to the species *H. neanderthalis* make their appearance. During this vast swathe of time, *H. erectus* had been adapting to a life outside of his native Africa. At times parts of Europe were not dissimilar to Africa with Hippos bathing in the River Rhine, rhinoceros grazing the plains and so on. But over this period of time the climate varied enormously, Ice Ages appeared and life became very different indeed from equatorial Africa. During these times *H. erectus* was well outside of his natural environment. Since well before *Ardipithecus* the Homo genus had evolved in a tropical climate. For the first time European *H. erectus* had to cope with a world covered in ice and snow. He had to change to survive, and change he did.

Illustration 16. Model of Neanderthal

The earliest Neanderthal-like fossils date back to around 650,000 BP, these are fossils which appear more similar to *H. Neanderthalensis* than to *H. erectus*. Sometimes these early Neanderthals are referred to as *Homo heidelbergensis* as if they were a separate species, rather than simply a species in transition. Currently there appears to be a gap in the fossil record between 300,000 and 243,000BP in which there are no Neanderthal fossils. There is general consensus that all fossil humans between than 243,000BP and roughly 35,000BP are considered to be Neanderthals. But this is more a matter of book keeping than of science. The advantage is that a convenient label can be attached to a fossil specimen without endless worrying about whether one feature or another in a mixed bag of characteristics entitles that fossil to an entirely different classification.

As we have seen in the *heidelbergensis* chapter, the typical *H. erectus* form of hominid in Europe started to evolve towards the Neanderthal type probably from about 800,000 BP and that evolution continued right throughout the existence of Neanderthals, including the period referred to as classic Neanderthals about 100,000 years ago (at which time the Neanderthal characteristics are considered typical of the species) up until around 30,000 years ago.

From the outset, it should be pointed out that study of Neanderthals is a fast-changing subject. Very many conclusions about Neanderthals taken as established fact in the last century have been proved inaccurate. Experts in the subject still alive today have seen their theories disproved, and there is still considerable debate over much of the area of Neanderthal study. Professional reputations, university chairs etcetera are at stake.

But what did Neanderthals look like? A single description of Neanderthal must be made with caution, as over the half a million years of his existence and over his geographical range he changed considerably. But there are features which are considered to be classical Neanderthal.

Perhaps the most important feature of Neanderthals was his brain, in the largest fossil specimens it was as large as 1700cc with an average of around 1600cc, being considerably bigger than our own. Males weight averaged around 77Kg and females around 66Kg, with respective average heights of around 1m66 and 1m54. Not very different from modern European populations, nor from the supposed *heidelbergensis*. The brain to weight ratio however is considerably greater. About 2.3% for male Neanderthals compared to about 1.4% for Caucasian males. So, from the outset we can dismiss the idea that Neanderthals were stupid, brutal cavemen with inferior intelligence to ourselves. Not so long ago it was considered that Neanderthals weren't even capable of speech because of the lack of fossil evidence of the small hyoid bone, considered essential for mastering the muscles of the larynx and tongue. Neanderthal hyoid bones have recently been uncovered, thus laying that argument to rest. But even without that discovery, the earlier chapters of this book, together with over 6 million years of evolution during which the brain size had grown to over three times its original size to a volume even greater than our own, it would be inconceivable that the Neanderthal was not from the outset of his appearance a master of vocal communication. He had language skills every bit the equal to our own.

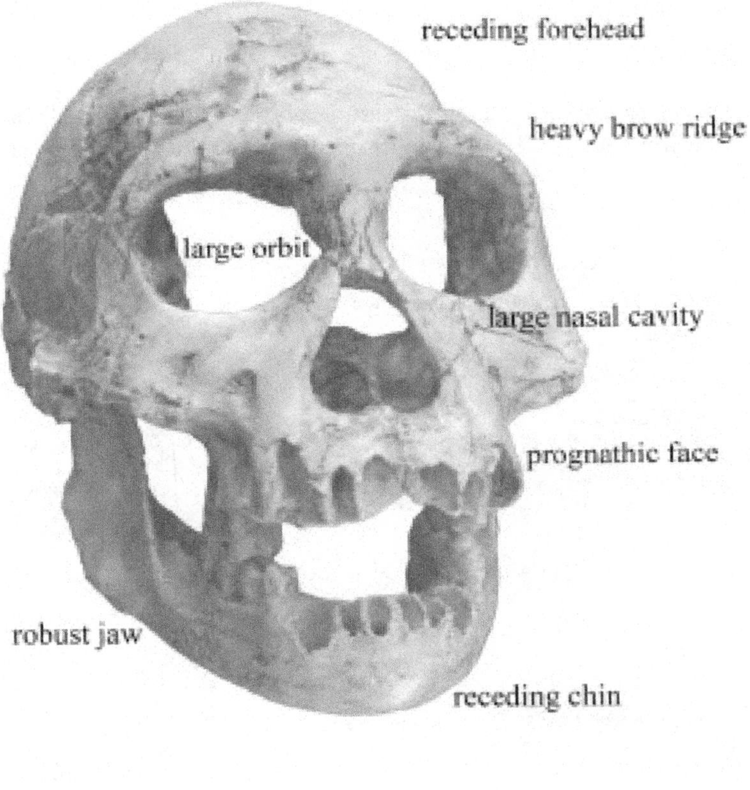

Neanderthals were muscular beings with stronger arms and hands than ours, which reflected no doubt the very physical needs of his daily life. And to some people the image of the jock athlete implies intellectual inadequacy. He had a powerful barrel chest, accommodating in all probability a powerful pair of lungs, filled via great air vents for nostrils. His facial appearance was similar to some robust people of European extraction today, a large head with a large nose, noticeable brow ridge and slightly receding chin and forehead. He had light skin, with often fair or red hair. Forensic reconstructions of Neanderthals dressed in modern clothes and given a clean shave have been made and they wouldn't particularly stand out in a crowd.

Closer examination of the typical Neanderthal skeleton do reveal features that are considered to be archaic and not common in the skeletons of modern Europeans. Let's start with the Neanderthal skull, with its large cranium.

Neanderthal Skull

This picture shows the salient features of the Neanderthal skull viewed from the front, followed by a comparison of Neanderthal and modern skulls.

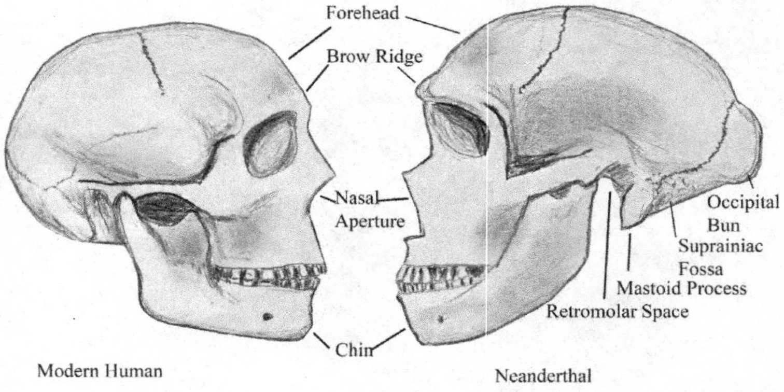

Illustration 18. Modern human and Neanderthal skulls

Comparison of the modern human (left) and the Neanderthal skulls (right), with labels showing the key differences.

During the period of Neanderthal evolution the size of the cranium increased considerably.

Specimen	Group	Cranial Capacity
Early European Neanderthal		
Ehringsdorf H		1450
Blache-St Vaast		1200
Lazaret		1250
Krapina 3		1255
Krapina 6		1205
Saccopastore 1		1245
Saccopastore 2		1300
Ganovce		1320
Guattari 1		1360
MEAN		1278
European Ice Age Neanderthal		
Engis 2		1362
Spy 1		1305
Spy 2		1553
La Chapelle-aux-Saints		1625
La Ferassie 1		1640
Neandertal 1		1525
La Quina 5		1172
La Quina 18		1200
Gibraltar		1400
Le Moustier 1		1565
MEAN		1350
West Asian Neanderthal		
Tabun C1		1271
Amud 1		1740

Shanidar 1		1600
Shanidar 5		1550
Teshik Tash		1525
MEAN		1540
Transitional		
Cro-Magnon 1		1730
Cro-Magnon 3		1590
La Chancellade		1530
Combe Chapelle		1570
Cap Blanc		1434
Bruniquel 2		1555
Predmosti 3		1580
Predmosti 4		1250
Brno 2		1600
Mladec 5		1650
Dolni Vestonice 14		1538
Dolni Vestonice 16		1547
Pavlov		1472
Sungir 1		1464
MEAN		1504
West Asian Transitional		
Skhul 1		1450
Skhul 4		1554
Qafzeh 6		1600
Qafzeh 9		1508
MEAN		1554
Modern human		
MEAN		1195

Illustration 19. Evolution of cranial capacity Neanderthal/ transitional/modern human

Credit: Data Sourced From Holloway, Holloway Et Al, Vicke And Vadermeersch

Supraorbital Ridge

The bony ridge over the Neanderthal eyes known variously as the brow ridge, the supraorbital ridge or supercillary arch is very noticeable in all primates, whereas in modern humans although present, is far less prominent. In modern humans it is located just above the eyebrows and is even less visible in women than in men, but within certain ethnic groups around the world it is more noticeable and it is more visible in certain individual Europeans than others. Within modern human populations the ethnic group with the largest brow ridges are the Australoids, followed by ethnic Europeans. Mongolids have imperceptible brow ridges in both sexes — although, interestingly, the Japanese also display prominent brow ridges.

The supercillary arch serves as a mechanical reinforcement to the skull, protecting it from stresses and fractures caused by the forces involved in chewing and biting with powerful jaw muscles. As the role of the jaw in tearing meat was reduced by the use of tools, so the jaw became less massive as we can see in the drawing above, and so the need for such bony structural reinforcement decreased. During the whole period of Neanderthal existence, they used increasingly efficient tools for both processing food and fashioning weapons. Over that period the robustness of their jaws diminished as did the supercillary arch.

The continued presence in Europeans and Australoids shows that the ancestral need for powerful jaws has not yet evolved away, and suggests the relative proximity in time of Neanderthal and *H. erectus* ancestors. In Europeans, the presence of the supraorbital ridge is an inherited trait from the Neanderthals, whereas in Australoids it is inherited more directly from *H. erectus* who only disappeared from South East Asia 30,000 years or so ago, which explains why they have the most prominent Supraorbital ridges in the world.

Forensic anthropologist Caroline Wilkenson said that australoids have the largest brow ridges, almost similar in size to that in caucasoids, "with moderate to large supraorbital ridges", caucasoids have the second largest brow ridges with "moderate to large supraorbital ridges". Caucasoids usually have a sloped forehead when the brow ridge is prominent. Negroids have the third largest brow ridges with an "undulating supraorbital ridge" and mongoloids are "absent brow ridges". Anthropologist Ashley Montagu said mongoloids are "absent brow ridges" and he said "such ridges are absent in the skulls of both sexes in Mongoloid peoples." Dr. Marta Mirazon Lahr of the Department of Biological Anthropology at Cambridge University said the "Paleoindian" has "proto-Mongoloid" "morphology" such as "pronounced development of supraorbital ridges" Anthropologist Arnold Henry Savage Landor described the Ainu from Japan as having deep-set eyes and large and prominent brow ridges.

Anthropologist Carleton S. Coon linked brow ridge prominence to other masculine skeletal traits and hairiness when he said, "brow ridges, and other bony excrescences of a hyper masculine nature, are closely linked with excessive pilous development of the body and beard, and with a tendency to baldness. Europeans, on the whole, are among the hairiest-bodied and heaviest-bearded groups of men, being equaled or exceeded only by the Australians and the Ainu. Both negroid and mongoloid skin conditions are inimical to excessive hair development except upon the scalp." Coon said that in "modern Finns" "brow ridges are usually only slightly developed."

(Coon, Carleton S. 153)

Pilosity

Peoples from around the world have very different amounts of body hair, whose presence is also significantly different between the sexes. The three racial groups with the most body hair are Europeans, the Ainu people and Australoids. Mongolids and negroids have very little body hair. There are a wide range of theories for the presence and absence of body hair in humans. Our remote ancestors were every bit as hairy as say a gorilla or a chimpanzee, but at some point in our history our hairiness decreased and to a differing degree between races, with women losing more hair than men.

Hair in mammals serves a very necessary purpose in thermo-regulating our bodies. As warm-blooded animals, mammals need to control their body temperature very precisely, and body hair helps to do this. There are several mechanisms that help us to thermo-regulate, amongst them the action of arector pili muscles which contract causing what we know as goose-bumps and raising body hairs which act together to trap a layer of insulating air around the skin, which in turn reduces loss of body heat. As bipeds most of our heat loss occurs through our heads, just as houses lose most of their heat through an uninsulated roof. So, humans as the only fully bipedal mammals produce far more hair on their heads than any other of the primates to ensure an optimal level of thermal insulation.

Hairs in other mammals are useful in the dark as extended touch sensors, and that is the function of eyelashes, giving advanced warning to the eyelid to close to protect the eyeball from physical damage.

Also, hairs in mammals act to protect the skin from damage from solar radiation. In mammals such as hippos, which possess hardly any body hair, this skin protection is achieved by exuding a reddish liquid which acts as a kind of sun screen. All other primates are quadrupeds, most of their bodies excluding the soles of their feet are exposed to the sun, whereas for bipeds the tops of the heads are mostly exposed to the sun. Once more, plenty of hair on the head protects us humans from ultra-violet radiation.

There is one more important role for hair in humans and that is how it affects our appearance. Hair color changes depending on genetic inheritance. Also, hair can be presented in very many differing ways and styles. These factors combine to help associate us with a group or tribe. Hair contributes to our social identity which is very important in a social creature such as the human. Also, hair can be arranged to greatly enhance the appeal of females, a useful ploy in attracting a male, or better still the right male.

Analysis of Neanderthal genes show that they had straighter, thicker hair, which tended to be more oily. This thicker hair helped with insulation in a cold climate, and was passed down to modern ethnic Europeans from the Neanderthals.

Skin Color

Another adaptation to the different conditions in Europe by European *H. erectus* and *H. Neanderthalensis* populations was paler skin. *Ardipithecus* and *H. habilis* had dark skin just like present day native Africans. This dark skin contains a high concentration of melanin which helps to protect the skin from the harmful effects of the tropical sun and simultaneously hinders Vitamin D synthesis. But in more northern latitudes where the sun is weaker, such protection comes at the cost of inhibiting even further the production of Vitamin D. Vitamin D is vital for the body's absorption of calcium necessary for bone growth, magnesium and phosphate, with low Vitamin D levels causing rickets in children and osteomalacia in adults as well as children. Osteomalacia causes the bones to soften increasing the risk of fractures and bending of the spine.

Geneticists have isolated the BNC2 gene which is one of the genes responsible the saturation of skin pigmentation. It is a Neanderthal gene which is present in Euro-Asian populations and in 70% of ethnic Europeans.

Although the initial waves of *H. erectus* 1.8 million years ago would probably have suffered from these diseases, especially as they migrated further north. The process of natural selection would have favored those with less melanin in their skin and so the slow evolution towards pale skinned Europeans started long before the first Neanderthals appeared, particularly in Northern Europe. This preferred selection of pale skin would have been less important for survival in Southern Europe where the power of the sun was still strong. Even with the first *H. erectus* arrivals in Europe 1.8m years ago, a slow divergence started to appear between darker skinned *H. erectus* living in Southern Europe and those with a paler skin in Northern Europe. It is becoming popular to portray Neanderthals with a fair skin and freckles, but that is only true of the northern Neanderthals, southern Neanderthals would have been every bit as dark skinned as Mediterranean peoples today.

Eyes

Looking at a Neanderthal skull, one of the most striking aspects is the sheer size of the eye sockets. They appear huge, and are significantly larger than modern human eyes. Even today amongst modern humans, eye size varies according to population, with the larger eyes belonging to people living closer to the Poles. Statistics show that people from Micronesia have average eye ball volumes of 22millileters, whereas Scandinavians have average eyeball volumes of 27milliliters over 20% larger than equatorial peoples. The reason is simple. The lower the light the larger the eyeball needed to gather enough light to produce a clear image. The largest eyeballs on the planet belong to those creatures which thrive in the deep, dark oceans, in our times the record belongs to the colossal squid with an eyeball diameter of 28cm. The average width of the Neanderthal orbit is 43.4mm compared to an average of 35mm for modern humans. The average eyeball size of early modern Europeans was however very similar to that of the Neanderthals.

The size of the cornea and the retina are limited by the size of the eyeball. The larger eyeball allows for greater sensitivity to light in low levels and greater acuity (i.e., precision) because it allows more light to form an image on the retina. The further north that Neanderthals migrated, the less light was available during the winter days. This was a significant departure compared to African living *H. habilis* and his ancestors as his days were of more or less equal length throughout the year. Without the benefit of refrigerators, and with the need of extra calories for maintaining body heat in the northern winters, northern Neanderthals would have been obliged to hunt in the twilight in which case natural selection would have provided an advantage to those with larger eyeballs. This slow evolution in the size of the eyeball for Neanderthals gave him an added advantage, he could also hunt in the dark, as well occupy deep caves where penetrating light was minimal.

All primates display a direct correlation between the size of the eyeball and the size of the visual cortex required to process the information. This is only to be expected, just as with a camera with more photoreceptors, a more powerful processing chip is required to deal with the extra information supplied by the increased number of photoreceptors. So, we understand why some Neanderthals have larger brains than modern humans: because they had larger eyeballs requiring a larger visual cortex. With the advent of artificial lighting from lamps, the need for larger eyeballs as a survival trait in the long winter months becomes less important, so the eyeball in modern populations has diminished, leading to a greater economy in cerebral resources devoted to image processing.

Eye color depends on the color of the iris, which is composed of two layers the epithelium and the stroma. The epithelium is just two cells deep and contains black-brown pigments. The stroma on the other hand is made up of collagen strands which sometimes contain melanin and sometimes contains excess collagen. It's the make-up of the stroma which controls the eye color. A large amount of melanin in the stroma gives the eyes their dark color and just like for the skin protects them from strong sunlight (a form of natural in-built sun-shade), so that the majority of peoples in the tropics have dark colored eyes. Blue eyes result from a total absence of melanin in the stroma which also have no excess collagen. The blue color is created by the same effect that makes the sky appear blue, the Tyndall Effect. This also has the advantage that the majority of the light falling on the eye also falls on the retina, an ideal situation for people living in low light conditions where the eye has to make do with limited light levels.

Not only have Neanderthals passed their larger eyeballs down to northern populations of modern humans but probably also the eye color. There is no conclusive evidence as yet, but it is more than likely that Northern Neanderthals had predominantly pale colored eyes. Geneticists reckon that it only takes about 10,000 years for human pigmentation changes to be fixed in the DNA. So, this is the sort of adaptation which would have occurred either with the first northern *H. erectus* or very early in the appearance of Neanderthals.

Another interesting aspect of the wide eye orbit which Neanderthals possessed is the width to height ratio, and the falling away of the outside wall of the eye socket (i.e., the right wall of the right eye and the left wall of the left eye). Animals which have forward pointing eyes perceive the world around them by combining and computing the images from both eyes, achieving a simulation of stereoscopic vision in the direction that they are looking, which helps in judging distances for an attack and the knowing the distance of a target allows the hunter to carefully weigh up timing and targeting data. This is a feature of predators such as felids, owls, bears and hominids. Whereas animals which are typically prey species such as bovids, ovids, etcetera have eyes placed on the sides of their heads for nearly all-around vision helping them to detect the advance of a predator. The inconvenience of the forward pointing eyes is that they don't give good lateral vision, essential for example when hunting a herd of large animals which may be dangerous in their own right, and counter attack, on a blind flank as it were. Lateral field of vision also helps considerably when coordinating an attack by several humans. Both early humans and Neanderthals developed an adaptation to enable them to be able to observe to the side almost at the same time as focus on a predator. This shows in the fossil record by measuring the width and the height of the orbit (Broca's Index). In many predators that ratio is close to 1, but with Neanderthals and indeed with modern humans the width is significantly greater than the height enabling the eyeball to swivel from side to side, which increases the field of vision considerably. The combined advantage of this evolutionary development is that eyeball movement from side to side is far quicker than head movement and speed in the hunt is of paramount importance. In addition, eyeball movement is less noticeable to an alert prey animal when stealth is required. Modern populations of humans still preserve to a degree the enhanced Broca's index. That of Europeans, the successors to Neanderthals, is still significantly larger than that of every other population with the exception of Australian Aborigines. Furthermore, the width to height ratio of eye orbits is the highest in humans of any of the primates. In yet another evolutionary development, human eyes protrude more than any other primates, thus further increasing the lateral field of view. With our closest relatives the chimpanzees the eyeballs are clearly sunk deep within the sockets. Studies on modern humans have shown that if something attracts our attention to the side our first instinct is to swing the eyeball around to see what is happening. These lateral eye movements which the wide orbits of the Neanderthals evidence, shows that they had developed into highly specialized hunters.

The map of eye-colors below shows where the areas of eye colors dominate geographically. As we would expect, pale eyes dominate in Northern latitudes where sunlight is less powerful, and equally predictably dark eyes dominate where the sunlight is the strongest and where the eye requires the greatest protection from melanin.

Given that it only takes about 10,000 years for the ideal eye color to adapt to the light levels available, and given that *H. erectus* was lived in parts of Northern Europe not covered by glaciers, and that Neanderthal his descendant lived for an additional half a million years or so in the same areas, then it is only to be expected that both *H. erectus* and Neanderthal had eye colors appropriate to their environment, and given the restrictions caused by glaciers at various periods, the eye color map for Neanderthals was probably similar to the one below.

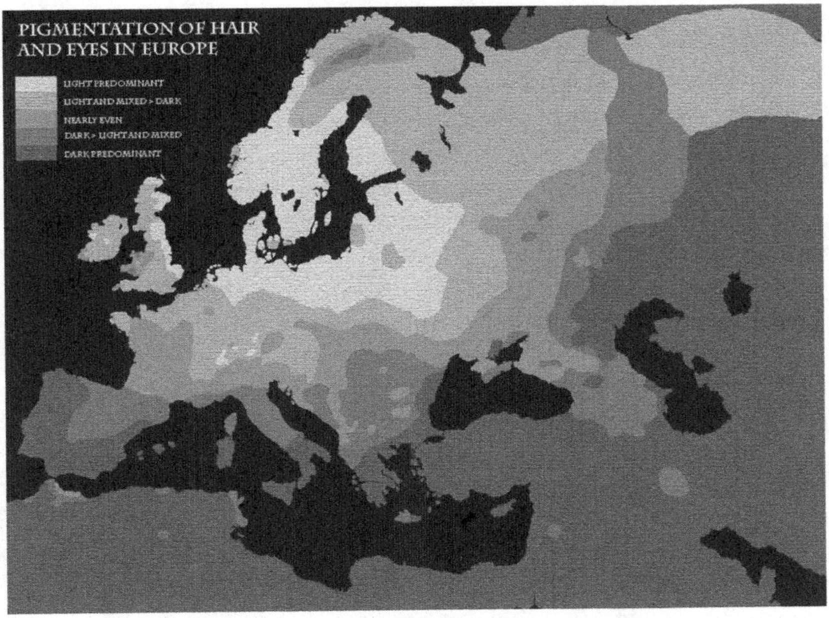

Illustration 20. Pigmentation of hair and eyes in Europe

Credit: Wikimedia Commons, Carleton S. Coon

The above map shows the pigmentation of eyes and hair as a result of research carried out by Carleton S Coon.

Light predominant: includes pure blue and gray eyes (12-16 in the Martin Scale)

Light and mixed: includes blue with gray, green, or gray with blue, light or light admixed with brown (14-12 in the Martin Scale)

Mixed: includes a mixture of light eyes with brown when they are combined in equal amounts (11-7 in the Martin Scale)

Dark Mixed: includes brown with some light coloring (6–5 in the Martin Scale)

Dark includes brown, dark brown or black (4-1 in the Martin Scale)

The combination of light-colored eyes, larger eyeballs and a large visual cortex Neanderthals, particularly northern Neanderthals were particularly well adapted for hunting in crepuscular conditions even during the night.

Chin

Neanderthals have lightly built chins compared to modern humans, but a far stronger mandible. The powerful jaw of the Neanderthal reveals that they still used their teeth as an implement to tear their food, particularly meat. As we shall see later, they were adept at making tools, but this didn't stop them also using their teeth, indeed certain Neanderthal teeth show scratches from tools where they held the meat in the teeth and cut it with stone knives, occasionally leaving scratches in the front teeth made by the tools. Interestingly these marks show that in all the cases studied, Neanderthals were right handed.

As tools become more and more efficient and the role of the teeth lessened, so the need for a stronger jaw diminished, especially as accidentally breaking teeth when exerting too much stress on a piece of tough meat could prove fatal. Using stone knives to cut and prepare meat was a sensible precaution against this potentially fatal mistake.

As the jaw muscles became less powerful, so did the jaw, to the extent that it risked breaking during normal chewing. The chin is a natural reinforcement to a lightly built jaw. But not all modern humans possess the recently evolved strong prominent chin. The old Neanderthal style chin still exists and is referred to as a weak or receding chin, resulting in what is called an overbite, where the upper teeth are unusually further out than the lower teeth. According to the Forensic Anthropology Training Manual, Europeans have more of a tendency of having an overbite than either Africans or Asians, once again revealing their Neanderthal heritage.

Examination of Tutankhamen's skull showed that he not only had a significant receding chin but also an elongated skull of typically Neanderthal shape, and has been classed as of Caucasian origin. We shall have cause later in the book to look at Neanderthal heritage in Egypt.

As we have seen the Neanderthal jaw was far more solid than modern human jaws, it also contained enough space to comfortably accommodate all of his teeth with space to spare behind the last wisdom tooth. As the role of the jaw has changed and it has become less robust it has also shrunk, causing the space available for the same number of teeth to become limited, to such an extent that it is common nowadays for people to have impacted teeth due to overcrowding. For modern Europeans who have a jaw with all four wisdom teeth and room to spare, they may well have a trait inherited from Neanderthals. The Neanderthal jaw was better suited for that number of teeth than our modern jaws.

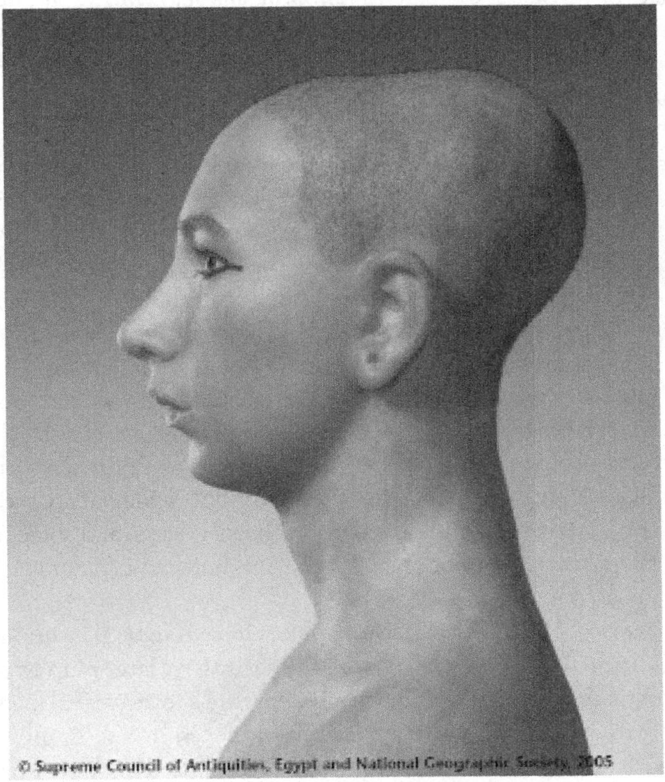

© Supreme Council of Antiquities, Egypt and National Geographic Society, 2005

Illustration 21 Reconstruction of Pharoah Tutankhamen' head

Credit: © Copyright Supreme Council of Antiquities Egypt

Teeth

Evidence from the Krapina Neanderthal site in Croatia show that Neanderthal had similar teeth issues to ourselves and was already using toothpicks to remove bits of lodged food from as early as 130,000BP. Various teeth recovered from the site show signs of toothpick grooves.

Studies of the outer covering on Neanderthal teeth, the dental calculus which accumulates remnants of food which hardens around the tooth have revealed some surprising information about Neanderthal life. Neanderthal living in the Spy Cave in Belgium were revealed to be probably the mostly vegetarian, living off mushroom, pine nuts and other vegetal matter. Whereas one young male from the El Sidon cave in Spain had DNA of a gastric pathogen in his calculus revealing that he was ill, but with that pathogen were traces of poplar bark which contains salicylic acid which contains aspirin, what's more he had traces Penicillium in his plaque. This individual was being treated 100,000 years ago with aspirin and penicillin for his gastric illness. This is the first evidence that we have of humans using natural sourced pain killers for medicinal purposes.

Neanderthal teeth from a wide range of locations have shown a curious phenomenon known as sub-vertical grooves on the facets between molars i.e., where adjacent teeth touch. In many cases these grooves are easily visible running from the crown of the molars in a slightly radial direction towards the root. These grooves have been the object of considerable study. The explanation for these strange grooves seems likely to be caused by intense forces at work in chewing hard vegetal matter. It would seem that the Neanderthal jaw muscles were so powerful that they could crush very hard material with the aid of robust well buttressed teeth, and that some tiny gritty objects were forced in between the molars, where variable compression from one tooth to the next created erosion causing these grooves. Similar grooves have also been observed in other fossil Homo teeth from Africa and some hunter gatherer peoples such as Aboriginal Australians, but are uncommon in most modern human populations.

The shapes of Neanderthal teeth are quite characteristic. The upper incisors are described as shovel shaped, and the molars have large pulp chambers or 'bull-toothed roots'. The image below compares a shovel shaped incisor on the right with a non-shovel shaped incisor on the left. Interestingly, recent studies have revealed that it wasn't only all Neanderthal fossil incisors that were shoveled but also all African fossil incisors of the same age were too. Indeed, it seems that in recent pre-history shoveling appears to have disappeared more quickly in European populations than in African populations. Shoveled incisors were inherited from distant Australopithecine ancestors and have only recently started to disappear.

Neanderthal upper canines are also described as slightly shovel shaped, being convex from top to bottom and from side to side. This is also true of African Homo fossils of the same age, so is not a distinguishing feature. But while early modern African upper canines continue to demonstrate shoveling, only 50% of European upper canines of the same age show shoveling, demonstrating that the early Europeans had developed their own dentition independently to a large degree from the early modern Africans. This is another significant element in the debate in the relevance of the Out of Africa Theory.

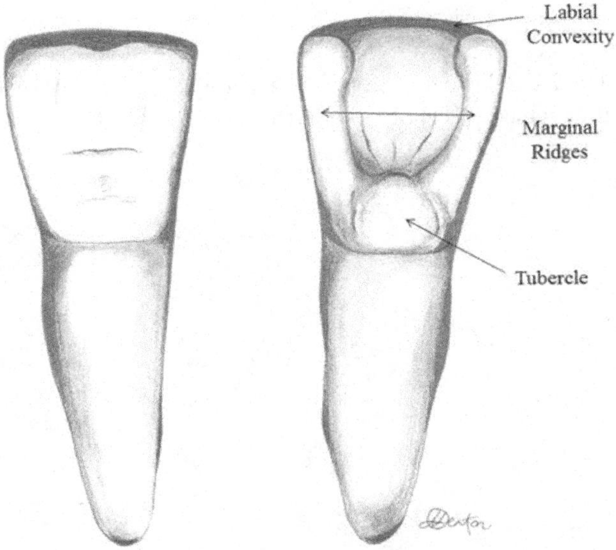

Illustration 22. Shovelling of incisors

Credit: Shovel-Shaped Incisors And The Morphology Of The Enamel-Dentin Junction: An Analysis Of The Human Incisors In 3 Dimensions. Lauren C Denton: Colorado State University 2011

Neanderthal upper canines demonstrate significant tubercles. Early modern Africans show a low degree (20%) of upper canine tubercles, whereas early modern Europeans show a significantly higher degree of upper canine tubercles (50%). There is a significant difference between early modern African lower canines and early modern European canines, who once again demonstrate an inheritance from Neanderthals.

The canine mesial ridge which is commonly observed in present sub-Saharan Africans is absent in early modern Africans, but present nonetheless in early modern Europeans, suggesting an influence of early modern Europeans towards Africa.

For both premolars and all molars, the majority of features of Neanderthal and concurrent non-Neanderthal are generally the same, and these archaic traits disappear gradually in early modern and today's populations. Neanderthal Molar M1 has at least five cusps, and 50% have cusp 6. Tellingly, all early modern fossils except for early European lack cusp 6 on this molar, yet another highly suggestive of a strong genetic link between Neanderthals and early Europeans.

Occipital Bun

The Neanderthal occipital bun is the protuberance at the back of the skull which is typical of Neanderthals.

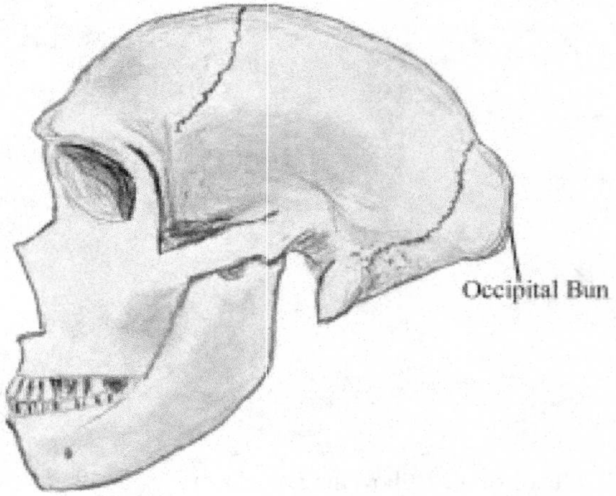

Illustration 23. Neanderthal skull with bun

Some scientists believe that the occipital bun provides space for the cerebellum, which is used to control movement and spatial reasoning. The cerebellum, or little cerebrum, sits below the brain at the back and just off the spinal cord. Although science today is not sure of all its functions, it's believed that although it doesn't instigate movement it does perform a management and coordination role due in part to its connectivity with signals exchanged with the spinal cord. It is also believed that it plays some kind of a function in language management, and possibly also plays a role in fear responses. People with damage to the cerebellum have trouble with the simple test of extending a finger to touch an object at arm's length. Those with cerebellum damage can reach the target with a hesitant wavering, often erratic movement, suggesting that the cerebellum refines and optimizes feedback loops involved with movement.

Viewed from the side the cerebellum is almost an isosceles triangular shape with the apex pointing towards the back. One could easily imagine this projection fitting into the inside of the occipital bun.

But it is more likely that the occipital bun provides space for an enlarged visual cortex which is located in the occipital lobe at the back of the brain. As we have already seen the larger eyes and larger retina require greater brain volume for processing the larger amount of information provided by the greater number of light sensitive cells on the retina. It would seem more than just coincidental that while in parallel the eye sockets shrunk with progressive generations, so did the occipital bun — while Neanderthals, with the largest eyes of our ancestors, had the most pronounced occipital bun.

The occipital bun is not found in all Neanderthals. It appears to be limited to just European Neanderthals, and even amongst those it is not always present. Tabun C1, Shanidar 1 and Amud 1 from Iran lack a developed occipital bun, but then they belong to the Southern Neanderthals where winters were shorter and general light levels greater; though amongst European Neanderthals it was present in some of the oldest Neanderthals and some of the youngest. Furthermore, it isn't noticeable in Neanderthal children, and appears to develop following puberty. Trinkaus and LeMay, two Neanderthal researchers, believe that skull development shadows brain development, and that the occipital bun develops as a result of the development of the occipital pole of the brain. To back up this theory they note that 80% of brain development is achieved in modern human babies in the first three years after birth. The remaining 20% of brain growth occurs towards the back of the brain, which would tend to cause an extension of the skull towards the back of the head.

Most early modern humans from Europe also possess occipital buns, inherited from their Neanderthal ancestors. So, do, some early modern humans from North Africa, which once again suggests that some Neanderthals migrated out of Europe into North Africa.

It was also a common feature in more ancient human ancestors, but has become quite rare in modern human populations. It was however very common amongst archaic European populations after the supposed disappearance of Neanderthal. Significant numbers of Finns and Saami people still possess Occipital buns, as do some regional populations in the UK. It is surely no coincidence that these are Northern populations. Elsewhere the Bushmen of the Kalahari are reputed to retain occipital buns.

In modern humans where the skull is somewhat narrowed but the brain is large an occipital bun can be produced to accommodate the necessary brain volume.

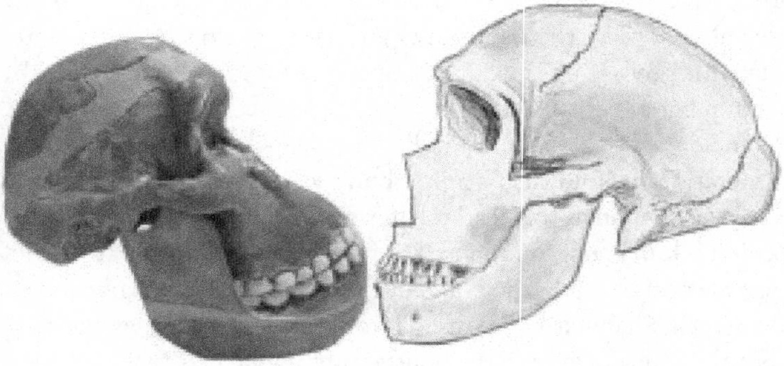

Illustration 24 Face to face: Australopithecus and Neanderthal

Suprainiac Fossa

The suprainiac fossa is a pitted elliptical shaped area at the base of the rear of the skull, located on the occiput above the inion. It is present on all European Neanderthal fossils (where the appropriate segment of the cranium is preserved) from the very earliest onwards. Also, it still exists in some modern Europeans.

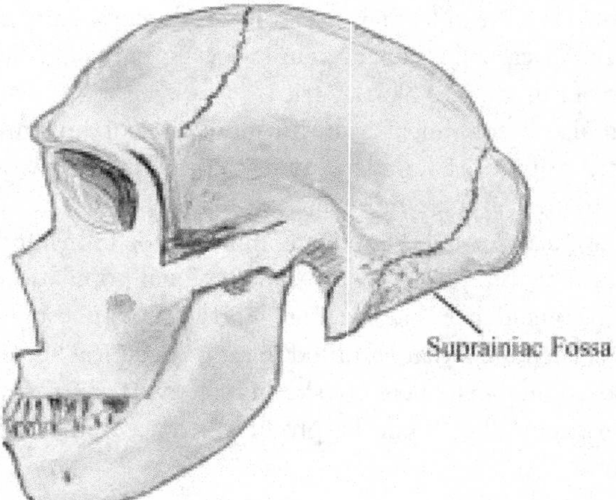

Illustration 25. Neanderthal suprainiac fossa

The fossa, as the name suggests is a depression with respect to the surrounding bone of the cranium, shaped in the form of an oval whose long axis roughly parallels the torus below it. The surface of this depression is characterized by pin-prick like pitting, which is where the nuchal ligaments rooted into the bone. In modern humans these nuchal ligaments root into an occipital protuberance and sometimes leave the same tell-tale pin-pricking. But in modern humans this nuchal ligament is concentrated centrally, whereas in Neanderthals it fanned out in the oval shape already mentioned.

The nuchal ligament which attached to the base of the rear of the skull runs down the spine and attaches to the bony process (or protrusion) of the 7th cervical vertebra at the base of the neck. Two muscles attach to this long ligament, part of the trapezius and the splenius capitis muscles. The trapezius is a large muscle which fans out from the shoulder blade connecting to various places along the spine, including the nuchal ligament. The splenius capitis muscle is a broad bandage shaped muscle which extends from the parts of the spine including the nuchal ligament and connects to the mastoid process. This latter muscle is used for lateral movement of the head and extension of the head.

The nuchal ligament doesn't exist in many animals including the great apes, as its main function is to relieve the weight of the head, particularly when running.

The broad attachment area of the nuchal ligament at the base of the Neanderthal skull gives us another clue about Neanderthal behavior. Neanderthal was a runner and with his large head he needed a strong nuchal ligament to take the stress off his neck muscles and reduce fatigue when running long distances. The shape of his femurs also testifies to Neanderthal being a powerful runner. We know that he was also a hunter from the bones we find in conjunction with Neanderthal bones, so we can conclude that an important part of his hunting technique involved running, and or chasing his prey. This development unique in the great apes is probably a result of the adoption of a bipedal lifestyle. We will return to his way of life in a later chapter.

The Nose

The Neanderthal nose was an imposing structure, dominating the face. Because it is a soft tissue structure we have no fossil evidence of the nose itself, but the skeletal structures which support the nose all testify to an object of some consequence. The broadness and vertical size of the nasal aperture in the skull is far bigger than in modern humans. The large nasal aperture is framed by projecting nasal bones and very prominent anterior nasal spines. Within Hominidae the projecting nose is a unique development, in other primates it is far more flattened, and appears to have performed a role in preserving heat and recovering moisture otherwise lost through respiration. This large nose was no accident of fate; it is a specific adaptation to a very cold climate. As we shall see in a later chapter the reindeer that most prolific of Arctic mammals has very similar nasal adaptations specifically to enhance survival in exceptionally cold conditions.

The prominent edifice which is the Neanderthal nose would have allowed him to warm the freezing air of periglacial Europe while inhaling to avoid a thermal shock to the brainstem. The added distance that inhaled air travelled would also have reduced heat loss to the brain case. Additionally, in a very cold dry climate, condensation within the bronchial tract would be recovered in the nose and swallowed, so the risks of dehydration in a very dry climate would have been reduced, and humidity recycled in the body. The cilia, which are the moving hairs which keep the airways clear, removing pathogens and dust from the lungs work more efficiently when moist. As the climate was particularly dry during the last Ice Age, the added humidification of air caused by a long nose would help protect Neanderthal from respiratory diseases.

It has been found that nostril size is a function of climate. In general, the larger the nostril the warmer the climate, and large nostrils were probably the norm with very early humans. Conversely smaller nostrils are typical of colder climates. The reason for the restriction in nostril size seems to be to enable the air to come into contact with the linings of the nose to improve the warmth and humidification of the air. The smaller the nostril the more air turbulence is created within the nasal passages causing the maximum volume of air to come into contact with the nasal walls.

In order for the nose to warm the freezing air, and not freeze itself, acting as a kind of heat exchanger, it needed a prodigious blood supply. Evidence of this is readily available in the fossil record with the very large infraorbital foramen (hole in the bone for a nerve to pass), on each side of the nose. This hole in the bone also allows for blood vessels to pass through the skull and supply the face from inside the skull. The Neanderthal infraorbital foramen is much larger than the modern human equivalent which can only mean that the blood supply to the face and the nose area was considerably greater for Neanderthals than for modern humans.

The result of this large nose was to give the front of the Neanderthal face a very prognathic appearance, i.e., the middle of the face projected noticeably forwards. This prognathism or Nasion Radius has been measured, (termed the NAR) and compared to overall head size with the NAR Index.

Sample	NAR	NAR Index
Neanderthal Mean	110.4	53.9
(N,SD)	(8,4.6)	(7, 2.1)
EUP mean	100.0	51.9
(N,SD)	(8,8.4)	(8, 2.7)
Norse mean	95.3	50.5
(N,SD)	(55, 3.4)	
Zalavar mean	94.7	51.1
(N,SD)	(54, 3.6)	
Berg mean	94.9	52.6
(N,SD)	(56, 3.8)	
African mean	92.8	50.1

Illustration 26 NAR indices

Credit: Data sourced from The human Lineage by Matt Cartmill/Fred H. Smith published by Wiley-Blackwell

N= number of samples
SD = standard deviation
NAR =nasion radius as defined by Howells
NAR Index = (NAR/max cranial length) * 100
EUP = Early Upper Paleolithic (early modern European)
Zalavar = Early European remains from the Zalavar site in Hungary

The prognathism of Neanderthals is part of a much longer-term process started from the early days of Homo and known as the zygomatic retreat. In early Homo the entire face was positioned well forwards of the rest of the brain giving a very elongated look to the skull. The overall appearance was of a more or less straight line from the brows down over the nose to the mouth. With Neanderthals however, the nasal bones and the nose itself projected well forwards, in addition the lateral parts of the face, the cheekbones regressed backwards, as did the vertical section of the mandible (lower jaw), creating the well-known retro-molar gap. The effect of this was to enhance the forward position of the center of the face, giving the tell-tale prognathic look. In modern humans the whole face and particularly the nasal structure has retreated backwards making the skull noticeably less long than earlier Homo species. This horizontal compression of the skull has forced the top of the skull upwards giving the typical modern tin-loaf appearance while allowing for a similar volume for the brain in the cranium. The front of the face meanwhile has become far flatter.

This zygomatic retreat can be seen in the above table. The most prognathic face is that of the Neanderthal and as Neanderthal transitioned to archaic European the Neanderthal prognathism diminishes from 110.4 to 100.0 and to the Zalavar early European remains of 94.7. All of which remain well above the African average of 92.8

General Build

Whereas *H. erectus*, Neanderthal's predecessor was tall and gracile, Neanderthal was stocky and well built. His chest was deep and powerful, his limbs were relatively short for his stature but heavily muscled, his finger bones were wider than modern humans lending them a somewhat spatulate appearance.

One suggestion for his strong build has been the need for energy conservation, following Allen's Rule, which states that warm-blooded animals living in colder climates tend to have shorter limbs in order to decrease the surface area to mass ratio, for the conservation of heat. The optimum surface area to mass ratio is a sphere and the least optimum a thin elongated body. In general, cold adapted humans tend to follow this rule. A rough approximation to quantify this rule in fossils is to measure the Brachial and Crural indices. The Brachial index compares the humerus length to the radius, and the Crural compares the tibia to the femur. The assumption being that the more gracile the animal the longer it's 2nd bone (humerus and tibia) in its limb.

Both Neanderthals and Eskimos have comparable indices. Southern and Northern Africans stand at the opposite end of the scale, and as Neanderthals gave way to archaic Europeans, so the index moves away from Neanderthals towards modern Europeans which approaches that of the Africans.

A ratio of combined member length to weight would be an even better comparison, but present research doesn't provide those numbers.

Another suggestion which seems eminently plausible is the large ribcage of the Neanderthal was required to accommodate two large lungs and a big heart necessary for processing the oxygen and supplying the energy required for his muscle-bound body.

In general Neanderthal joint surfaces are larger than modern humans, as are the areas of bone where ligaments and tendons attach, confirming the notion of a heavily muscled body designed for a heavy workload and resistant to physical stresses. However, when scaled allometrically to body mass, these joint surfaces become comparable to modern humans.

Neanderthal Way of Life

We've learnt quite a bit about Neanderthals now from the evidence of their fossil remains and the characteristics that they inherited from their forbears. We've learnt that they were highly social and mastered the spoken language. They occupied all ice-free Europe and had colonized wide swathes of Western Asia, and even colonized parts of North Africa. They were powerful hunters with strong limbs and were adept at running. They had adapted to life in an extremely cold climate, although some of them also lived in warm climates as well. They could be fair skinned, pale eyed, and have light or reddish colored hair or darker skinned when living in the Southern parts of Europe or the Middle East. They had eyes adapted to life in low light levels and because of that were well equipped for hunting at night, dawn or the evening. As with their ancestors they fashioned stone tools and weapons.

Let's take a closer look at their tools. For most of the existence, Neanderthals used tools which belong to a category of lithic technology which has been labeled Mousterian. In many locations where Neanderthal bones have been discovered so have Mousterian tools and this has led to the two being considered as synonymous. However, as we shall see later, Neanderthals used and even developed more advanced technologies. But before we look closely at Mousterian, let's take a look at *H. erectus*' tool kit which is commonly known as Acheulean and which preceded Mousterian.

Acheulean (Mode 2)

Acheulean tools first appeared in Africa about 1.76 million years ago, and appear to have been used until the disappearance of *H. erectus* and also in some cases by his ancestors. As such Acheulean technology often appears wherever *H. erectus* was present (Africa, Europe, parts of Asia), although bamboo tools are thought to have replaced Acheulean in parts of China. But whereas *H. erectus* arrived in Europe 1.8 million years ago it would seem that he brought Oldowan technology with him initially, and that that was replaced gradually by Acheulean around Europe from 1.5million years ago to 800,000 years ago.

The chief difference between Acheulean and the earlier Olduwan technology is in the Acheulean edges that are knapped on both sides to make what is known as a bi-facial tool, compared to often just the one worked side of the Olduwan. In general Acheulean tools take the form of pear-shaped hand axes knapped from hard stone, but they also exist in different forms, such as elongated spear points, tapered spear points, circular scrapers, and triangular spear points. The hand axe has a rounded base which fits comfortably into the palm of the hand, and tapers to a point. When the hand holding the hand axe is brought down on say a bone, it concentrates all the force of the blow into the point, allowing the point to break into the bone. It could be used for many other purposes such as delivering a lethal blow to an injured animal or breaking open bone to access the nutrient rich marrow inside.

Some hand axes required a considerable amount of knapping with a hammer stone to produce the desired shape. The technique used in Acheulean tool manufacture was to prepare a core by knapping flakes off it, until the desired shape was achieved. In general, the finished product was symmetrical. Acheulean technology employed more precise hammers. Instead of the Olduwan hammer, Acheulean used bone or more often in Europe deer antler. So, although the broad term hand axe is often used to describe Acheulean tools, there were a large number of stone tools that could be shaped by the simple process of chipping away at a promising looking core. As we have seen chimpanzees fashion spears, as probably did our last common ancestor with chimpanzees. So, it is not surprising that 5 million years further down the evolutionary path, these spears had become tipped with stones with very sharp penetrating points. The earliest wooden spears so far discovered come from Schoningen in Germany where a collection of them with pointed ends have been dated back to 300,000BP, i.e., fashioned by Neanderthals. Unfortunately, to date no older ones have been found, although they no doubt existed, as the wooden shafts would have rotted away without trace, within the first hundred years or so.

Mousterian (Or Mode 3)

This technology appears to date back as far as 300,000BP and lasts until around 40,000BP, although there is still some debate about its first appearance. It covers a range more or less equivalent to Neanderthal's geographical range, that is to say Europe, Western Asia, the Near East, North and East Africa. These stone tools were for the most part made from flint and are characterized by the production method which is known as Levallois.

The Levallois technique employs a particular form of stone knapping, which creates the tool in three essential stages. Firstly, small pieces are chipped away from the core stone, which has been selected because of its appropriate size and shape. Chips are firstly removed right around the edges. Once the edges have been chipped away then more chips are removed from the domed remainder of the core.

Illustration 27. Neanderthal Mousterian point

Then, the blunter end of the core is chipped away vertically, to create what is known as a striking platform, this is an entirely new development in human technology. Finally, a substantial strike is made down onto the striking platform and if done correctly, this removes a thin slice of the flint which reflects the general tear drop shape of the original core but is far thinner and with sharp edges. Some of these Mousterian tools are objects of considerable beauty. Many can be observed, displayed in painstaking detail at the Les Ezies Museum in South Western France.

Depending on the shape of the core various different tools can be produced, each with their particular uses. Spear heads, scrapers for skins, awls, chisels etcetera. The preparation of the striking platform was crucial in the choice of what kind of finished tool was intended.

Curiously perhaps over the wide span of time that they were used and huge geographical area, Mousterian tools are remarkably similar, testifying to a systematic process of teaching and learning on a far-reaching scale throughout the Neanderthal world.

Illustration 28. Mousterian scraper and cutter

Contention has swirled around Mousterian tools and still does to a degree. Initially, there were two schools of thought, the Frenchman Francois Bordes considered that Mousterian varied according to the tribes that used them. The American Louis Binford preferred the idea that the variations depended more on the raw materials available as well as the effects of resharpening and reshaping, as the original shape became blunt or damaged. The main and important problem with the French position is that it can lead to serious misunderstandings such as have arisen at the end of the Mousterian period. For example, in places where Mousterian technology evolves to Aurignacian then so too must the people responsible for those tools. So, the heated debate over Mousterian has spawned an even more heated one over Aurignacian and who used that.

Illustration 29. Mousterian scraper

In recent years studies on flint knapping have managed to reproduce Mousterian tools and videos are available on the internet which demonstrate the Levallois knapping technique.

A subset of Mousterian tools is the spear tip technology known as Aterian. The main difference of Aterian is that they display a tang, used for hafting onto spears. There is a lot of debate about whether these spears were thrown or not. As we know, chimpanzees are perfectly capable of throwing projectiles at their prey or enemies. Once again, 5 million years of evolution, a brain over three times the size of a chimpanzee's and with a perfectly throwable weapon to hand, it would seem inconceivable that some of these spears weren't thrown at an animal that was just out of thrusting range. Indeed, how much more likely is it that prey animals on their guard would be out of touching distance of the Neanderthal hunters, leaving the Neanderthals little option but to throw their spears? Despite these seemingly self-evident statements, there is a forceful body of opinion which refutes the possibility that Neanderthals threw their spears.

A lot of the functions of the Mousterian tools appear to revolve around the daily necessities required for survival of hunting, preparing food and clothing.

For hunting we have spear points. For preparing food there are backed knives with one sharp side for cutting and a blunt side allowing finger pressure. There are hammers for breaking the bones and accessing the calorie rich bone marrow. There are scrapers for stripping the flesh off skins to prepare them for clothing, bedding and shoes. There are very sharply tipped awls for drilling holes, to make flutes from bones and piercing skins in preparation for sewing them together to make clothing. Some of the axes may have also been used as mattocks for cutting wood for fires.

Illustration 30. Mousterian cutter

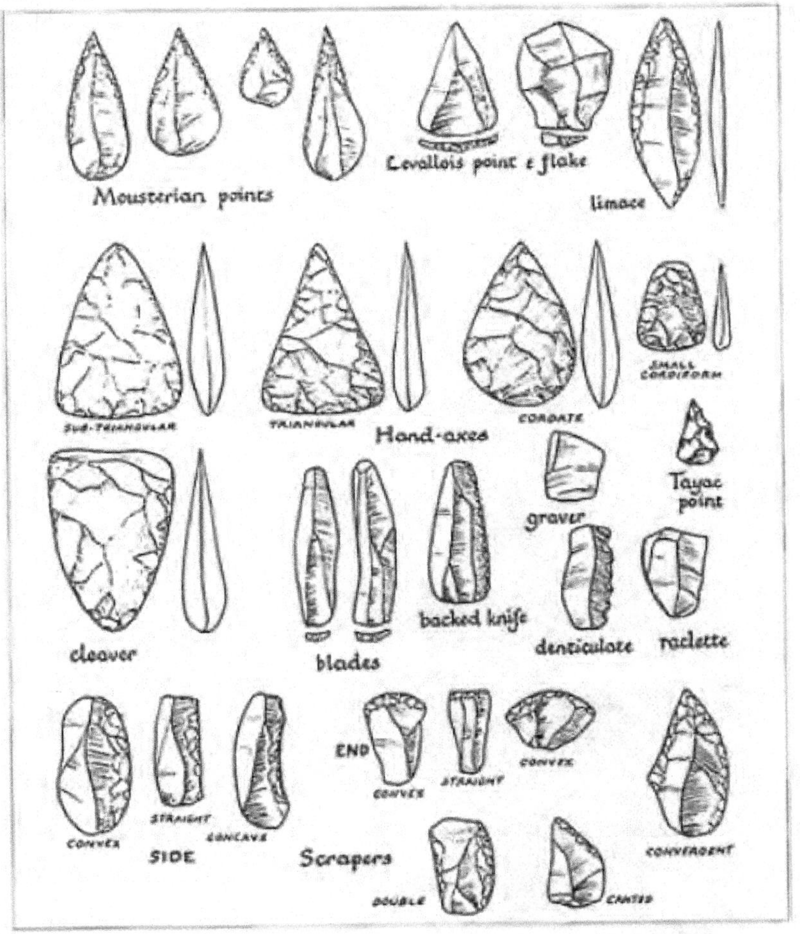

Illustration 31. Mousterian tool kit

Credit: The Mousterian Toolkit from Neanderthal Tools and Weapons. https://www.neandertals.org/tools.html

Neanderthal Population

Neanderthals occupied exclusively all of ice-free Europe, Western Asia, Central Asia, and the Near East for the best part of 400,000 years, a huge swathe of time and a vast geographical area. For an idea of the Neanderthal population we can look at North American Indians before the arrival of Europeans, who for thousands of years had a similar level of technological advancement, and who occupied vast regions in the Northern Hemisphere at similar latitudes.

Illustration 32. Mousterian spear tip

According to the Smithsonian's *Handbook of North American Indians*, the population around AD 1500 (after no more than 15,000 years to adapt to and expand in the continent), yet before there was a significant presence of Europeans on the continent, is estimated at 1,894,350.

The size of the North American continent is about 24.7 million km^2 including the arctic tundra of Alaska and wide swathes of Canada, giving an average population density of around 0.07 people/km2,[2] otherwise put, 7 people in a 100km^2 area. By today's standards of urban society, a very low figure indeed. The size of Europe is 10.8 million km^2 and Western Asia covers about 6 million km2^2, making a total of nearly 17 million km^2. If the population density of Neanderthals was similar to North American Indians then excluding any populations in the Near East, and Central Asia, the population would have been around 1.2 million. This must be seen as a very conservative figure as Neanderthals had 20 times as long to adapt and colonize their continent.

This figure may have diminished during the glacial maxima, and it may have increased well beyond that number during the inter-glacial periods when tropical conditions prevailed in Europe and Western Asia. From the fossil remains so far discovered, Neanderthal people didn't live to a ripe old age, and 40 may well have been the average life span. So, over a conservative 300,000 year period there may well have been in excess of 9 billion Neanderthal people who roamed Europe and Western Asia (a little over the current world population).

So what happened to all the bones of these 9 billion Neanderthals? Bones can decay within decades, they are composed principally of collagen which like the rest of the body decomposes naturally. During the Pleistocene when Neanderthals occupied Europe they shared it as we have seen with a large number of megafauna some of which preyed on Neanderthals both alive and dead. Indeed, many Neanderthal bones have been found in cave hyena dens. Any Neanderthal who died in the open would very likely have been eaten by any one of the large predators or scavengers (which we will focus on in a subsequent chapter), leaving no trace at all within months of death. But what about those that weren't eaten by carnivores? If the Neanderthal body is exposed to either water, air, insects or highly acidic soil then bacteria and funghi can invade the bones seeking out the proteins of the collagen as a food source, after which the bone will simply become dust.

However, if the body is buried in a warm, arid climate then it is more difficult for the bacteria and funghi to survive, and so the body is likely to be better preserved for longer, and possibly last for thousands of years even.

Only an extremely small fraction of living organisms manage to become fossilized, and even if we call these fossils 'bones', that isn't actually the case. Instead of decomposing, minerals from the surrounding materials slowly replaced the living material, transforming it into rock. So, the few bones of Neanderthals that have been recovered are exceptional cases where particularly rare circumstances have contrived to preserve the bones, or fossilize them. Neanderthals themselves have helped to a degree in this, by deliberately burying some of their dead, in the first deliberate practice of this kind carried out by humans. There are various places where deliberate Neanderthal burials have been performed. One of these is Shanidar Cave in the Zagros Mountains in Iraq. In one of these burials, the body showed signs of healing after serious injury. The body known as Shanidar 1 (or 'Nandy' to the excavating team) had suffered a brutal blow to the side of his face crushing his orbit and no doubt rendering him blind in one eye. Nevertheless, he survived this terrible injury which shows signs of bone fusion, and lived to a ripe old age by Neanderthal standards, into his 5th decade. He also suffered from several severe breakages to his right arm, which had also healed but had withered. This poor individual also appears to have suffered from deformities to his legs, possibly caused by partial paralysis.

Shanidar 2, appears to have met a grizzly end by been crushed in a rockfall judging by the number of crushed bones in his body. Nevertheless, his body was recovered and buried together with stone tools.

Shanidar 3 appears to have died a violent death, showing evidence of a stab wound to his 9th rib, although bone growth around the wound, suggests that he lived on for at least a few weeks before succumbing to complications from his wound, and was then buried.

Shanidar 4 also known as the flower burial was an individual laid to rest in a fetal position, and surrounded by flowers. There is contention over whether the flowers, all of which appear to have particular medicinal properties, were placed there by Neanderthals or by a gerbil.

In the case of Shanidar, when other members of the family group survived, burial appears to have been routine, and thanks to the warm dry climate the bones have survived. The dating of the 10 burials discovered cover the period between 65,000 and 35,000 BP.

At the far distant site of Chapelle-les-Saints in France, Neanderthals also buried their dead in a cave. In other locations in France, Neanderthal burial sites exist and the pits are covered with large protective stones.

The use of burials which was to become a widespread human tradition was probably initiated by Neanderthals for two reasons. The dead could simply not be left to rot in the cave which was also the primary home for the family, so it had to be disposed of in some way. The simple expedient of removing the corpse from the cave and leaving it to the predations of the surrounding carnivores would have had the unwelcome consequence of attracting dangerous predators to the area, and also may have been upsetting for the rest of the family to discover the mutilated remains of their loved ones strewn around the immediate area. Two possibilities remained open to them to avoid this situation. Put the body in the nearest river, as Indians do in the Ganges today, or to bury it. In some cases, they chose to bury it. In places where starvation took the whole group, then the chances are that cave lions, hyenas, cave bears or other carnivores feasted on the remains, and the remains were scattered over the surrounding land to rapidly decompose, and disappear entirely from the archaeological record.

Other Neanderthal remains have been found due to cave roof collapse, where Neanderthals were unfortunate victims of the natural process of cave development, and were buried under heaps of rock which managed to keep the bones free from predation and decomposition.

Thanks to the unique conditions that prevail in some caves, it is in these places where we find the majority of Neanderthal remains, sheltered from the elements and equally from hungry carnivores. Thanks to the careful ministrations of a few long-dead Neanderthals, a small number of their relatives have been preserved and testify to their occupation of Europe and Asia for a vast period of time.

Neanderthals' ancestors from *H. erectus* backwards in time, as we have seen in some detail, evolved in a world where tropical temperatures prevailed. Neanderthals on the other hand had to adapt to a very cold climate, which for great periods of time were periglacial, this required a considerable amount of adapting. Whereas African *H. erectus* and his ancestors could happily have slept on a nest of leaves or grass in the open savannah, this would not have been possible for Neanderthal in the winter and in periglacial conditions. Fire was one of the solutions, but not the only one, shelter from the rain, the snow and the howling gales was essential. Overwhelming evidence from caves in Europe shows that Neanderthals considered them as the perfect home, which is fine for areas where there are caves, i.e., in limestone regions, where caves are abundant, but what about all the areas where there is no limestone and therefore no caves? And what did Neanderthal people do when all the caves were full? The obvious solution was that they built his own shelters, and fortunately we have plenty of evidence of these shelters.

Neanderthal Buildings

When ready-made cave dwellings weren't available, Neanderthals made their own buildings for shelter. In some cases these were very large. Most of the wooden buildings that they built have long since decayed, but remains of those that they made from mammoth bones and tusks remain as evidence of their capacity to build. In the Ukraine, close to the Dnestr River, five of these mammoth bone buildings have been found to date. The outside dimensions of Moldova 1 measured about 10m x 8m the frame was constructed of wood and mammoth bones, with skins for a covering. Roughly 180 mammoth bones were used in the construction, most of them the largest bones from the animal. Using the same method of construction that was used in Europe until quite recently for wood framed houses; the long bones were inserted into purpose drilled holes to provide stability for the rest of the structure.

Excavations in the area reveal that this was not just a single dwelling but part of a settlement or village. So here we have evidence of a Neanderthals choosing to live together in communities. An interesting feature of the settlement which is repeated in other Neanderthal settlements was a purpose dug pit into which were thrown bones that all show signs of butchery. One interpretation of this pit was that it was the communal dump for waste material, another is that it was used as in Siberia today as a storage area for food in the winter. This pit demonstrates a degree of collective organization, to dig the pit in the first place, and then to use it for a well-defined purpose.

Within the mammoth bone building various hearths have been located and also dedicated areas used for tool manufacture.

It was inhabited for a substantial period of time with several layers of occupation and numerous hearths.

At Nice in southern France, a site known as Terra Amata is an important archeological location for early Neanderthal structures. At the time, 380,000 BP, the sea level was about 26m higher than today attesting to a warmer climate and the site was located on the shore of the Mediterranean. There is some controversy over the dating of the site; some have put it as late as 230,000. Evidence of lines of rocks and associated holes in the ground suggest that the habitations were apparently made by placing poles against one another creating a sort of tent shaped structure covered by skins, with a hole in the apex to let smoke from the fires out. The huts were of impressive dimensions: between 7 and 15m long and between 4 and 6m wide.

Each hut found had traces of a hearth, testifying to Neanderthal use of fire, and if the earlier date of 380,000 BP is correct, then it is one of the earliest signs of the controlled use of fire in Europe. 29 different layers of habitation testify to a very lengthy period of occupation with 28,000 objects discovered, belong mostly to the Acheulean technology.

Despite there being a very large number of animal bones from elephants, rhinoceros, giant deer, wild boar etcetera there don't seem to be any human remains which strongly suggests that the dead were disposed of deliberately elsewhere, possibly sent out to sea on rafts.

The site is now buried underneath an apartment block, but some of the artifacts are on display at the local prehistory museum.

Other evidence of fire in Europe dating back to around 400,000 BP comes from Beeches Pit archaeological site, Suffolk in the UK.

At another site in France, Menez-Dragan in Brittany, which is essentially based around a cave, archaeologists believe that the living space was extended by use of tented structures outside the cave forerunners of awnings, in order to accommodate an expanding population. Again, this attests to communities living together rather than just isolated family units. In just the latest layer of occupation a grand total of 14,909 stone tools were found, itself also suggestive of a considerable number of occupants. This final layer of occupation is dated to around 223,000BP. Given the large number of tools, it is highly likely that the community swelled beyond the capacity of the cave to house the population so that the community rather than splitting up to find another propitious site, they decided to create sheltered extensions.

Man's Best Friend

A considerable amount of doubt swirls around the origins of dogs, not just in terms of where they first occurred, but also by what specific pedigree of species, and exactly what happened when. But the first animal species to become domesticated, and by a large margin is the dog.

There are various contenders for the ancestor of the modern dog. The Eurasian wolf, the Paleolithic dog (Canis c.f. familiaris – c.f. indicating uncertainty), the Pleistocene wolf, the Eastern wolf and the Western wolf. To add to the uncertainty of the ancient origins of the modern, it would seem that interbreeding at various stages between the various contenders has further muddied the waters.

What is becoming clearer however is the general process of domestication. At some point probably after 50,000 BP, some wolves became familiar, just as some garden birds do when regularly provided with food. This was probably a widespread process over time. Some researchers believe that the earliest dogs date back as far as 130,000BP.

Familiarity over generations would have led to a form of symbiosis where in exchange for food the wolves performed certain useful services such as guarding the camp from other predators, particularly while the Neanderthals were sleeping, and eventually in helping with the actually process of hunting. Wolves that proved aggressive or troublesome would be driven away or killed, so that over time selectively only wolves acting in a friendly manner to humans would be tolerated close to the camp. Over generations through this form of selection and possibly rearing orphaned pups, human tolerant wolves would become friendlier and friendlier until domestication would be achieved.

We will look more closely at experimentation in Russia in the field of domestication, which throws considerable light on how quickly domestication of some species can occur, and the surprising results that domestication produces.

From 36,000BP onwards it was the Paleolithic dog bones that were most frequently found close to human habitations. This new species of the domesticated dog had been selectively created, and man had found his closest and most reliable ally in the animal kingdom, a close and lasting partnership which endures to this day. By this time the Paleolithic dog had diverged significantly from the wolf, becoming smaller (average 36Kg compared to 42Kg) with a shorter snout, reduction in number and size of teeth and wider head. It would appear that the closest modern dog to the Paleolithic dog is the Central Asian Shepherd. A realistic cave painting whose date is estimated at 19,000 BP from Font-de-Gaume in France shows what the Paleolithic dog looked like, with erect ears, and a fur free face and lower legs, but with thick fur covering the rest of the body from the ears and neck back.

Affection that human ancestors had for their dogs has come down to us touchingly from the distant past, by a dog burial from Predmosti in Moravia, where a dog was buried with an animal bone placed carefully in its mouth, dated to somewhere around 32,000BP. At this site, dogs were buried with humans, quite possibly their owners.

In an evocative image a 50m long trail of footprints in a cave in Vallon Pont d'Arc in France shows evidence of a 10-year-old walking alongside a large canid (either wolf or dog). Soot from the torch that the child was carrying date this partnership to about 26,000BP.

Analysis of bone collagen from a camp in the Czech Republic indicated that the Paleolithic dogs had a different diet compared to their people in their camp. Whereas the humans had a diet of uniquely mammoth meat, the dogs fed on musk ox and reindeer. The reason for this different diet isn't clear, but certain peoples living in the Arctic today give their dogs different meat to that which they eat themselves. The origin of this differentiated diet may be a deliberate choice to avoid domesticated dogs competing with humans for human food, thus reducing the risks of potentially dangerous conflict.

Neanderthal Art

For a long time, it was considered that the Neanderthal mind was incapable of the abstract thought necessary to create art, which is after all a uniquely human expression of feelings. Over recent years, and despite considerable resistance from the old school of paleoanthropologists, various examples of Neanderthal art have been discovered.

In Gibraltar at Gorham's Cave, a series of intersecting lines were uncovered beneath 39,000-year-old sediments, making them at least that old. The engraving is found 100m inside the cave in a place thought to have been used as a Neanderthal bed chamber. Admittedly these scratches in the rock are a far cry from what we would call art today, but it is a small step in that direction.

In Slovenia overlooking the Idrijca River at the Divje Babe cave, a flute manufactured from a cave bear femur has been found, unfortunately broken in two, but in an excellent state of preservation, with carefully drilled holes. This flute has been dated to 43,100 BP. A lot of controversy has swirled around the classification of this flute as Neanderthal, for the usual reasons; a reluctance to accept that Neanderthals were capable of creating such sophisticated instruments. They certainly had the tools for the job, there is no shortage of Mousterian awls available capable of drilling these holes. The inevitable implication of the existence of this Neanderthal flute is that they were also interested in performing and listening to music.

Further hints at Neanderthal's passion for music comes from mysteriously notched bird bones. Neanderthals hunted birds, 41 species of which have been identified in Ukrainian Neanderthal sites alone. Many of these bird bones bear witness to Neanderthal carvings. Some of these have regular saw tooth marks cut into the sharp edge of crow radius bones, such as the one from Zaskalnaya VI. The points of the notches are slightly rounded suggesting wear. This is consistent with the bone used as a modern Guiro, just one of a number of similar instruments used today around the world.

The guiro is made from a hollow gourd with parallel notches cut in one side. The guiro is played by rubbing a stick along the notches producing a rhythmic ratcheting sound, which resonates in the gourd, much as it would resonate with a hollow bird radius. The guiro is played often by the singer in Puerto Rican and Cuban folk and dance music. Similar designs include the Guacharaca, Quijada (cow jaw with teeth) and charasca. Previously it was thought that the origins of the Guiro came from Africa, whereas this crow radius instrument dates to around 40,000BP, together with the cave bear flute the earliest musical instruments in the world.

In Spain at the Nerja caves, a line of 6 seals have been drawn vertically on a stalactite by charcoal. The carbon found at the base of the stalactites has been dated to 42,000BP.

These examples of Neanderthal art are far from isolated. Painting from 11 other caves in Spain including outlines of hands, red dots and horses make up the subject matter. Previously attributed to anatomically modern humans (purely on the basis that Neanderthals were considered incapable of art of any form), advances in the technique of dating of uranium and thorium in layers covering the paint have pushed back the dates of these paintings well into the classical Neanderthal period. This improved dating method which relies on the covering material rather than the carbon content of the paint itself means that the painting itself isn't damaged by removing samples. Now the paintings can be left intact, by simply dating very small amounts of the covering material which gives a minimum age.

This new method also opens the doors for many other cave paintings to be dated more accurately some, if not many of which, will probably be reattributed correctly to Neanderthals.

Neanderthal creativity wasn't restricted to painting on walls, they also created jewellery and there are several examples of this around Europe. In Croatia they used the talons of white-tailed eagles as personal decoration, which were found in the Krapina Cave, and dated to around 130,000 BP. The talons show signs of improvement by Neanderthals, cut marks made probably during the extraction of the claws from the eagle's feet have been smoothed over and the claws have all been burnished to enhance their appearance. 130,000 years later and eagle talon jewelry is still made showing how some tastes from European Neanderthal past remain unchanged.

At Arcy-sur-Cure a variety of ornaments were found including beads fashioned from shells, animal teeth and mammoth ivory. These have been dated to about 42,000BP contemporary with the Nerja paintings.

Also, in Spain at two different sites in Murcia, sea shells have been found with traces of pigment on them, suggesting that they were probably used as paint holders. Amongst traces of the pigment were lumps of yellow pigment, red pigment was also found together with flecks of a reflective black material. Professor Joao Zilhao who led the archaeological studies into these finds considers that these shells were used for storing and also for mixing pigments to use as body paint. The shells were dated to approximately 50,000 years ago. A later chapter on ochre looks into just how useful this mineral was.

The oldest form of Neanderthal art (indeed art of any kind at all around the globe) comes from Israel. The Berekhat Ram Venus was found in an archeological layer dated to between 280 and 250,000BP. It would seem that this earliest form of sculptural art found anywhere was inspired by the resemblance of the original pebble to a female figure. This suggestive pebble inspired the artist to chisel away to enhance the likeness. The stone is a piece of light tuff, a porous volcanic material and measures 35x25x21mm. The Berekhat Ram Venus could well have been overlooked as just an ordinary small stone if it wasn't found in a layer of Acheulean tools comprising burins, Levallois flakes, end scrapers and borers made from local flint. Such is its general lack of distinction that it is easy to imagine that other such sculpted stones from the same period with equal or lesser degrees of likeness to reality may easily have been overlooked in other archaeological digs.

Very careful examination of the Berekhat Ram Venus has revealed which features of the stone are natural and which have been worked through impact and scraping. For example, scraping around the neck has managed to distinguish the head from the neck. Attention by way of deliberate smoothing around the chest area has accentuated the breasts, a feature which was to become a trademark of later European Venus figurine sculptures as we shall see later.

Neanderthal Navigation

The stone "mousterian" tools are unique to Neanderthals and have been found on the islands of Zakynthos, Lefkada and Kefalonia, which range from five to twelve kilometers from mainland Greece. Some researchers, such as Paul Pettitt from the University of Sheffield, suggest they could have swum that far. But that doesn't explain how similar tools found on the island of Crete got there. That would have meant swimming forty kilometers, which seems extremely unlikely, especially since such swimmers wouldn't have known beforehand that Crete was there to find.

Ferentinos et al suggest the evidence shows that Neanderthals not only figured out how to build boats and sail but did so quite extensively long before modern humans appeared. They say that because the tools found on the islands are believed to date back 100,000 years (and the islands have been shown to have been islands back then as well), Neanderthal people were sailing around that long ago. Thus far, evidence for humans sailing dates back to just 50,000 years when they made their way to Australia. If true, this would push back the invention of sailing by fifty thousand years earlier than previously thought.

Neanderthal Clothing

No clothing from Neanderthal times survives and no painted images from Neanderthal times have been found to date to give us more of an idea of the clothing that they wore. *H. habilis* and African *H. erectus* living in Africa had no need of clothing to keep warm. However, living in Europe and Asia required this tropical species to adapt to the cold conditions. This meant finding artificial ways of staying warm. The further North he went the colder it got, and the more he relied on clothing to keep warm. But what did Neanderthal wear?

The only clues that we have come from the bones of animals close to camp, scraping tools, awls, needles and lice.

There was no weaving of cloth, flax, or wool in the Pleistocene, the only sheet like material that could be used for clothing was animal skin. The larger the animal the better it could cover the person. An aurochs or reindeer skin would be useful as a bed covering. A bear skin would be large enough to cover a human. Larger skins could be cut to become smaller. Skins of smaller animals could be sewn together to make larger coverings and footwear requiring more careful preparation.

In the Pleistocene, if you didn't use the skin of an animal, you discarded it. But one of the most common stone tools found not just in association with Neanderthals but also with *H. erectus* is the stone scraper used for preparing skins. Scraping all the excess tissue from a skin is a tedious business requiring considerable energy. Stone scrapers were part of the habitual tools in the Acheulean toolkit and have been found over 1.5 million years ago in Europe. By Neanderthal times, the preparation of skins for clothing and bedding had been the custom for over a million years (as evidenced by the scrapers). But by Neanderthal times the Acheulean scrapers had become more sophisticated and better adapted, using the sharper Mousterian flint edges. Working of animal skins both in terms of scraping the skin and cutting it to shape were done more efficiently.

Why go to all that effort to scrape a skin? Were Neanderthals simply vain and fussy? Were they repulsed by stinking animal skins? Probably the primary reason for scraping the skins properly was to preserve them. The fat in animals contains bacteria and as soon as the animal is killed, these bacteria begin to break down the natural tissues of the animal, causing the hair in the skin to fall out so that it loses its natural insulating properties. In addition, the warmer the skin, the faster this bacterial action begins. It is important to cool down the skin as soon as possible after the kill. The proximity of a nearby river is important in this role. It is no accident that so many of Neanderthal settlements are found close to water which was vital for drinking and washing but also for the preparation of the skins.

Different skins of different animals possess different thermal properties, and it is no surprise that mammals which live in the coldest regions have the best thermal insulation. Reindeer which are adapted to life within the polar circle would have been one of the best animals to choose for clothing. Reindeer hair consists of thick guard hairs which offer mechanical protection to the thinner more fragile under fur. Both guard hairs and under fur are hollow and woolen in aspect helping to trap an insulating layer of air against the body in the same way that double glazing maintains a layer of gas between the sheets of glass to reduce the loss of heat. The density of guard hairs on the reindeer differs considerably depending on the thermal requirements of each part of the body. The legs have a density of 2,000 hairs/cm^2 the abdomen 1,000 hairs/cm^2 and the back 1,700 hairs/cm^2. Reindeer calves that have less body mass and are more prone to death from the cold have an incredible 3,200 hairs/cm^2. By contrast hairs on the scalp vary from 160–220cm^2

Reindeer are so well adapted to the cold that the last Ice Age is also sometimes known as the Age of the reindeer. Reindeer herds were vital to the survival of many Neanderthal groups. There are reindeer fossil bones in many caves inhabited by Neanderthals. Reindeer feature in cave art throughout Northern Spain and France. We'll look into reindeer and other animals of the last Ice Age in more detail in another chapter.

The vast numbers of skin scrapers found in Neanderthal camps and caves bears witness to the importance of animal skins to the Neanderthals for clothing and bedding. Not only could large skins be cut down to the appropriate size and shape, but smaller skins could be sewn together with gut or vegetal cords. The holes for sewing were initially large and roughly made by flint awls. Later, elegant bone needles, similar in size and shape to modern needles were used and which economized the process of drilling the hole and sewing into one action. Not only did these needles allow Neanderthals more precise sewing of skins, but stronger joins also, especially when it came to sewing skin boots from the toughest of hides.

In the Levantine Neanderthal Caves of Kebara II, III, IV and V the number of scrapers found were 149, 283, 235 and 206 respectively. Research by Bordes in France showed that in what he called Quina Mousterian locations up to 80% of the tools found were scrapers, used for preparing skins or wooden tipped spears. But, curiously this high percentage wasn't the same everywhere. In certain levels and locations, the percentage of scrapers was far lower. Sites that he classed as Acheulean Mousterian had very few scrapers.

The following table shows just how important scrapers were in the Neanderthal toolkit and in their lives, taken from a large number of sites in South West France, with well over half the tools found in Ferrassie and Quina sites being scrapers.

Variant	Side Scrapers %	Quina Retouch	Hand Axes
Charentian Quina	50-80	14-30	Absent/rare
Charentian Ferrassie	50-80	6-14	Absent/rare
Typical			
Mousterian Acheulean A	25-45	Very low	8-40
Mousterian Acheulean B	4-40	Very low	Absent/rare

Illustration 33. Presence of scrapers amongst other tools

[credit : Encyclopedia of Human Evolution and Prehistory / by Delson, Tattersall and Van]

Indeed, the Quina Mousterian sites are defined as such because of the dominance of scrapers in the tools found on site. The dates of these sites vary according to Geographical location. Quina Mousterian in Southern France is around 70-60,000BP, while Quina Mousterian sites in Belgium to around the period 60-45,000BP, while Quina Mousterian sites in Northern Spain to a little later still. Equally, Charentian in Western France is defined also by the dominance of scrapers in the tools found. Acheulean as we have already noted is a more primitive mode of tool manufacture and with a far lower proportion of scrapers.

The oldest needle so far discovered dates back to about 50,000 BP and although is not directly associated with Neanderthals is attributed to his close cousins the Denisovans. It was found in a cave in the Altai mountains a region of Southern Russia not far from the borders of Kazakhstan and Mongolia. An incredibly fragile looking implement, it is 7cm long with a small eye just like a modern needle which was drilled with considerable precision. Apparently, it was made from the bone of an as yet unidentified bird.

Illustration 34. Awl point (left) for working holes in skins

Other tools used in the preparation of skins suggest a far more elaborate scale of work, for a more delicate finish. These are lissoirs, or smoothing tools, made from bone by repeated grinding and polishing to produce a smooth face and sharp edge and are used in the final preparations of leather. Four of these tools have been found at two sites in South West France: Abry Peyrony and Pech-de-L'Aze. We know that they were used in the preparation of leather because microwear on the bone surface is identical to microwear on leather working tools used in modern times. The Abry Peyrony bones were well preserved and maintained in their correct archaeological context by cementing caused by deposition from the roof and walls of the cave. The age of these bones given by 7 mass spectrometry measurements is put at between 47,700 and 41,130BP. The bone smoothing tool from Pech was dated even older at 51,000 +/- 2,000BP. These bone tools were made from the ribs of deer, probably a red deer. Each smoothing tool was manufactured in the same way to produce a similar end product, and to palaeoarcheologists the tool can thus be called standardized, meaning that it was a tool made to the same specifications in different physical places, and not just a one off or an accident. We will meet this standardization again and again across Neanderthal territories to a surprising degree.

To understand the importance of these tools, it's necessary to have some understanding of the preparation of leather. So far, we have seen the preparation of skins by scraping the flesh from the inside of them using the standard and ubiquitous Mousterian scraper. This leaves the skin with its insulating hair intact, ideal for warm clothing and bed covers. But much more work is required for the manufacture of leather which could be used for pouches, water bottles, shoes, underclothes etcetera. In addition, un-cured skin will eventually rot when wet, whereas leather is far more resistant.

To make leather, the skin needs first to have the flesh removed with the flint scraper. Once this is done the hairs need to be loosened by soaking it in a basin of lime water. After a couple of days, the hairs will loosen, and can be carefully scrapped off with a scraper or sea-shell. With the hair removed the two further layers need to be removed; the epidermis on the hair side and a membrane on the flesh side. These need to be removed with a very sharp scraper used perpendicularly to the skin. The importance of a the sharp, carefully made Mousterian edges repays the extra time in tool manufacture by enabling the manufacture of longer lasting, better quality clothes.

The skin needs to be tanned by soaking it for months in a basin of water and hemlock or oak bark. Finally, the skin needs to be smoothed and worked with the lissoir or smoothing tool by drilling holes in the edges and stretching it out over convenient branches with cords. This process is called sleeking and requires hours of working the leather to make it pliable and supple. The better the leather is sleeked the more workable it becomes. The smoothing tool can also be made of wood, but any wooden sleeking tools from this distant age will have long since rotted away, leaving only the bone sleekers to be found today.

These smoothing tools tell us that in South West France Neanderthals had developed leather manufacture, in order to make finer clothing, hoods, belts, shoes, leather tongs, water bottles, pouches etcetera. Yet another first in Neanderthal's impressive very long list of technological innovations.

Whether or not Neanderthals employed all the above stages used in leather manufacture isn't clear. It may be that they didn't use lime to loosen the hairs on the skin, and relied on the scrapers to do that. It may be that they didn't cure their leather for as long as we do now. Alternatives for tanning agents instead of oak bark that were readily available to the Neanderthals were faeces and animal brains.

Given that all the skins and leather that they made has long since disappeared, we shall probably never know — leather typically decomposes naturally unless carefully protected within 25 to 40 years. The use of bone tools in itself is a technological leap forwards. After several millions of years of using stone tools, man was now diversifying and becoming more sophisticated. This step to using bone for tool manufacture opened the flood gates to a whole new range of tools and weapons which were to rapidly become astonishingly well worked with wonderful designs. Another great leap forwards in tool technology which we will look at in more detail later.

The combination of the availability of leather and of reindeer skin, allowed Neanderthals to make boots designed for periglacial conditions such as the traditional Mukluk boot of the aboriginal Eskimos whose origins go stretch back into the mists of time, but which are still in use today. These Mukluk boots, made from reindeer or seal skin are so light that they don't need lacing and friction alone allows them to stay on the feet. The absence of tight lacing reducing the chances of frostbite due to the restriction of blood flow to the feet and toes, and also allow the feet to breathe ensuring that they remain dry. They are also specifically appropriate for hunting for which they are still used because they make very little noise. Mukluks are made with a wrap-around sole, so that the seam is above the foot and not in contact with the ground, reducing the chances of leaking. For warmth, Mukluks use the fur side of the reindeer skin on the inside of the boot, which as we have seen has excellent insulating properties.

The Neanderthals created other bone tools, marking an even further departure from the Mousterian technology which they had used for so long. Initially these bone tools were associated with anatomically modern humans, but there have been Neanderthal bones associated with this new technology which has now cemented it as a Neanderthal technology, and it is called Chatelperronian. In particular and relating to their increasingly sophisticated clothes manufacture they started to make bone awls. Many of these have been discovered at the Chatelperronian site of the Grotte de la Reine at Arcy-sur-Cure in Burgundy, France. These bone awls being about 10cm long and tapered to a point at one end for piercing the skin, were up to 1cm or so at the blunt end, which was rounded. So, with very many scrapers, bone smoothing tools and fine bone awls, Neanderthals were capable of making a wide variety of clothing, boots, pouches and bedding from the animal skins of animals that they routinely hunted. Together with their mastery of fire they were now well equipped for facing the worst of the great Ice Age.

Neanderthal Nomads and Their Diet

Evidence of large quantities of bones around Neanderthal camps and DNA in the enamel of Neanderthal teeth shows that a large part of their diets was mammoth meat. But how did they procure so many mammoths to eat?

Scientists from the Seckenberg Center for human Evolution and Palaeoenvironment at Tubingen have researched the Neanderthal diet based at two sites in Belgium, where they had a vast quantity of bones from the camps to analyze. They used the isotope levels in the collagen in the Neanderthal bones to determine what they fed on. In the immediate vicinity of the Neanderthal camp were found bones of reindeer, wild horses, European bison, cave bears, lions and hyenas. In the 20th century it was suggested that Neanderthal was a mere scavenger eking out a pitiful survival from the leavings of more successful predators. Later in the 20th century it was assumed that Neanderthals fed on many of the smaller mammals that the other predators fed on, such as reindeer and wild horse. However, the Neanderthal bones show that over 80% of the Neanderthal diet was from the woolly rhinoceros and the woolly mammoth, the largest and most powerful herbivores around in Pleistocene Europe. Far from being scavengers Neanderthals preferred to feed on some of the most powerful and dangerous animals in their world and were the Pleistocene apex predator. Less than 20% of their diet was based on plant matter.

The reliance on mammoth and rhinoceros meat provokes questions over the presence of so many bones of different animals. It is possible that cave hyenas occupied these Belgian caves during Neanderthal absences and brought their kills to the cave. It is also possible that Neanderthals killed other animals to feed their domesticated wolves, just as some Eskimo peoples feed their dogs on different meat than what they eat themselves. Or simply they enjoyed a varied diet depending upon which animals they encountered on their hunting trips.

Mammoths, like elephants, were gregarious animals moving around in large and well-knit family groups, which was necessary for the protection of the mammoth calves. Woolly mammoths are cousins to elephants and we know that elephants eat several hundred kilos of vegetation daily, which takes them between 16 and 18 hours to consume. A group of say 10 mammoths would munch through well over 1 ton of vegetation daily, and given the energy expenditure required in keeping warm probably much more than that. In Europe, fertile grassland produces between 12–14 tons of grassland (made up of oat grasses or lucernes) per hectare. Steppe or periglacial grassland produce a lot less. A herd of 10 mammoths would strip the grass from a fertile 1 hectare area (100m x 100m) of grassland in less than two days. Wherever the quality of grass was less than optimal, then the mammoth herds would have been obliged to remain on the move permanently.

This should come as no surprise, as that is the natural behavior of large herbivores in the wild throughout the world, but it does mean that Neanderthals feeding almost exclusively on mammoth meat would have been obliged to move with them. In other words, they were nomads. This dependence on mammoth meat supplies us with a vital clue about Neanderthal behavior and is borne out by evidence in the caves which shows that although Neanderthals may have inhabited the caves for tens or even hundreds of thousands of years, there were frequent absences.

There is no evidence that Neanderthals had yet domesticated horses and so their nomadic lifestyle would require them to carry all their necessary belongings on their backs; clothes, weapons and tools essential for their daily chores. They may well have divided the roles between the women and children bringing the necessary elements of camp life and the hunters moving ahead following the mammoth herd. Evidence from bones around Neanderthal camps is that the Neanderthals hunted either young or female mammoths, and stayed clear of the large and dangerous males. An adult female mammoth would have weighed around four tons, at least half of which would have been edible, i.e., at least two tons of meat and probably 3. If we look at traditional Native American Indian practices while hunting buffalo, it may give us a clue as to how Stone Age cultures hunted large migratory herbivores. This is a description of hunting practices of the Plains Indians.

Once the buffalo had been harvested, the carcass had to be fully butchered and processed into usable food fairly quickly or it would spoil. In a communal hunt, such as a buffalo jump, processing the carcass was done with an assembly line. Removing the hide and emptying the stomach were crucial in cooling down the carcass and ensuring that the greatest amount of food could be saved for future use. In butchering a buffalo, the tongue and internal organs were removed first. These were taken to the camp's medicine people and then eaten as delicacies. As the people butchered the carcass-a process which would go on around the clock until it was done-they would smash the big marrow bones with heavy stone hammers to extract the tasty and nutritious marrow. This would help replenish the energy of the workers.

The body would be cut into 11 pieces to facilitate transportation: the four limbs, the two sides of ribs, the two sinews on each side of the back bone, the brisket, the croup, and the back bone.

The dried meat would be stored in hide containers known as parfleches. Parfleches were made from stiff, untanned hides that were folded into a large envelope. The food would be packed in the parfleche as tightly as possible to keep out as much air as possible, thus reducing spoilage. Properly cured and packaged dried meat could last for months, and even years. (Ojibwa)

Bison meat is about 65% water, so the Indians would dry it to make it lighter and easier to carry and allow it to last longer without spoiling. The meat would be cut into thin strips and hung up on wooden racks made from branches, thus increasing the surface area to speed up dehydration. This method was also used for preserving fillets of fish.

A common method of cooking amongst American Indians, was to dig a pit and line it with a buffalo skin, placed flesh side upwards, to make the hollow water-tight. This would then be filled with water and heated stones placed in it until the water was hot enough to cook the food without burning it.

As we shall see later, the nomad way of life continued through to the Mesolithic in Europe and Asia, from where some of these nomads migrated to North America carrying with them the culture, so there is very good reason to suppose that the North American Indians hunting methods were derived from their nomadic ancestors in Eurasia.

For tribes such as the Blackfeet, the bison was the principal source of food, every piece of it was used for either food, clothing, decoration, utensils, weapons and medicine. Their religious beliefs maintained that it would offend the Creator to waste any part of the buffalo, which He had provided for them. This aversion to any waste is identical to the attitude of Ice Age Europeans who relied on the reindeer for sustenance and used all parts of that animal once they had killed it.

The Blackfeet with their nomadic hunter traditions inherited from the Eurasian hunter nomads illustrate how they prepared their food, their hunting methods can also prove illuminating. The buffalo hunt was a special event. The men would set off in hunting parties with the women and children following behind carrying with them the tools for butchering, preparing and transporting the meat. The Blackfeet used three methods of killing, the first was hunting with the bow and arrow from horseback, the second was driving them over a cliff and the third was corralling individuals onto frozen lakes, where they would fall through the ice and die from hypothermia. Because they depended so much on the buffalo to sustain them, they had to follow them, never making permanent camps, but always temporary camps never far from the buffalo herd.

Preserving mammoth meat might have been necessary for survival during times of hardship, and also for members of the Neanderthal group incapable of following the migrating mammoth herd. The Blackfoot Indians had this recipe for the preservation of bison meat.

> 'Pemmican — Ingredients — Choice Cut bison Meat, Wild Cherry Paste (Optional)
>
> Pemmican was a very important food to the Blackfeet because it is very dense, hearty, and nutritious. Pemmican is a mixture of choice cut bison meat and occasionally crushed wild cherries gathered by the Blackfeet women. Once prepared, pemmican was a staple food taken on hunting trips by the Blackfeet men as it is a very filling food. One pound of pemmican is equal to five pounds of meat. The berry form of pemmican is prepared by first crushing the berries into a paste, then selecting the best cuts of bison meat to dry. The marrow from boiling bison bones is collected and used to prevent burning the meat. The meat is then minced and mixed with the berry spread and sometimes peppermint for flavor and then held over a fire. Once cooked, the meat goes into a bag for storage and is edible at any point forward for the hunter for many months.' (Partridge Dennis)

If each Neanderthal in the group ate 2Kg of meat per day the two tons of mammoth meat from a carcass would keep a 10 person strong group going for three months if they could keep it fresh for that long. Drying the meat would possibly halve that weight, but the nutritional value would be similar, so the rough calculation would probably remain consistent. If the group was 40 people strong, it could keep them going for nearly two weeks on a single mammoth carcass. The larger the group, the more warriors it could put in the field, which would be a considerable advantage when attempting to single out a mammoth and kill it with the minimum of losses to the warriors. But a group that was too large would be forced to hunt more often, this would cause a rapid decline in the mammoth herd with the risk of it becoming extinguished and too regular hunting would cause it to be spooked permanently, both of which would be counter-productive. For groups of Neanderthals dependent on a woolly mammoth herd all year round, the size of the group would be dependent on the size of the mammoth herd.

If the woolly mammoth was similar in its reproduction to the modern elephant, then each female once mature enough would only produce a mammoth calf every five or 6 years and it takes about 18 to 20 years for an elephant to reach adulthood. A cow elephant stops producing calf elephants at about 50 years old, meaning that on average she will produce roughly 6 calves in her life time, with elephant's mortality rates of young calves is about 30%, this would result in only four of those young being likely to reach adulthood.

In a group containing 20 female mammoths only those from 20-50 would be of breeding age, meaning about half or 10 of them. If each breeding female bred every five years that would mean that there would be only two new calves in the group per year. Statistically 1/3 of these would not reach adulthood. So, the group would produce 1.3 new adult mammoths a year. As the average elephant dies at about 60 years of age, in a group of 20 females, one would die every three years. In those three years the herd would grow by 4 and lose 1 to death; in other words it would grow at 1 per year. That is without considering predation. If the Neanderthal group killed just one mammoth a year, the herd would remain roughly stable. Obviously, a group of Neanderthals would not be able to live off one single mammoth kill every year.

If each Neanderthal ate 2Kg of mammoth meat every day of the year, and there were 10 Neanderthals in the group, that would equate to about 7 tons of mammoth meat, meaning at least two mammoths. But for that mammoth herd to be sustainable and not be rapidly killed off, a herd of at least 40 animals would be necessary to maintain a group of 10 Neanderthals. In the wild elephants breed young males and females in approximate even numbers. So that for 20 females another 20 males may well exist, although because of herd dynamics only a few of them might be present in the herd. For a Neanderthal group to live off its mammoth herd, it would wherever possible select immature males for hunting, in order to maintain a healthy number of breeding females. This approximate ratio of 4 mammoths to every 1 Neanderthal gives an idea of the maximum numbers of Neanderthals living off mammoth herds. It also serves to highlight the very close dependence that Neanderthals had on the mammoth herds and how much it was in the Neanderthal interest to protect their herd from other predations be they any of the other great mammalian hunters such as saber toothed cats during the Ice Age or even other Neanderthal groups. Just as today's farmers protect their flocks of sheep from wolves and foxes so the Neanderthals are likely to have protected their main and sometimes only source of food from other predators. This may well have led Neanderthals groups to hunt and kill these other big predators to protect their own food supply. This in turn may well have contributed to the demise of the great Ice Age predators such as the cave lion and the saber-toothed cat. We will come back to the extinction of the great Ice Age carnivores later in the book.

A group of Neanderthals that overhunted its mammoth herd would be putting its very existence in peril. It was very much in the Neanderthal's interests to maintain a harmonious balance between the number of members in its group or tribe and the number of mammoth that it followed. Given how they survived for hundreds of thousands of years, they must have developed an acute sense of the balance in nature. Wasting mammoth meat would mean having to hunt another one, reducing unnecessarily the size of the herd that they relied on to survive. Knowing that mammoth calves arrived infrequently, they must have realized what a precious resource each mammoth was. The dependence on the delicate natural balance between hunted and hunter is probably one of the crucial factors in the development of their religion which we will look at in detail later.

Whereas a group that was too small would probably struggle to be efficient in effecting a mammoth kill with the added risk that injury or incapacity due to illness to a small number of hunters might put the very survival of the whole group in danger. The maintenance of an optimum group size in Neanderthal nomadic society was probably of paramount importance.

Sedentary Neanderthals

Various Neanderthal remains in a roughly central belt of Europe reveal a mixed diet which includes mammoth and other animals such as wild horses and reindeer. In these cases, it is likely that these peoples lived in areas where there was a large enough supply of wild animals to maintain their populations based in one area throughout the year. Many of these camps lie along river banks which could have been migration routes for migratory animals such as mammoth and bison. Some riverside caves in France have revealed fish bones indicating that the rivers also supplied Neanderthals with fish as a source of food. During times when animals were scarce, particularly in the winter, it is likely that Neanderthals managed to store meat packed in snow deep in their caves, just as meat is stored in permafrost cellars in Siberia still today, and in Northern Italy up until very recently food was preserved in glacier bored holes around the alpine town of Chiavenna and elsewhere. Long term storage of meat outside of the caves would not have resisted the predations of wolves, bears and hyenas, all capable of digging up any meat. But

Neanderthals guarded their caves against predators; anything stored deep in the cave was as safe as anywhere could be in the Pleistocene. So, not only did caves offer protection from the elements and from large predators, but also represented a secure place to stow food for long periods.

In Neanderthal camps where there were no caves, pits were dug and partially filled with snow and ice; and covered over, offering a lesser degree of protection for long term storage of food. Many Neanderthal settlements are accompanied by these pits which today have been discovered still filled with animal bones. This practice of snow pits was continued as a form of primitive but effective freezer well into Roman times. One such food pit can still be visited at Martigny in Switzerland. This storage of meat allowed Neanderthals to profit from times when wild animals were plentiful enabling them to see through the difficult lean months.

Sedentary Neanderthal Settlements

Whereas many Neanderthal groups in the Northern two thirds of Europe were nomadic, there were others along the shores of the Mediterranean who could live off a combination of produce procured from the sea and mammals in the surrounding countryside throughout the year. These groups were settled mostly in one place and had a very different lifestyle to their nomadic Northern cousins. In Gibraltar for example, two caves (Gorham and Vanguard) show extensive evidence of Neanderthal occupation from 45-26,000BP containing various layers of Neanderthal food remains most of which has been burnt, cut or deliberately broken. These caves reveal a combination of feeding from the sea procuring animals such as monk seals, dolphins, sea-shore mollusks and fish, supplemented by migratory birds, ibex, red deer, wild boar and bear. With such a wide range of food sources they were less dependent upon any one species for survival, and from current research they would appear to be the very last classic Neanderthal group to have survived anywhere.

Other southern Neanderthal populations have had their diets in the last years of life analyzed by studying the contents of the collagen in their bones. Two Neanderthals bones were analyzed revealing that 'their overwhelming diet was of meat'. Furthermore, the carbon 13 isotope levels indicate that they mostly ate free ranging herbivores rather than forest species, in particular, preliminary findings suggest that even these southern Neanderthals focused on woolly mammoths which demonstrate a signature high N15 value. This collagen analysis has been compared to analyses of Neanderthal collagen from Scladina Cave in Belgium and Marillac in France and have been found to be remarkably similar.

At the Moldova 1 site in the Ukraine, the mammoth diet was supplemented by hunting also red deer, bison and reindeer.

It would seem that even some of the Southern Neanderthal populations were dependent partially at least on the migrating mammoth herds.

The nomadic Neanderthal depended almost totally on mammoth meat whereas the more sedentary Neanderthals in the warmer south although still feeding on mammoth when it was available, diversified their diet depending on what was available. In all probability, they ate mammoth in the winter and non-migratory smaller species during the winter.

The Ice Age

One of the most important factors to shape the modern European was the last Ice Age. In mainland Europe this is known as the Weichselian Ice Age. It covered the period from 115,000 BP to 10,000 BP, and we are still emerging from it today in what is known as an interglacial period. A slight shift in the earth's orbital configuration led to a significant decrease in the summer sunlight in the Northern hemisphere, lowering temperatures, and the northern ice sheets started to grow. This led to the beginning of the Geological Epoch known as the Pleistocene an epoch characterized by repeated glaciations. The period of the Pleistocene is now considered to begin about 2.58 million years ago and end roughly 10,000 years ago. The current Geological Epoch which followed on from the Pleistocene is the Holocene.

The impact on the lives of our ancestors of the Ice Age was immense. For the majority of the time the climate was very extremely cold, dry and dusty. Survival was a constant battle in the face of cold, scarcity of water, need for warmth and shelter, and avoiding the predations of large and very dangerous animals, in conjunction with omnipresent issues such as malnutrition and disease. All these challenges shaped the ancient Europeans and enhanced their resourcefulness and capacity for survival.

The Weichselian Ice Age was preceded by the Eemian interglacial period. This was a period lasting from 130,000BP to 115,000BP. The climate was comparable to our own Holocene epoch, but somewhat warmer. The increased warmth meant that sea levels were up to 9m higher than today's levels, due in large part to reduced ice retention at the poles. The effect of this was to make Scandinavia into an island which was free of any ice cap, as was a reduced British Isles. Hippopotamus could be found on the Rhine and the Thames together with water buffalo. Various large carnivores were present too in this period, the lion and leopard, various species of bear, hyena, and lynx. There were gigantic herbivores too, including the largest land mammal ever to have existed the Paleoloxodon estimated to weigh in at an impressive 24 tons. A staggering 3 ½ times the weight of the largest of African elephants today. Neanderthal man hunted all over Europe and was already present in the British Isles, having arrived during the previous Ice Age, the Riss Glaciation (300–130,000BP), also known as the Wolstonian Stage in Britain when Britain was linked to the continent by Doggerland (a vast area of the North Sea that was above sea level at the time). In Britain as in other parts of Northern Europe, Neanderthal, as with all the other land animals, was forced to flee into Southern Europe at various times, for thousands of years at a stretch, during this period by repeated advances of the great northern ice sheets which covered even greater areas in Europe than the last great Ice Age. At the coldest point during the Riss Ice Age most of Britain was engulfed in the Sheet Ice with the exception of the South Coast. Permafrost dominated all land between the great ice sheets and Southern Europe, rendering life all but impossible north of a line drawn from Bordeaux on the Atlantic Coast to the Black Sea.

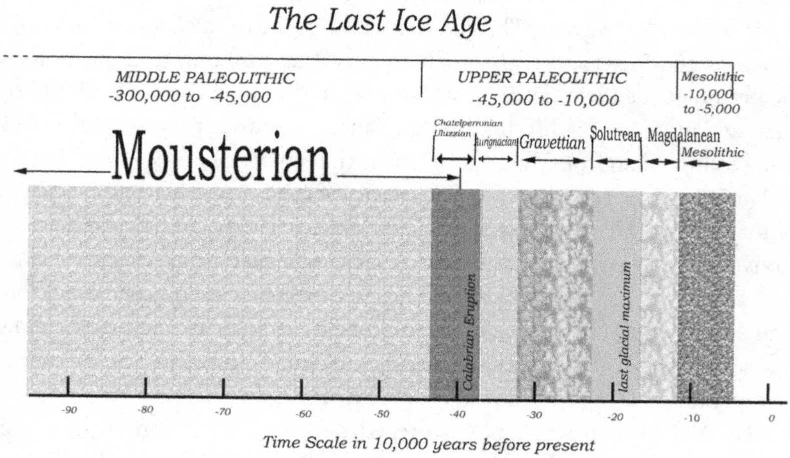

Illustration 35. European cultures during the last ice age

It is in Britain, right at the end of the Riss Ice Age that we find at 130,000BP the first ever intentional human burial. Indeed, Britain had already been inhabited by hominids for over 800,000 years already during periods when the Ice sheets had retreated northwards. Each subsequent Ice

Sheet advance wiping away all traces of human activity apart from those preserved in caves underground.

The Eemian interglacial was the brief period between the Riss and the Weichselian Ice Age (the last great ice age in Europe).

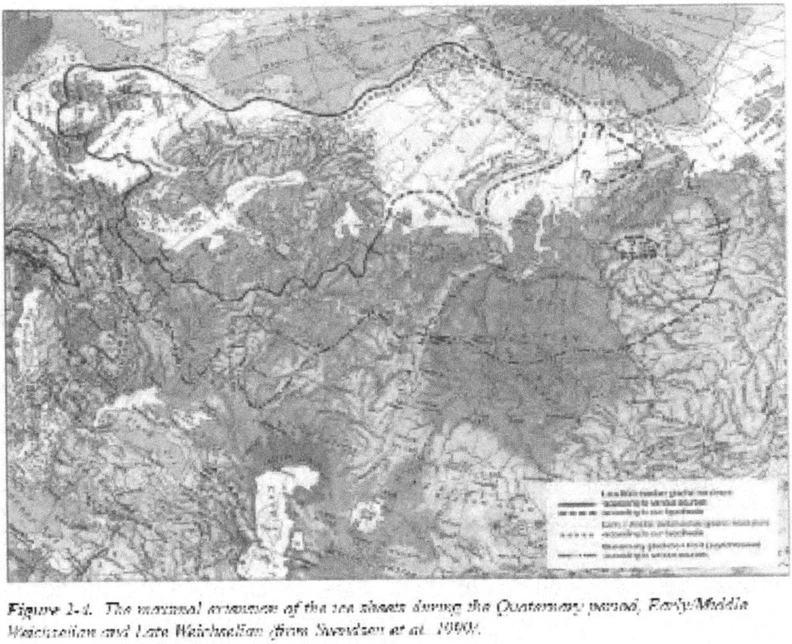

Illustration 36. Extent of ice sheets during the quaternary

Credit: Technical Report: Ice Marginal Fluctuations during the Weichselian glaciations in Fennoscandinavia. By Hanna Lokrantz, Gustav Sohlenius. Geological Survey of Sweden (SGU) 2006

When the climate suddenly started to become colder about 115,0000 years ago, ice sheets started to form in Scandinavia and glaciers coalesced in the Alps. One problem with providing precise dates and lines for the various limits of the ice caps in Europe during the Weichselian, is that subsequent ice sheet advances tend to completely eradicate all evidence on the ground whether it be surface fossils, tree spores, or soil. Indeed, all soil, plants, trees and even the rock itself was ground into huge quantities of dust, by the great weight and grinding power of the ice. The material produced, called loess, was made up of extremely fine dust just micrometers in diameter, so light that it was easily blown around the continent and accumulated in places to depths of over 100m.

The glaciers effectively wiped the archeological slate clean in large swathes of Northern Europe again and again throughout the Pleistocene, obliterating without trace, all human remains with the exception of scarce remains deep in caves. Many caves themselves, and particularly their entrances where human activity tended to be concentrated were also destroyed by the glaciers, reducing our ability to uncover human activity during these glacial times.

The dating methods used for the various periods mentioned in this chapter have been arrived at by extensive research throughout northern Europe, including dating mollusk shells, and Greenland ice cores, as well as sea bed deposits. We have far more precise data concerning the late Weichselian ice sheets. When the ice sheets retreated they left behind great moraines which leave clear indications of where the ice sheets remained for some time, as they gradually retreated.

Looking at the Weichselian Ice Age from a great distance in time, it is easy to imagine a long period of great cold, but the reality is very different indeed. It was a period of cold but of a changing climate, and within it were many different climatic phases, which in turn changed the flora and fauna immensely. The cold phases are referred to as stadials and the warm interludes as interstadials. A list of the stadials and interstadials is given in the Appendix. During the Weichselian Ice Age a period of roughly 100,000 years, there were about 27 swings from temperate to cold and back again each one evidenced by a radical change in the flora and fauna. During the stadials the conditions were similar to arctic and subarctic conditions today. The dates in this list are approximate and differ between geographical locations and not all authorities agree on the interpretation of the evidence. But for the scope of this book, it is sufficient to understand the dramatic extent of the climatic swings and the effect that they had on all the fauna and flora of Europe.

In essence during the Weichselian, there were two ice sheets on the continent. The northern one, with a fluctuating southern border, with the ice sheet stretching down from Scandinavia reaching at its greatest extent a line drawn from roughly half way across the British Isles, through the middle of Germany and Poland and into Russia. The second ice sheet covered the Alps, and stretched beyond the mountainous areas for sometimes hundreds of kilometers into the surrounding plains.

During this Ice Age, as with the previous one, large amounts of the earth's water were locked up in glacial ice around the globe; the result was a lowering of sea levels to roughly 120m below present sea levels. This lowering of sea levels extended the continents and changed the contours of the world map considerably. In Europe, much of the North Sea was land, known as Doggerland. The land bridge sometimes referred to between continental Europe and Britain is somewhat misleading, suggestive of a narrow defile linking Dover and Calais. In reality, Britain was more of a simple extension of the continental landmass projecting further into the Atlantic Ocean. Whereas the North Sea was mostly a land of hills and marshes, partially covered by the northern Ice sheet, the English Channel was a huge river valley, where the Rhine draining the Alpine ice sheet joined with other rivers such as the Thames draining the northern ice sheet, and flowing down the present course of the English Channel into the Atlantic Ocean well beyond present Cornwall and Brittany.

This surprising state of the land was first suspected when North Sea trawlers started to bring up curious objects from the sea bed far from land, such as pieces of Neolithic worked deer antler.

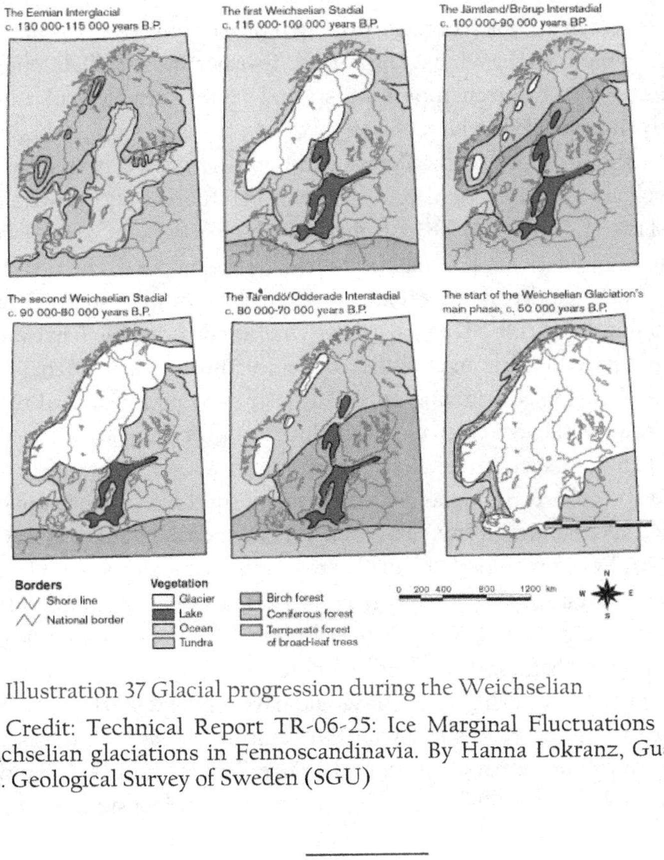

Illustration 37 Glacial progression during the Weichselian

Credit: Technical Report TR-06-25: Ice Marginal Fluctuations during the Weichselian glaciations in Fennoscandinavia. By Hanna Lokranz, Gustav Sohlenius. Geological Survey of Sweden (SGU)

The shallow sea currently at the northern end of the Adriatic was also land. The Baltic changed considerably during this period, from a fresh water ice lake which at times spilled over through Sweden and fed the great river which flowed through the English Channel. As the ice sheets retreated at the end of the Ice Age, the form and content of the English Channel changed considerably, slowly becoming more brackish and finally becoming a salt sea linked to the North Sea.

At the start of the Weichselian Ice Age sea levels were 4-5m higher than present, with the size of the European land mass smaller than today. With lowering temperatures, ice slowly started to accumulate in the coldest regions, at the northern end of the continent and over the Alps. The first stage lasting from 115,000 to 60,000BP is known as the early glacial period and was milder than the second half.

In this first half of the Weichselian, lasting roughly 55,000 years there were two fairly distinct cold phases or stadials and two fairly distinct warm phases or interstadials. Each of these principal phases however was made up of considerable climatic swings. During the warmer interstadials much of Europe was covered by birch or pine forests and during the colder phases the trees largely disappeared to be replaced by grassy tundra.

North of the Alps, during the Eemian, the continent was covered by pine forest to well above the Arctic Circle, further north than today. However, at the onset of the Weichselian, the first phase of which is known as the Herning Stadial was so intense that the majority of the forests north of the Alps were killed off, and the landscape was dominated by arctic tundra, steppes, hardy grasses and juniper shrubs. This must have caused considerable hardship for animals unprepared for life in an extremely cold climate. Neanderthals who had become accustomed to living outside in camps would have had to find protection against the extreme cold of the Ice Age winters. They would have been forced to seek shelter particularly during the winter, migrate south or perish from the cold. Caves would have been a natural refuge from the cold, where they could maintain a fire. But other animals such as the cave bear, Cave lion, and cave hyena would also have been seeking shelter from the intense cold and competing for these caves. It is likely that north of the Alps there would have been a general depopulation, coupled with an increase in the population of Neanderthal migrants from the north, fleeing to Southern Europe. Resident populations south of the Alps would have mixed with their northern neighbors, causing a degree a sharing of DNA, culture, diseases and resistance to diseases. In the far north of Europe, the Scandinavian and Greenland ice sheets advanced as far as the coast. The ice sheet started to spread over the high Alps. This forced migration southwards is one of the contributing factors that ensured that Neanderthal technology and DNA remained remarkably homogeneous over Europe and Western Asia.

The Brorup interstadial, or brief warmer interlude around 107,000BP provided some relief to Europe. All the ice sheets started to retreat, and forests started to grow over the tundra. The first tree to establish itself was the birch, then over several thousands of years; pine and larch forests started to cover the land interspersed with summer grasses. The latter would have provided summer pastures for large herbivores. As a consequence, for a period of nearly 6,000 years, large animals and large predators would have spread northwards over Europe. In their wake would have followed groups of Neanderthals. But even if north of the Alps the summers were pleasantly warm the winters were still very cold with mean minimum temperatures between -8c and -14C. Warm summers and a lengthy growing season would have favored migrations of herbivores north in the summer, and then south to warmer climes in the winter, and the Neanderthals would have followed them for the most part. This pattern of northward summer migrations followed by southern fall migrations was one that was to continue right throughout the Ice Age. Then the temperature dropped again.

Curiously, there is a growing consensus that the Scandinavian and Russian ice sheets were expanding and contracting out of synchronization, and that it was in the early part of the Weichselian that the Russian ice sheet was at its maximum and not in the High Weichselian 60,000 years or so later. Conversely, during the High Weichselian, when so much of Europe was under ice, Russia was less so, allowing animals and Neanderthals to escape to the great Asian plains to the East. One explanation for this seeming anomaly is that when the ice sheets covered northern Europe the air was cold and dry preventing snow fall from penetrating further east into Russia. Whatever the cause, this desynchronization of the glacial maxima between Europe and Russia allowed animals to displace to regions where life could continue.

The onset of each stadial cold period was accompanied by a gradual evacuation of Northern Europe as food sources depleted. Although many animals may have migrated to warmer climes with more available food supplies, some will have remained and eventually starved. Scavengers such as cave hyenas and possibly bears will have survived for substantial periods on the remains of the bodies of dead animals including Neanderthals which had accumulated in caves amongst other places, so that a sort of clearing out of a good deal of archeological evidence occurred in caves at the onset of each stadial. One can easily imagine the sad scene of Neanderthal families starving to death in caves as the animals which made up their food sources disappeared. And then the cave hyenas move in to scavenge the remains. This end of interstadial phenomenon of scavenging while food sources become depleted, explains the paucity of remains of Neanderthals as well as other animals.

This intense scavenging for survival as each stadial sets in, coupled with the forced abandonment of caves may well have been the trigger to cause Neanderthal to protect the bodies of loved ones, for the first time by burying them under heavy rocks. Thus, creating the custom of human burial, which occurred for the first time with Neanderthals.

Although most species of European mammals struggled to adapt to the extreme stadial conditions in Europe, some species such as the reindeer and the Polar bear evolved and became cold climate specialists. Those that moved south beyond the permafrost region encountered sedentary Neanderthals, and competed with them for resources. But tough as life was during the first half of the Ice Age, it would get far tougher still as Europe entered the High Glacial Period.

The middle of the Weichselian Ice Age, called the High Glacial Period, from 57,000–15,000BP, had far colder conditions. It too has been subdivided into different phases of alternating cold stadials with advancing ice sheets with pollen free deposits indicating a polar wasteland and warmer interludes or interstadials sometimes dominated by tundra conditions at other times dominated by sedge grasses, dwarf birch and even temperate forests.

The same cyclical process of freezing stadials interrupted by warmer interstadials continued through the 2nd half of the Last Ice, but was far colder than the first half, right up until the last glacial maximum 24-12,000 BP. The most extreme part of the whole Ice Age occurred at around 21,0000 BP when the ice caps reached their greatest extent and sea levels dropped to their lowest levels, exposing more land, normally covered by the sea.

As the glaciers reached their maximum extents and locked up a maximum amount of the world's fresh water in the ice caps, sea levels dropped to around 120m below today's levels. The topography of Europe's coastlines changed dramatically. Britain had long been a peninsula of Europe, linked by a wide swath of chalk stretching from South East England to France and Belgium. However, around 500,000BP, it is considered that this soft rock was breached by the glacial flood water escaping from the Scandinavian Ice Cap. As the glaciers from the Scandinavian mountains retreated they left behind vast areas of moraines in the North Sea which created a wide landscape of low hills.

During the Eemian interglacial (before the start of the Weichselian) some of these moraine hills projected above the sea, as low-lying boggy islands. As the Weicheselian Ice Age advanced the sea levels lowered until these islands joined up and a vast area of the Southern North Sea from Jutland to Scotland

and down to southern England was above sea level. This large area is called Doggerland, named after the Dogger Bank off the Dutch coast, which in turn was named after the Dutch dogger boats. The Southern end of Doggerland, was dominated by the vast river created by the joining of the Rhine, Thames and Seine, which once joined flowed down the dry English channel to reach the Atlantic somewhere well to the West of Cornwall. Doggerland was indeed land long enough for substantial thicknesses of peat to have been created, some samples of which have been dredged up from the North Sea bed by fishermen. Peat thickness grows at 1mm per year. So, a 1m thickness of peat will take 1,000 years to create.

Inside one clump of peat was found a deer antler worked into a barbed point. Over the last 100 years trawlers have dragged up many prehistoric tools, as well as remains of mammoth and lions and also Neanderthal remains.

The northern end of Doggerland was a country of lagoons, rivers and lakes, and is considered to have been a land of rich natural resources, and an area where humans thrived in numbers.

As the ice sheets retreated in the last Ice Age, and once again sea levels started to rise, slowly Doggerland started to disappear below the waves. By 10,000 BP parts of it were still dry land, but by 6,500 BP Britain had once again become an island, together with other islands in the North Sea. By 5,000 BP, within the historical record the last of these, quite possibly the Dogger Bank, had disappeared too. Today the submerged sandy Dogger Bank covers 17,600km^2 measuring roughly 260km west to east and nearly 100km from North to South and is only about 15m below current sea level. Because of the shallowness of the sea it has been identified as a key location, albeit right in the middle of the North Sea for a huge wind farm installation.

By the time that Doggerland had disappeared under the sea however, links between Britain and the continent were maintained by boat travel. Off the coast of the Isle of Wight in 11m of water there is a Mesolithic boat yard, implying the systematic manufacture of boats for fishing and travel in a world where water was invading the land. This discovery was made thanks to a lobster, which divers observed removing worked flints from its burrow in the mud. This boat yard is estimated to be about 8,000 years old. However, boat yards in deeper water may yet be discovered by chance, and of far greater antiquity.

Interest is growing in Doggerland because of its potential for revealing key information about Europe's past. The shore line has often been a favorite location for habitation, because of the ready availability of food sources such as fish and shellfish. The entire area of Doggerland has at some time in the last 100,000 years been a shore line, and so potentially is a rich source of archeological material, which may well be in an excellent state of preservation.

The final period in the Weichselian Ice Age is known as the late glacial period from 12,000-10,000BP. It marked a warming of the continent as it emerged from the Ice Age, but was interrupted by a sequence of cold phases. Three of these stadials Oldest Dryas, Older Dryas and Younger Dryas (in chronological order), were characterized by a disappearance of trees and the appearance of the arctic flowering plant the dryas (*Dryas octopetela*), a small daisy like flower of the rose family with 8petalled flowers, whose pollens dominated these stadials.

The Barents and Kara ice sheets never reached the Russian mainland during the late Weichselian. The Scandinavian ice sheet did however spread into North West Russia, and reached its maximum in the Dvina basin around 17,000BP

Between 18 and 17,000BP the Scandinavian ice sheet had started to recede, whereas the Baltic section advanced somewhat and reached Denmark. In Germany and Poland, a fairly stable ice front was created along the line of Frankfurt–Poznan–Pomerania. The ice sheet retreated in Sweden between 18 and 13.000BP

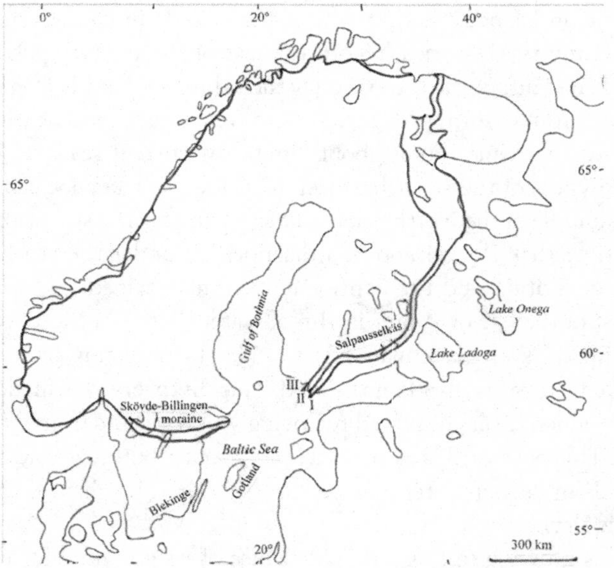

Illustration 38. Scandanavian ice sheet during the Younger Dryas

Credit: The Younger Dryas Age Of The Salpausselka Moraines In Finland. By Joakim Donner. Bulletin of the Geological Society of Finland, Vol 82, 2010, pp 69-80

At 10,000 BP there was a rapid rise in atmospheric temperatures, which marked the end of the Pleistocene epoch and the start of the Holocene. The Holocene, our present age is considered an inter glacial period, as the remnant glaciers of the Pleistocene, concentrated mostly in the Alps and in Iceland continue to retreat.

Despite the inhospitable conditions in Europe, particularly close to the ice sheets, where there were extensive areas of permafrost, as in Siberia today, life hung on, adapted and continued to survive. Life in northern Europe might have been wiped out entirely, if the two ice sheets had expanded to the point where they had united, covering most of the continent in a single ice sheet. Fortunately, however this never happened, and although arctic or subarctic conditions reigned between the two ice sheets and to the West in France, Europeans continued to occupy wide swathes of the continent.

There were extensive periods during the Ice Age, when tundra conditions in northern Europe prevailed, with only hardy grasses poking through the snow. As temperatures fluctuated, forests appeared in various guises, sometimes dominated by coniferous sometimes by hardy deciduous like willow and birch. As described above there are about 20 phases where conditions changed radically over the 100,000 year period of the Weicheselian. Each phase presented new challenges for ancient Europeans, with new threats to survival. When grasslands prevailed, large herbivores grazed them, such as the aurochs, megaloceros, and woolly mammoths, providing potentially ready supplies of meat to Neanderthals and other carnivores. When the grasses disappeared, the grazers would have died or migrated south. This would have forced ancient Europeans to follow the herds or starve. In places where the temperatures were less extreme particularly around the Mediterranean, grasses could grow around the year, herbivores could become sedentary, allowing humans to remain in situ. In colder areas where the grasses were seasonal, and only visited by migrating herds of herbivores during the warmer months, Neanderthals would have had to adopt a migratory life style. Where permanent human life was possible, they would have been able to establish permanent settlements in caves, a precious resource. But in the colder regions populations of humans would have tracked the herds of herbivores. This would have been a more challenging life style requiring early humans to keep on the move, survive in cold conditions with no permanent shelter. Camps would have been temporary and mobile. The ability to maintain fires was essential. Life would have been harsh. It would have been extremely difficult to care for the elderly and sick. Those that couldn't keep moving would have died. Only the fit and strong would have been able to survive. Thus, the few Neanderthals remains that show life threatening wounds that have subsequently healed during this period belong to the southern sedentary Neanderthals such as in Iraq.

Although many writers have glossed over this period of human evolution as one single homogeneous trend; closer inspection reveals a diverging evolution. On the one hand in warmer climates sedentary populations living in caves in relatively warm conditions with access to year-round supplies of food would have thrived with relative ease compared to their northern cousins. The Northern Europeans were nomads having to be constantly planning the next move, making life and death decisions about where to go next, ensuring that women and children were fed, to ensure the future of the family group or tribe.

Northern Europeans living in areas without permanent grazing would not have had the same sense of territoriality, or belonging to a particular place. Their lives would have been closely synchronized with the seasons and with the animals that they needed to live off. As the animals underwent their annual migrations, returning year after year to the same places, so the northern Europeans would have done the same.

When tundra conditions prevailed over the northern plains, the herbivore herds and the Neanderthals would have been forced to move south, and come into contact with their southern territorial cousins. Desperate life and death conflicts over the ownership of precious food resources would have followed. Even though conflict may have been a regular occurrence there was also a beneficial side to the Southern migration of the nomads. The nomadic lifestyle was the cultural glue that kept Ancient Europeans from across the continent broadly in step.

The Rapidly Oscillating Climate

The last Ice Age as we have seen was a period of rapid cyclical climatic changes, with temperatures oscillating from extreme cold to mild. Records of the changing flora show that the pace of change was too fast for trees and so tree and other vegetal species were wiped out from vast areas of Europe on a regular basis, before re-introducing themselves when the climate became more favorable. As the climate and the flora changed so did the fauna. Just to take one example; reindeer are adapted to tundra conditions, but not forests, whereas red deer are adapted to forests but not tundra. Throughout Paleolithic excavations at human settlements we see alternating layers of differing fauna, with reindeer dominating during tundra conditions, and horse and aurochs in others. Although the majority of species were incapable of changing fast enough to adapt to these cyclical changes, our human ancestors were an exception. We find Neanderthal remains present continuously whatever the flora and fauna profiles of the Ice Age.

The one great advantage that hominids had over all the other species of fauna was his very large brain, allowing them to adapt to the conditions with considerable success. As the climate and the fauna changed, Neanderthal adapted his target species to ensure survival. As the colder parts of the Ice Age spread over Europe he relied on fire and clothing to keep warm and used shelters, either provided by nature or built by his own ingenuity. For each fresh challenge he found a solution, for those that didn't, they perished, only the most resourceful, careful planners survived. This harsh process filtered out the weak, and ensured that those that did survive were the strongest, smartest individuals.

By way of contrast, if we look at sharks. The evolution of sharks shows how a successful design can remain unchanged for vast periods of time, if the environment remains largely unchanged. Sharks first appeared around 455 million years ago, 450 million years before the first bipedal hominids. The basic torpedo shape of many sharks has remained more or less unchanged since then. Around 200 million years ago in the Triassic age the dogfish type of shark evolved which remains with us today. Various other types of sharks share a similar ancient pedigree such as ground sharks, the most widespread of sharks, lamniform sharks and carpet sharks, which represent over 200 million years with very little change in the basic form. This is testament to the success of the initial design of shark, how well they were originally adapted to their environment, but even more so, to the relative stability of conditions in the oceans compared to on land.

As the saying goes, 'necessity is the mother of invention'. The more stable an environment the less the need to evolve and so the less evolution occurs or even needs to occur.

The European Ice Age was the diametric opposite of the stable oceanic environment. Temperatures and conditions fluctuated wildly, and Neanderthals had to adapt fast to survive. So, we see in Europe over the last 100,000 years the increase in size of the brain, and a vast number of changes to the way of life, such as language, farming, art and building, which culminate in the modern humans of today. The Ice Age was a harsh training ground for survival. Adapt or die, and adapt they did, changing the way of life beyond all recognition from the start of the last Ice Age to the end of it, the pace of development was unprecedented in all human history, until the most recent times.

By contrast environmental conditions in tropical Africa, indeed life in tropical South Asia remained relatively stable, so there was no pressing need to adapt and change fast. It is no accident that in these places the perfectly well-adapted peoples of tropical Africa retained their Neolithic life styles well into the last century, as it was perfectly adequate for all their needs.

In Ice Age Europe relying on old successful traditions to hunt particular animals was no guarantee of success in the future. With each violent swing of the climate an old species would disappear and a new one would appear or maybe not at all. Clothing that is appropriate for temperatures 10°C is not appropriate for temperatures of -20°C that and many other aspects of life had to change also.

Ice Age Europeans were forced to think of new solutions to new problems which created a very long list of culture changing technological innovations some of which are with us still today, and we will look at these in more detail in later chapters.

Changing Times

About 40,000 years ago after nearly 1.8 million years of slow evolution in Europe, big changes started to sweep through the continent in quick succession as we leave the Middle Paleolithic and enter into the last phase of the Paleolithic, the Upper Paleolithic. Innovations in tool manufacture started to appear replacing Mousterian technology which had been the Neanderthal mainstay for hundreds of thousands of years. In France this took the form of innovations called Chatelperronian; in Italy it was Uluzzian and in the Black Sea basin Streletskaian. Neanderthal people were beginning to express themselves artistically, creating music, sculpture and wall art. The hunters were becoming more efficient, with better clothing, better weapons and hunting dogs.

Chatelperronian

For most of the 20th century the prevailing view amongst the international palaeological community was that in Europe Mousterian and Neanderthal were synonymous. It is true that for the majority of the occupation of Europe and Western Asia by classic Neanderthal his remains were accompanied by Mousterian technology. The implication being that Neanderthal was incapable of thought processes sufficiently complex to invent more advanced technologies, that he was stuck in an intellectual and technological rut. A further assumption was that post 40,000 BP Europe was occupied by anatomically modern humans (AMH) who had all arrived from Africa. These two assumptions together went some way to explaining the rapid series of changes that we are about to look at now in Europe.

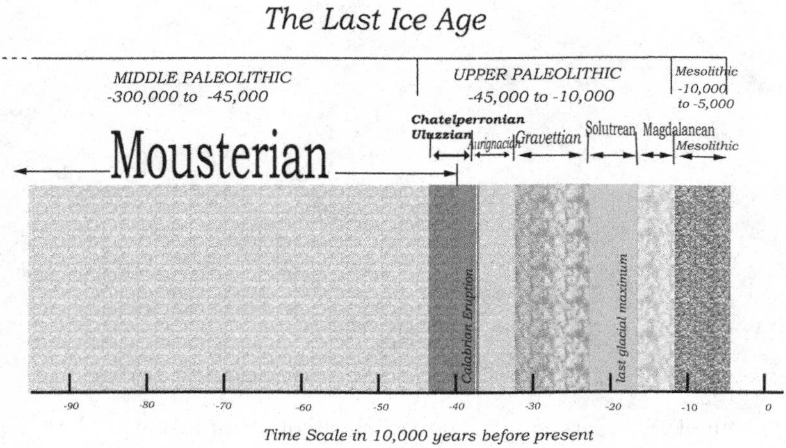

Illustration 39. Chatelperronian in the Ice Age

They had become accepted to such a degree that archaeological levels which dated to more recently than 40,000BP or held tools post-Mousterian were automatically associated with AMH. It is rare to find complete human skeletons from this period, usually the human bones recovered are just unattributable fragments which when examined will not necessarily reveal any traits that permit the identification of classic Neanderthal or otherwise, and often haven't any salvageable DNA to analyze. In the absence of a firm basis for identification of the people who accompanied the finds, the above assumptions are used to fill in the gaps.

To further muddy the waters many skeletal remains from this period display features common to both classic Neanderthals and to modern humans. Nevertheless, the discipline requires that an archaeological layer be pigeon-holed, for example Mousterian, Aurignacian, etcetera.

Thus, many archaeological sites and or levels around Europe have been associated in a binary fashion with either Neanderthal or modern human occupation without any hard evidence to establish one or the other. Most levels post-40,000 BP were inevitably labeled modern unless there was clear evidence of Mousterian tools and so following this circular logic, the Out of Africa II theory became overwhelmingly accepted with virtually no hard science to underpin it.

For a more detailed discussion on the Out of Africa II theory, please refer to the Appendix. Various technologies were discovered around Europe demonstrating greater technical advancement than Mousterian, such as Uluzzian, Chatelperronian and Aurignacian. Following the processes of classification mentioned above all these technologies were associated with the new African immigrants known as anatomically modern humans. Such was the situation for much of the 20th century.

But this comfortable situation was thrown into disarray by discoveries made in the Grotte des Fees in Chatelperron, France which revealed flint tools with denticulate (serrated) edges, a flint knife with a single cutting edge and a blunt back to allow finger pressure as well as worked mammoth ivory and two mammoth tusks over 2m long as well as drills and scrapers. This was clearly not Mousterian technology; indeed, it closely resembled another French technology called Perigordian. Perigordian is roughly dated to between 35 and 20,000 BP sitting easily inside the period attributed to AMH, thus Chatelperronian must equally be an AMH technology even though no identifiably modern human bones were found there. The three caves at Chatelperron gave this culture its name, Chatelperronian. Little did the original archeologists realize that their discoveries were to be the focus of a heated debate which has raged for 30 years or more and still continues today.

The most revealing finds came from a network of caves in Arcy-sur-Cure, Burgundy and from Saint Cesare in Charente Maritime, France. The former is a complex of caves and galleries containing a wealth of prehistoric artifacts and some very old art, dating from before 200,000BP (containing Neanderthal, hippopotamus, beaver and tortoise remains). The most famous levels are Chatelperronian (VIII, IX and X) from the reindeer Cave in the network. The artifacts found in this level contain symbolic ornaments, pierced animal teeth, human bone fragments, awls and pendants. Then at Saint-Cesare in 1979 a burial was discovered of a young Neanderthal woman (nick-named affectionately Pierrette) with a partially healed, severe cranial wound 6cm long, which was inflicted apparently by a severe blow and considered to be the result of inter-personal violence. This body was discovered in conjunction with Chatelperronian tools and dated to 36-35,000BP.

The assumptions mentioned at the head of this chapter were blown wide open by these extremely inconvenient discoveries. The Chatelperronian artifacts in the three Chatelperronian layers also contained unmistakable Neanderthal teeth associating Chatelperronian incontrovertibly with Neanderthals. In addition, these artifacts have been dated to 42,000 BP, well before the supposed arrival of the Africans otherwise known as Anatomically Modern humans in France. There wasn't enough DNA in the human remains in the Chatelperronian levels to allow a solid identification thus allowing enough wriggle room for some who still believed that Neanderthals were incapable of producing new technologies. Chemical analysis of the protein content of a bone sample was compared to known protein profiles in modern humans and classical Neanderthals, and it was confirmed that not only was the bone Neanderthal but that it belonged to a baby being breast-fed. The process of scientific analysis and identification of the bones in the Chatelperronian layers as Neanderthals as described by Bob Yirka are as follows:

> We identified 28 additional hominin specimens through zooarchaeology by mass spectrometry (ZooMS) screening of morphologically uninformative bone specimens from Châtelperronian layers at the Grotte du Renne. Next, we obtain an ancient hominin bone proteome through liquid chromatography-MS/MS analysis and error-tolerant amino acid sequence analysis. Analysis of this palaeoproteome allows us to provide phylogenetic and physiological information on these ancient hominin specimens. We distinguish Late Pleistocene clades within the genus Homo based on ancient protein evidence through the identification of an archaic-derived amino acid sequence for the collagen type X, alpha-1 (COL10α1) protein. We support this by obtaining ancient mtDNA sequences, which indicate a Neandertal ancestry for these specimens. Direct accelerator mass spectrometry radiocarbon dating and Bayesian modeling confirm that the hominin specimens date to the Châtelperronian at the Grotte du Renne. (Yirka)

So, there we have it. This new culture with all its significant improvements over Mousterian was unambiguously Neanderthal with not a shred of evidence to suggest that it was imported from another continent. This association between personal decoration, worked ivory, denticulate tools and Neanderthals is proof that by 43,000BP the latter were starting to advance beyond the traditional Mousterian techniques that they had used for most of their history. What's more, Chatelperronian technology is very closely associated with Aurignacian, which is sequentially the next technological classification in Europe, as we shall see later, making it overwhelmingly likely that there was a smooth transition between Chatelperronian and Aurignacian.

Chatelperronian is differentiated from the Mousterian from which it emerged by a number of advances. In terms of tools, serrated edges appeared for the first time which were used as saw blades. Backed flint blades, like modern knives with a sharp cutting edge and a thick edge on the opposite side to allow for finger pressure, appeared for the first time, and were to feature in Aurignacian culture and beyond. Tools made from bone and ivory started to appear, including bone awls (see photo below). Typically, in Chatelperronian, the blanks would be chosen from naturally pointed bones such as horse metatapodials, and shaft bones broken to access the bone marrow from a wide variety of animals. Whereas later during the Aurignacian the blanks were taken from a substantially smaller subset of bones. Microscopic examination shows that Chatelperronian awls were used as drills possibly tens of thousands of times for each one, and when they became blunt were re-sharpened on a stone, until they were completely exhausted at which point they were discarded. Various sizes of awls were used for different types of skins, from large robust bone awls used for bovid hide, to smaller ones better adapted for thin skins such as bird skins. This indicates that the Chatelperronian Neanderthals were prodigious clothes makers.

The debate over whether Chatelperronian was a Neanderthal or AMH technology was addressed in a scientific paper, "Many awls in our argument. Bone tool manufacture and use in the Châtelperronian and Aurignacian levels of the Grotte du Renne at Arcy-sur-Cure," by Francesco D'errico, Michèle Julien, Despina Liolios, Marian Vanhaeren and Dominique Baffier.

In this study they focused on the large number of awls found at Arcy-sur-Cur made from various animal bones. One of the intriguing aspects of this cave is that it has a sequence of layers from Mousterian to Chatelperronian to Aurignacian. The bone awls from the Chatelperronian layers conveniently differentiate the different technologies. Mousterian is an almost exclusively lithic technology. Bone tools appear in Chatelperronian and continue through to the Aurignacian, but the manufacturing techniques change from one to the other. Crucially, and very unusually, two bone awls were found in the late Mousterian levels. Although these two bone awls have been somewhat overlooked in the heated debates focused on the Chatelperronian, they are of great significance. These two awls show the first tentative experiments during the Mousterian period in bone tool technology, while still relying on the tried and trusted stone tools which had been in use for hundreds of thousands of years. These two bone awls in the Mousterian levels show how Mousterian Neanderthals were starting to experiment with a totally new raw material for tool manufacture, and this experimentation was happening in France. By turning to bone as a raw material that was readily available, man had discovered that he could shape his tools with great precision. He could use the old flint chisels of burins to roughly split bones to the approximate size that he needed, then he could use his new denticulate knives to cut down the piece more precisely. Then, using a variety of scrapers he could plane away the bone to achieve the right shape. Once the shape was achieved he could smooth everything down on a grinding stone to achieve a polished finish. Not content with just a nice shiny finish he would add decorations to the tool, in the form of inscriptions. Some of these may have been utilitarian, for example parallel lines to incise a form of grip on the tool, or they may also have been decorative. With the advent of Chatelperronian we had arrived at a stage where decoration, not only for tools but for people had become very important indeed.

This is why the Out of Africa II apologists have drawn up their battle lines at this point in time, and defended them so relentlessly. Chatelperronian technology crosses the line between purely utilitarian, basic tools to ornament and artistic expression, in other words into the world of humanities and the sure signs of unmistakably modern behavior. To admit that Neanderthals are capable of modern human artistic expression is to open the flood gates on a range of other innovations which begin to appear from this period onwards in European pre-history. If you can't prove that the Neanderthals never reached this level of technical sophistication, where can you prove that they weren't responsible for even greater achievements?

The claim that Chatelperronian is an African innovation is now proved groundless, there is no great step change from Mousterian to Chatelperronian and the only remains associated with Chatelperronian in Western Europe which have been positively identified have been identified as Neanderthal. Further excavations have shown other Chatelperronian sites such as Saint Cesare is definitely linked to Neanderthals.

The two key assumptions at the start of this chapter now having proved false all the conclusions that have followed on from them need to be reconsidered, and this involves rethinking large parts of European pre-history for the next 30,000 years. The implication for text books, professional reputations of well-known experts, educational films museum displays and the general understanding of European pre-history is very significant indeed.

In the light of these recent discoveries, it seems surprising that some experts still cling to the idea that Chatelperronian was African in its origin, even despite the fact that it first appears in France in the Neanderthal heartland rather than thousands of kilometers away in Africa. A little more credence could be given to the African origin of Chatelperronian if there was the slightest shred of evidence of it having first appeared in Africa, but there is no such evidence.

The implication of the now undoubted association of Chatelperronian to Neanderthals has widespread impact in the world of paleoanthropology, as it removes the key stone in the Out of Africa Hypothesis. But the Out of Africa II Theory was intended to explain a series of great changes that were about to occur in Europe. If the Out of Africa Theory II does not explain these changes, then what does?

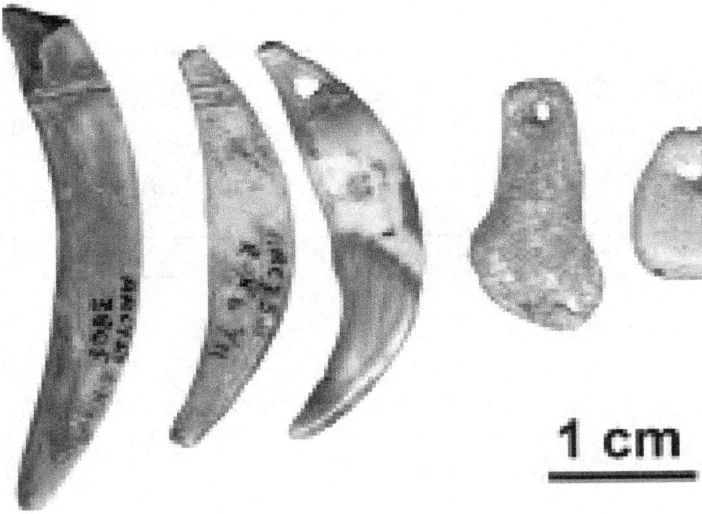

Illustration 40. Chatelperronian claw pendants

Credit: Chatelperronian Neanderthal Body Ornaments From The Grotte Du Renne (Arcy-Sur-Cure, France) Credit: Marian Vanhaeren & Michele Julien

Bone awls were used principally for piercing holes in hides to sew them together along their edges or seams. They form part of an extensive toolkit essential for the manufacture of Stone Age clothing from animal skins which we shall look at more closely later in this book. Other tools include very sharp knives for cutting the skin to the right shape, various scrapers for removing flesh and membranes and smoothers. Tendons and guts were used to sew together the skins into the correct form. A hole pierced in skin by a sharp pointed, but smooth sided awl will not suffer from cracked edges from which splits will start to appear eventually causing the seam to rupture and ruining the precious garment.

The proliferation of these awls in the Chatelperronian layers shows just how important clothing manufacture was to these people living in the middle of the Ice Age. We have already seen the special thermal qualities of reindeer skin, but equally essential was that the clothing was made to fit properly, that parts of the clothing weren't flapping open allowing heat to escape and cold air to chill the skin.

The following chart shows the number of awls per archaeological layer in the reindeer Cave at Arcy-sur-Cure.

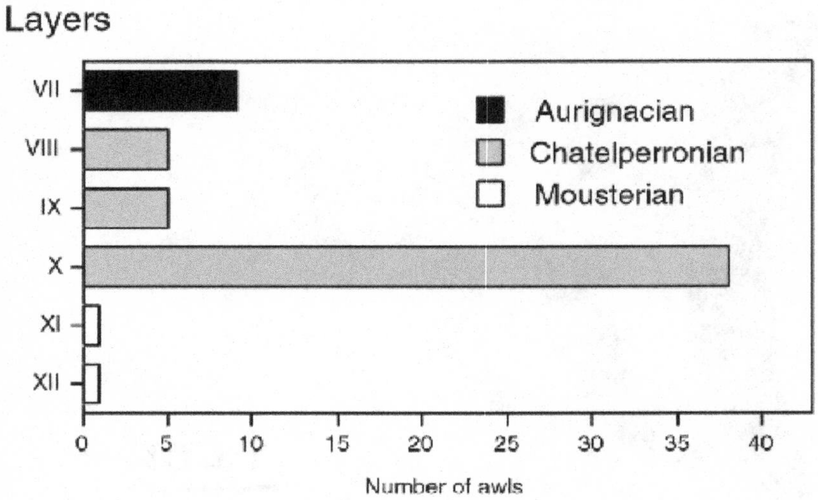

Illustration 41. Awls in the Grotte du Renne

[Credit: Francesco D'errico] *Awls In The Grotte Du Renne*

Of crucial significance are the 38 bone awls in the Chatelperronian layer X compared to 1 in each of the previous Mousterian layers. Given that each bone awl was estimated to be capable of piercing around 200,000 holes before being worn out and discarded we can begin to appreciate just how much clothing was being created during the time period of level X, and how that compares with previous levels. The manufacture of well-made clothing was becoming an activity of the utmost importance to the Chatelperronian Neanderthals.

We have already seen how Neanderthals' bodies were specifically adapted to life in a cold climate, from their general build to their hairiness and the size of their noses. But now, with the advent of well-made clothes, they no longer needed to rely on specific modifications of their morphology to stay warm, they had invented warm clothes to do that job. These specific adaptations to extreme climate which had differentiated Neanderthal from his ancestor *H. erectus* were now no longer as necessary as they had been. The latent gracile build genetically inherited from *H. erectus* could now return without it being selected out. This is one of the most important missing links in the Neanderthal puzzle.

Until recently interpretation of DNA evidence was offered up to show how there was no living trace of Neanderthals in the human genome. In recent years however, this interpretation has been proved to be wholly wrong as just about all modern Europeans carry with them Neanderthal DNA. So, what really happened?

Anatomically Modern Humans Or Transitional Humans

While Neanderthal had been evolving in Europe and Asia, his distant cousin, another descendant of *H. erectus* had been evolving in Africa, and it is this descendant who is often credited today as being the principal ancestor of all modern humans. The term given to this ancestor is Anatomically Modern human or AMH for short. From a classification point of view, *Homo sapiens sapiens* or modern man is considered to have evolved from *Homo sapiens* around 10,000BP. The oldest fossil officially classed as AMH is from Jebel Irhoud in Morocco. Earlier AMH remains come from Omo in East Africa dating to about 195,000BP. Included in this group are various remains from the Levant such as at Skhull dating from around 95,000BP. But applying the term anatomically modern to these skeletons is very misleading suggesting that these people were identical to us today – they were not. They demonstrate a rich variety of characteristics both modern and archaic. To be more precise these people are also in a transitional state.

Qafzeh Skhull Remains

These fossils come from the Es Skhull and Qafzeh caves in Israel, on the migration route between Africa, Europe and Asia and have been dated to between 120 and 80,000BP. Although officially classed as AMH, the details tell a different story. The braincase has a modern appearance often described as 'tin loaf', rounded on the top and no occipital bun. But they possess Neanderthal brow ridges and Neanderthal prognathic faces. The best preserved of the skulls from Qazfeh, Qazfeh 6 has massive brow ridges and cheek bones with a low and wide Neanderthal like forehead. The accompanying tools at these two sites are Mousterian.

Curiously, classical Neanderthal remains post date these transitional Skhull and Qazfeh at nearby Kebara Cave. So, it would seem that at some time from 120 to 80,000BP these transitional humans were living in Skhull and Qazefeh, then between 61,000 and 48,000BP Neanderthals were living at nearby Kebara. What to make of this enigma?

Closer inspection of the remains reveals a more nuanced story. KMH5 from Kebara is a mandibular fragment from a two year old. One of the few diagnostic features that we can observe from this fragment is a straight chin rather than a typically receding Neanderthal chin.

Researchers at Skhull and Kebara published results in their study. Referring to both sets of skeletal remains: - 'The Skhul 1 child is a very good illustration of the mosaic of features possessed by immature Middle Paleolithic skulls.' (For 'Middle Paleolithic' read Neanderthal-like). The foot bones of KMH9 and KHM10 are gracile and most resemble modern humans. KMH 1 child's skull is of a similar thickness to modern skulls for children of the same age. Whereas many of the teeth found show the sort of shovel shaped characteristics associated with Neanderthals.

In other words, in the Levant, not only at Skhull, Qazfeh but also at Kebara we are looking at humans in a transitional state, with some archaic features and with some modern features. So, what is the correct interpretation from this rather confused situation?

Already we have some modern features appearing in Africa nearly 200,000 years before the Levant transitional people. In Europe and Central Asia, we have Neanderthals who are slowly changing, but certainly not yet to the degree of the remains in the Levant. Earlier official classifications have placed Qazfeh and Skhull squarely into the AMH category, and Kebara into the Neanderthal category and by doing so have made themselves an unnecessary problem to solve. Why did these seemingly superior modern humans disappear to be replaced by the more archaic Neanderthals? Various convoluted theories have been proposed with no solid basis in underlying facts to explain this Gordian knot.

We have already seen that Neanderthal characteristics have appeared in North Africa, which means that Neanderthals had migrated South through the Levant into Africa. It is equally not surprising to see some Africans migrate north from Africa. Indeed, whenever you look at the borders of racial regions you see a combination of features such as on the borders of China and Central Asia today, where the features of Mongoloid and Caucasian produce a fascinating blend of different races. This is only to be expected on the border of the African and European populations. No surprise therefore that with the ebb and flow of populations within the three continents, people at any one time were closer sometimes to one population and sometimes to the other. This is only to be expected and certainly doesn't go more than half way to explain what happened in Europe after 40,000BP. If at some point shortly before 40,000 there was an abrupt transformation in both the physiognomy of the fossils and the technologies associated with them in favor of African types then we could lend some credence to the Out of Africa Theory, but that evidence doesn't exist.

Does what happened in the rest of Europe and Asia shed any more light on the debate?

Uluzzian

The Uluzzian is described as a post-mousterian transitional techno complex mainly found in Italy and Greece marking the transition from middle to upper Paleolithic. The same debate that has raged over the identity of the Levant remains at Skhull and Kebara has also erupted over who were the people responsible for Uluzzian technology: Neanderthal or modern humans? The dates generally given for Uluzzian are 45–39,500BP, although these vary by plus or minus 2,000 years — more or less contemporaneous with Chatelperronian

Uluzzian is characterized by stone implements in the main comprising of backed knives and backed bladelets enabling more finger pressure and cutting power being applied to the blade with less damage to the wielders hand. These tools are still manufactured using the Levallois technique of flake manufacture which was already employed by the Neanderthals.

As with Chatelperonian technology, Uluzzian sites reveal pierced shells, which are considered to be personal decorations worn on some form of cord around the owner's neck. Also, like Chatelperronian, there are bone implements such as the awl found at Grotto del Cavallo and Castelcivita, or bone points. And in common with other Neanderthal sites, blocks of ocher are found.

Post holes indicating wooden buildings have also been found in Uluzzian sites as have been found at various other Neanderthal sites around Europe.

There are few human fossil remains associated with Uluzzian, the most important is one incisor found in the Grotto de Cavalho which show Neanderthal characteristics such as Neanderthal wear patterns.

However, the general lack of more fossil evidence allows for a certain ambiguity about who the Uluzzian people were. Reflecting the Chatelperronian debate, many researchers have seized on this lack of hard evidence to conclude that because Uluzzian shows a slight improvement over Mousterian, that the Uluzzian people must therefore have been AMH. This logic is unconvincing, but it is seen to corroborate the Out of Africa II theory.

There are disagreements about just how tightly to define Uluzzian, some stating that it only truly existed in the Southern third of the Italian peninsula, which at the time was a cold bare steppe. Northern Italy by contrast had a warmer more Mediterranean climate and is considered to have been a refuge for Neanderthals escaping the cold conditions north of the Alps. Thus, there is general recognition that the Northern Italian sites contemporaneous with Uluzzian in Southern Italy were occupied by Neanderthals. One of the characteristics of Uluzzian is an increasing variability in tool design and manufacture dependent in part on the raw materials available.

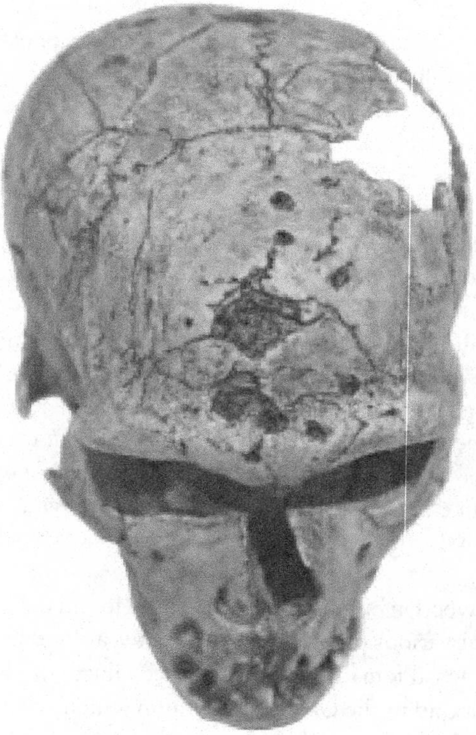

Illustration 42. View from above of Neanderthal skull from Chapelle aux Saints

Let's remind ourselves of the characteristics of the Chatelperronian technology. It lasted from roughly 45-38,000BP the same period as Uluzzian. Chatelperronian is found is central and South Western France as well as in Northern Spain. It featured blunt backed denticulate knives enabling the users to exert more finger pressure while minimising damage to the hand, as did the Uluzzian. It used the Levallois stone flake production technique. Using one or two striking platforms long thin blades were flaked off from the core block. It is considered that softer hammers were used such as deer antler for greater precision and finer finished tools. Also bone and ivory tools and adornments become regular features of Chatelperronian sites.

There is little if anything to differentiate Chatelperronian from Uluzzian. The main difference between the two is that different researchers in different countries were responsible for the discovery of each one, even though the geographical regions of Chatelperronian and Uluzzian are adjacent, separated by no more than a couple of months walking. The only skeletal remains associated with Chatelperronian are those of Neanderthal, and the areas covered by both were occupied by Neanderthals for hundreds of thousands of years. It would be fanciful indeed to imagine that Uluzzian was anything other than another Neanderthal Chatelperronian.

The use of pierced shells as necklaces is merely another use of mollusk shells which were initially used as a food source, most frequently, although not uniquely, where Neanderthals lived close to the coast. Most of these locations have now disappeared beneath the waves as the sea-level during the Ice Age was up to 120m lower than today. Only in places where there were high cliffs close to the sea can we hope to find sea-side Neanderthal remains during the Ice Age above present sea level. These conditions exist in Gibraltar and Nerja as we have seen and with those remains can be found considerable quantities of shells. These shells were also used as impermeable containers for paint used on their bodies and for cave decoration and also as skin scrapers. The advent of awls with sharper points allowed Neanderthals more precise tools for more careful work on delicate materials such as mollusk shells. As with bone musical instruments Neanderthals were finding secondary usage for the remains of products that were initially sought after only for nutritional value.

Two teeth have been found in association with Uluzzian layers in Italy which bear some modern characteristics and which have been associated with modern humans. Some researchers believe that these teeth are evidence of a wide scale African colonization via the Levant, but there is no other evidence of this which fits the timeline between Africa and Italy. So, who did those two modern looking teeth belong to?

With the great improvement in cutting using both the denticulate backed knives of Chatelperronian and finer knapping methods producing sharper edges, the dependence on powerful buttressed teeth previously used for tearing meat and skins was greatly reduced. Natural selection which previously would have relied on Neanderthals needing strong reinforced teeth no longer weeded out those with finer teeth and less powerful jaws. From the Chatelperronian and Uluzzian onwards, knives did the cutting, enabling those with less powerful teeth and jaws to survive. The slow change to our modern lightly built teeth and jaws had begun; indeed, it had probably started well before 40,000BP. The full transformation of teeth and jaws to modern dimensions would take another 15,000 years or so, but there was no going back to the massive jaws of previous eras once knives became part of European culture.

Teeth uncovered from 40,000 onwards had an increasing tendency to be less bulky with lighter if not non-existent buttressing of the type typical in classical Neanderthals. This change was a gradual one, and didn't happen all over Europe and Asia overnight. The two Uluzzian teeth with a more modern appearance fit into this category, in other words they are teeth belonging to transitional Neanderthals.

The Jaw

As the jaws became lighter in construction so did the powerful muscles that operated them and as a result many aspects of the skull changed.

Opening and closing the jaw is a surprisingly complex process and simulations of the mechanisms in the field of bio-mechanics have been developed which reveal just how many muscles and processes are involved. The structure and pivot comprise the temporomandibular complex (TMC) involving the mobile lower jaw (mandible, the fixed upper jaw (maxillar) and the temporal bone on the side of the head. Collateral, capsular, temporomandibular sphenomandibular and stylomandibular ligaments are used to control movements of the jaw. On each side of the head, each of these ligaments attach the lower jaw to various parts of the skull at a variety of anchor points, and each one works in concert during the activity of chewing and biting. The more powerful the bite the bulkier the ligaments and more bone is needed to anchor them.

Also, a complex shock absorption system exists in the jaw pivot, known as the articular disc which is a non-ossified disc of bone, located at the pivot of the jaw in a recess called the mandibular fossa. Made of collagen, it bends and compresses during loading of the jaw, the natural elasticity of the collagen then pushes the jaw back when the bite relaxes. The more powerful the bite the more strongly built this shock absorbent system needs to be.

The jaw is capable of movement in all three axes, and this requires the coordination of seven different main muscles: temporal, masseter, medial pterygoid, lateral pterytoid, digastrics, suprahyoid and infrahyoid. Each of these muscles attaches at various points of the lower and upper jaws, as well as the hyoid bone and even to the distant sternum and clavicle. These muscles operate together in the process of chewing, but also in swallowing and talking. It is the power in these muscles which determines the strength of the bite. When Neanderthals used their teeth to tear meat from dead animals these muscles were necessarily very powerful indeed. But in order to exert force during a bite, these muscles exert an equivalent force on the jaw and the bones of the skull. Some of these muscles are attached across wide areas of the side of the head on the temporal bone and exert forces there. Indeed, the whole skull is used to distribute and absorb the forces required in operating the jaw. Because there are so many muscles at work these forces operate in different directions according to the vector of each muscle. The result is a highly complex distribution of forces within the structure of the skull, each force requiring strong enough bone to not break when operating the jaw. Even the process of opening the jaw exerts powerful forces on the skull. If you try opening your mouth to its fullest extent you will feel strains right around the side of the head. The most powerful of the muscles involved, the anterior temporalis can exert over 300 newtons in modern humans, and three others can exert over 200 newtons.

For the classic Neanderthal with his powerful jaw, the skull was heavily buttressed to absorb these forces and provide the necessary strength in the structure of the skull. Not only was the Neanderthal jaw necessarily powerful but the bones of the skull were also strong. Some of these reinforcements to the skull included the powerful continuous brow ridge as well as processes for muscle anchor points. Indeed, the very shape of the skull was designed to be structurally strong.

With the invention of the sharp knife to replace the tearing action of the teeth, there was less of a requirement for such a powerful jaw and less growth investment is such a powerful apparatus. As the ligaments and muscles became finer so the corresponding bone buttresses became finer too. Not only did the teeth become less robust requiring smaller roots, the jaw become considerably lighter, but so did the rest of the skull, the great buttresses started to disappear. The whole aspect of the human skull started to change dramatically.

A good if rather extreme example of the effect on bone growth on the skull is the Sagittal Crest which is found on many animals including primates and distant human ancestors. This is a high sometimes very high ridge of bone than runs centrally along the top of the skull from front to back, along the line of the sagittal suture, similar in appearance to the crest on a Spartan's helmet. This crest exists as an anchor point for a very wide muscle (temporalis muscle) used to operate very powerful jaws for chewing tough foods. Among modern primates the Sagittal Crest occurs among male gorillas, orangutans, and some male chimpanzees.

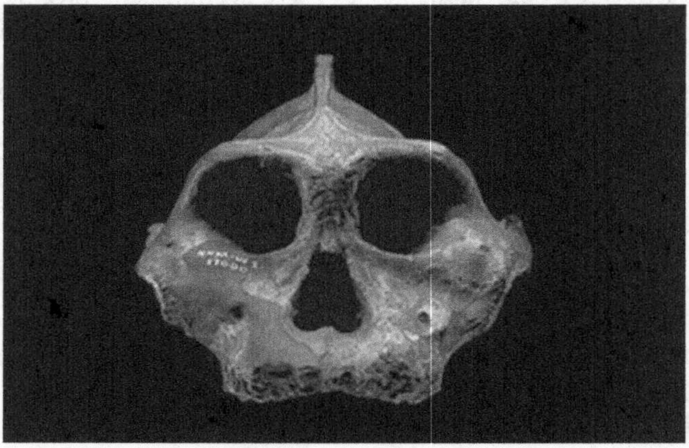

Illustration 43. Example of Sagittal Crest in Paranthropus

Credit: Sagittal Crest: Hominid Lab Report Period 6. Jennifer Bilker, Sophia Swartz, Trish Grove, Scott Shanfield.

Even some modern humans show the vague remains of a sagittal crest.

The change in prominence, even the disappearance of the supercillary arch has the same explanation.

So, what was the purpose of the supercillary arch? Endo developed a biomechanical model to analyze the forces involved in chewing.

By applying pressure similar to the type associated with chewing, he carried out an analysis of the structural function of the supraorbital region on dry human and gorilla skulls. His findings indicated that the face acts as a pillar that carries and disperses tension caused by the forces produced during mastication. Russell and Oyen et al. elaborated on this idea, suggesting that amplified facial projection necessitates the application of enhanced force to the anterior dentition in order to generate the same bite power that individuals with a dorsal deflection of the facial skull exert. In more prognathic individuals, this increased pressure triggers bone deposition to reinforce the brow ridges, until equilibrium is reached.

Oyen et al. conducted a cross-section study of Papio anubis in order to ascertain the relationship between palate length, incisor load and Masseter lever efficiency, relative to torus enlargement. Indications found of osteoblastic deposition in the glabella were used as evidence for supraorbital enlargement. Oyen et al.'s data suggested that more prognathic individuals experienced a decrease in load/lever efficiency. This transmits tension via the frontal process of the maxilla to the supraorbital region, resulting in a contemporary reinforcement of this structure. This was also correlated to periods of tooth eruption.' (Endo, B. 275)

In other words, the powerful, longer jaws of our ancestors had a less efficient lever effect and required more muscles to create the required forces. These powerful muscles exerted strain on the skull, by pulling down on the front of the face. A way of picturing this effect is to imagine the front of the face as a sort of nutcracker with the lower jaw being one jaw of the nutcracker and the upper part of the skull (where the muscles anchor) the other jaw of the nutcracker. During a powerful bite, the two jaws of the nutcracker close exerting force on the nut, the analogy here being that the nut is the front of the face, which in order not to crack must be reinforced. In order to cope with the extra strain, reinforcement built up above the eyes in the supra-orbital region. Just as for those people who have a very physical lifestyle their bones become bulkier and stronger by a natural process called appositional growth where osteoblasts on the bone surface secrete bone matrix, strengthening the bone.

The important point here is that role of the jaw and eating habits is a primary factor in influencing the shape of the skull. If the jaw is required to do more work, chewing harder food, tearing skin and meat, then the whole skull will change to accommodate the stronger muscles and ligaments. If on the other hand the jaw is required to do less work, then the whole skull will become less robust and the bone structures finer. This is what happened to Neanderthals during the course of the Ice Age. Well made, sharp knives replaced many of the functions fulfilled by the jaws, and the whole skull became finer as a result.

This fact is almost always overlooked when it comes to identifying human remains post 40,000BP. The more gracile skull shapes that started to be found around this time were attributed to a different species of human ancestor, whereas in fact, these more gracile, modern looking skulls were a result of the changing habits of Neanderthals which in turn was brought about by the improved quality of their tools, in particular their knives. It is no accident whatsoever that the first sign of rapid change in the middle of the Ice Age was the advent of the Chatelperronian toolkit with its sharper more precise tools and knives with serrated edges. These two events are inseparable.

Of course, the changes to the skull were gradual and occurred over generations, and were not synchronous all over Europe, as knowledge of this new tool culture slowly spread over the continent. This is exactly what the fossil record reveals, a mixture of classic Neanderthal and modern features, slowly becoming less Neanderthal and more modern over the continent.

We can point to this time in human history and say that this is the beginning of 'cuisine' as we know it today, the deliberate preparing of food with implements prior to eating, this included cutting the meat to an appropriate size and cooking it. Previously hand axes had broken parts of the animal away from the body which had then either been eaten directly from the bone using the teeth to tear the meat away, or thrown on the fire to cook. Now we see systematic preparation of meals begin with tools and soon we will see pottery arrive to augment the cook's kitchen implements.

Clothing

These changes to Neanderthals were not limited to teeth, jaws and skull shape. As we have seen the Chatelperronian and Uluzzian ushered in a new age of the manufacture of quality clothing to deal with the ever increasingly bitter cold of the Ice Age as evidenced initially by finely made bone awls. These new tools allowed thermally efficient reindeer skins cut well to size, to be sewn together and exclude drafts minimizing heat loss, which in turn helped preserve precious energy when hunting.

All mammals that lived in Europe throughout the Ice Age evolved their own features to cope with the arctic conditions. Woolly mammoths and rhinoceros developed thick insulating coats. Reindeer developed a variety of strategies which we shall focus on in a later chapter. Neanderthal developed a strongly built thick-set body, a huge nose equipped with copious blood supply to heat the cold air and thick body hair to trap a layer of insulating air close to the skin, a very common mammalian strategy when adapting to cold conditions. But above all, Neanderthal developed excellent clothing and the tools that he needed to make it. He also had fire. Hearths from now on are almost always found in conjunction with Neanderthal habitation.

His clothing was so good that the other strategies became less vital to survival. Slowly, the large nose with its bony foundations began to recede; slowly the thick set body began to revert to the old *H. erectus* form, becoming more gracile. Some of these features would linger on to the present day, but as the generations passed they would become less prominent.

The sum total of all these changes is readily visible in the fossil record. With each millennium that followed 40,000BP the tendency would be for various characteristic Neanderthal traits to begin to disappear, and the shape of modern man start to come to the fore.

Starting with improvements to tools leading to better clothing and different eating habits, Neanderthal had begun to change, a great transition had begun, and there was much more to follow.

Denisovan

Very little indeed is known about these mysterious people more than what can be gleaned from a few paltry teeth and bones. What little we do know can be quickly summed up. They occupied a region in Central Asia around the Altai Mountains in Siberia. The length of time that they existed isn't known but they occupied some caves in the Altai mountains around 41,000BP on the eastern edge of Neanderthal territory Indeed intermittently Neanderthals also inhabited the cave. The name Denisovan comes from the Denisova cave, where a finger bone of a juvenile female was found, and the name of the cave itself from a Russian hermit who lived there in the 18th century.

The sum total of fossils relating to this apparent sub-species of human is 5; and 4 of those are from different levels of the Denisova cave. The oldest is a tooth whose age is estimated at over 100,000 years. In total the only remains currently identified as Denisovan are three teeth, a toe and a bit of a finger.

Some DNA has been extracted from the bone and the results are interesting. It is estimated that Deniso big vans and Neanderthals had a common ancestor around 400 and 600,000BP, more or less when Neanderthals were becoming a distinct sub-species themselves. But that both Neanderthals and Denisovans had şimilar DNA. It was also observed that the DNA of the oldest Denisovan specimen was significantly different from the later ones. Indeed, the oldest Denisovan specimen was a close descendant of *H. erectus*.

Morphologically the toe bone is similar to that of a Neanderthal, leading some to suggest that it belongs to a Denisovan-Neanderthal hybrid.

In terms of Mt DNA, the difference between Denisovans and Modern humans is 385 nucleotides out of 16,500, whereas the difference between some Neanderthals and modern humans is only 202, clearly suggesting that Neanderthal is a lot closer to modern humans than Denisovan is.

Curiously a DNA sequence from a 430,000-year-old so-called *heidelbergensis* from Spain revealed a closer relationship to Denisovans than to Neanderthals.

What to make of this riddle?

The literature often refers to Neanderthals and Denisovans as species. But in reality, they are sub-species. What does that mean?

A subspecies is 'a category in biological classification that ranks immediately below a species and designates a population of a particular geographic region genetically distinguishable from other such populations of the same species and capable of interbreeding successfully with them where its range overlaps theirs.' (Merriam-Webster: subspecies)

But in this case, the Neanderthals expanded their geographical range eastwards until it butted up against the range of the South East Asian *H. erectus* Populations also known as Peking man. Peking man (a branch of the *H. erectus* sensu latu family) occupied parts of South East Asia from roughly 800–350,000BP. Just as Neanderthal adapted to the cold European climate had evolved from *H. erectus* who had originated from Africa, so the *H. erectus* populations expanding north from sub-tropical South East Asia towards the center of China where the weather is considerably colder, adapted in the same general manner, thus Peking man was a cold weather adaptation of *H. erectus*, analogous to Neanderthal.

When the two sub-species (Neanderthal and Peking man) met inter-breeding was inevitable. It is no accident that Denisovans are found right at the very edge of Neanderthal and Peking man territory where the two populations met, very close to the current Mongolian border.

It is no surprise either that there are significant differences in the DNA of the earlier and later specimens of Denisovan. Some groups of Denisovans would have more Neanderthal heritage and other groups would have more Peking man heritage, as continual contact with both groups would have constantly changed the amount each contributed. Thus, there are other finds in the region that are similar to Denisovan (in demonstrating mixed heritage), but there is debate about what basket to put these finds in, so in official classification terms these unexplained people are in limbo. Examples of this are the Dali skull dated to around 200,000BP originating from the Shanxi Province of China which shows mixed characteristics, with the sagittal crest of *H. erectus* but the large cranium of Neanderthal. The Maba skull from Guangdong Province is another example and is described as resembling Neanderthal.

So, in Central Asia on the borders of Peking man and Neanderthal territories we have various small groups of hybrid peoples showing different characteristics of both sub-species.

Although we have little information on these peoples, they have left their legacy amongst modern populations. Indeed, 20,000 years later, we'll be meeting their descendants again, once again on the edge of Neanderthal and Peking man territories, this time around Lake Baikal. These are the Mal'ta people who we'll look at in the chapter on the Gravettian Period.

Meanwhile it is worth noting that some modern populations still carry Denisovan DNA who made a significant contribution to modern Melanesians from where they also contributed to the DNA of people in Papua New Guinea and Australian Aborigines. They also contributed to the DNA of the Manamwa people, Negritos in the Philippenes. And to a lesser degree they also contributed to a portion of Native American DNA. Also, Tibetans share some DNA with Denisovans, particularly parts relating to their adaptation to air with rarified oxygen content.

In 2012 an updated version of the Denisovan genome revealed that they possessed dark skin, brown eyes and brown hair. Even more recently still, in 2016, DNA analysis (confirming yet further the hypothesis above) has shown that there has been multiple interbreeding between Neanderthals and Denisovans.

Denisovans may not have left many bones for us to study, but the few that they did have enabled us to fill in a crucial part of the human jigsaw in the last half a million years.

AURIGNACIAN

At about the same time as the Chatelperronian and Uluzzian innovations changed the Neanderthal world in France and Italy similar technological changes known as Aurignacian began to appear in Eastern Europe. The earliest examples so far found have been in Eastern Europe around 43,000 BP from where it appears to have spread to Western Europe around 40,000BP, by which time it almost totally replaced Mousterian throughout the Neanderthal world in Europe. Chatelperronian and Uluzzian technologies may not have reached all Neanderthal communities in Europe and Asia, but Aurignacian did, with the possible exception of just a few communities living on the fringes of the Neanderthal world.

Aurignacian is characterized by bone and antler points which differed only slightly from Chatelperronian due to the presence of a grooves in the bases. The flint tools were prepared using the Levallois technique still i.e., producing flakes from cores, but with greater care in the preparation of the core, making for finer more precise tools, some taking the form of fine flint blades with carefully worked teeth as in a modern saw.

The artistic expression that made its first appearance during the Chatelperronian phase now started to blossom right across Europe. Cave paintings become more prolific, and the first 3-dimensional sculptures in the world appear in the form of various figurines of animals some of which are now extinct, such as mammoths, woolly rhinoceros and tarpan (extinct wild Eurasian wild horse). Some of the figurines are beautifully made, even to the modern eye accustomed to photographic images and scale model replicas.

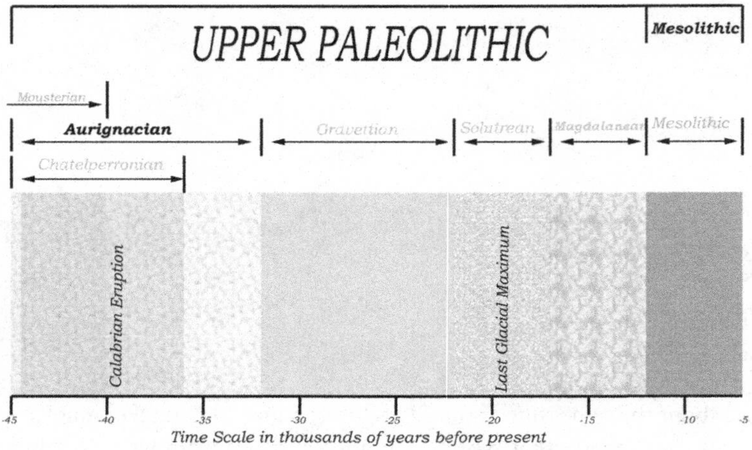

Illustration 44. Aurignacian in the last ice age

Other objects start to appear whose functions are debated by some, such as perforated rods. These pieces of antler contain one or two well drilled holes located close to the branch in the antler and are frequently decorated with designs of animals on the shaft. Amongst the many curious explanations for the use of these objects include dildos, symbols of fertility, midwife's calendar, but the most likely by a wide margin is as a spear thrower. Spear throwers are sometimes still used by Inuits and experiments have found that when used correctly can more than double the range of a thrown spear. Various methods have been proposed, but the most likely one appears to tie a piece of leather or gut as a thong through the hole and wrap the thong a turn or two around the middle of the shaft of the spear. The length of the rod acts as a lever to increase the momentum imparted to the spear and the unwrapping of the thong during release imparts a spin to the spear in the same way that rifling in a gun barrel imparts spin to a bullet, which improves stability of the spear in flight and therefore accuracy. The length of thong adds yet more leverage during the throwing process.

In North America the Aztecs used the spear thrower and called it an Atlatl. The spear is more properly termed a dart as it is made of slightly flexible wood and is of a lighter construction than a spear. Tests with Atlatls reveal that they can kill deer at 40m but can achieve distances of 200m, which is two times the distance of the Olympic record for the javelin. Aztecs used Atlatls against the Spanish invaders who were dismayed to discover that the

Atlatl darts could penetrate their armor. The Atlatl employs two finger loops on either side of the shaft to improve the grip.

Australian Aborigines also used the spear thrower and called it the Woomera. The Woomera doesn't have the drilled hole but uses a marsupial tooth at the end for a spur at the end which locates the butt of the spear an improvement to the design which will appear shortly in Aurignacian Europe.

As prowess in carving improved in Europe beyond the Aurignacian, spear throwers were made with increasingly elaborate and inventive carvings which we shall see later.

The second drilled hole in the spear thrower was most probably used to tie a leather thong around the wrist to ensure that the spear thrower wasn't lost during the action of throwing, which would have been particularly problematic if several spears needed to be thrown in quick succession.

The antler shafts of the spear throwers were often carefully engraved with images of animals, which would have helped to identify the ownership of the weapon, and may also have served as a form of associating the weapon with the prey, just as modern day hunting rifles often display engravings of their intended targets such as bears or ducks or even the names of targets written onto bombs before being loaded onto the bombers. Alternatively, these animal forms may have had some shamanistic significance, which we'll learn more about during the later Gravettian period.

The existence of these sophisticated tools to enhance the distance and accuracy of thrown spears implies that simple spear throwing had been practiced long before this new design had been invented. Although there is no archaeological proof of spears earlier in the fossil record, because any wooden objects from this time wood have rotted away and quite probably within the lifetime of the owner of the spear. Indeed, *Australopithecus* was already throwing objects as weapons 5 million years earlier. Indeed, if it wasn't for the spear thrower there wouldn't even be proof of the use of spears during the Aurignacian.

It is quite possible that the principal of the spear thrower design evolved from the sling, a powerful weapon used well into Roman times and prior to that used all around the world with the exception of Australia. The sling is very easy to make from two pieces of thong attached to a pouch for the projectile or sling shot. On one end of one of the thongs a loop is tied for hooking round one of the fingers. On the end of the other thong a tab for holding is attached. In the Aurignacian period and earlier this may simply have been a wider cut of thong. With a finger in the loop, the tab held in the same hand and the projectile in the pouch the sling is swung around rapidly and at a precise moment the tab is released which causes the projectile to be flung at great speed from the sling. This form of weapon is ideal for downing birds from flocks and for many tens of thousands if not hundreds of thousands of years in prehistory was the weapon of choice for killing flying birds. The sling had the added advantage of being easy to carry, and as long as pebbles were readily available the ammunition there was no need to be encumbered with excess ammunition, particularly along river banks, where water fowl could also be found. In classical Greek times, sling shot with Zeus lightning bolt design imprints, cast from lead have been found in great quantities. In the Neolithic period sling shots were made from baked clay, particularly in locations where appropriate pebbles were scarce.

In Roman times the Balearic Islands were famous for their slingers and even as late as the Spanish Civil War, slingers were used to hurl hand grenades considerable distances and over high obstacles such as buildings. In the Old Testament David famously felled the giant Goliath with a single sling shot. A sling shot can be projected over 400m and ancient writers repeatedly emphasize the advantage in terms of distance of sling shot over arrows. Even today in the Levant, Palestinian rioters still use slings against Israeli troops.

Thus, when a group of Neanderthal slingers encountering a flock of birds they could maintain a considerable distance from them without needing to disturb them and simultaneously unleash a number of sling shot at the flock with a reasonable expectation of maiming one or several of them.

But sling shot would have been little use against animals such as woolly mammoth or woolly rhinoceros thus the spear thrower was used to cause deeper penetration of the spear, which in turn would speed up the immobilizing of the targeted animal, which in turn would reduce the danger to the Neanderthal hunters.

A combination of the spear thrower and the sling was used in early history and might also have been used by ancient Europeans, this is known as the staff sling, where the chord and pouch were attached to the end of a staff thus increasing the lever effect and thus potentially the release velocity of the projectile. In yet another variant on the principal, the staff sling was scaled up greatly to form the standard medieval siege weapon the trebuchet, capable of slinging boulders or burning projectiles great distances.

Manufacture of slings from hide or leather would have been one of the many uses of the increasingly sharp and precise backed knives that were being made in the Aurignacian period. Because of the biodegradable nature of leather none of this material has been preserved in the archaeological record.

It has also been suggested that the holes were used to straighten spears by holding parts of them in a fixed position and applying heat to straighten the spear.

The Neanderthal's aptitude for artistic expression first appears in a Chatelperronian context and flourished in the Aurignacian. (Recent advances in dating wall paintings may push back the first appearance of Neanderthal painting by as much as 20,000 years before the Chatelperronian.) The main art forms are grouped into three categories: personal decoration often in the form of shell and talon necklaces, wall painting and 3-dimensional sculptures. Neanderthals were fascinated by two subjects; naked women and the animals that they hunted; and they rarely deviated from these two themes. The female form still fascinates artists 40,000 years on (although modern day nude sculptors may not appreciate being told that they are continuing in a Neanderthal tradition) and modern hunters frequently have paintings or photos of their favorite prey decorating their walls. Some things just don't change.

The Neanderthal world was one where survival was the overriding preoccupation. All the tools that we find today are tools necessary for their survival. The wild animals that they painted and carved replicas of were equally necessary to their survival. The Neanderthal world was the natural world. Their food, their tools in the Aurignacian, their clothing all came from the animals that they hunted. These wild animals were absolutely vital for the survival of Neanderthals and they well knew it. It isn't surprising therefore that the wild animals that they hunted would be the principal subject of their art. What may be more surprising though is that from the earliest days of Neanderthal art the sculpted figurines were not just of animals but of part animals -part humans. These zoomorphological figurines were creations from the Neanderthal imagination. This tells us something of the subtlety of their thought processes, that they could create fantasy figures. These figures were not just one-offs or passing fads that appeared occasionally and were forgotten about, they remained a key subject of both sculptural art and painting. Indeed, some of these fantasy subjects created at the time accompany human history down to Hindu and Ancient Egyptian times. And in both these cases they appear in a religious context. We have now come across the first unmistakable signs of religion in the world. We will return later to this theme, but first let's look at some of the wonderful art created by these early Europeans.

Some of the earliest sculptural artwork in the world dates from this period and was discovered at the Vogelherd Cave in South West Germany carved from mammoth ivory. The earliest of these is a 40,000 year old cave lion figurine with cross hatching detail for its mane, bearing a regal countenance. Another is an entire, unmistakable and evocative 35,000 year old woolly mammoth sculpture with curved trunk and powerful legs just 3.7cm long. Another figurine found in Vogelherd is a wild horse with its legs broken off. According to the bones found in the Aurignacian levels the two main animals hunted for food were wild horses and reindeer.

Illustration 45. Venus figurine from Hohle Fels, Germany

Illustration 46. Mammoth ivory woolly mammoth

Another very old sculpture and to date the oldest of its type is the Venus of Hohle Fels in South Western Germany dating to between 40 and 35,000BP and also sculpted from mammoth ivory. Venus figurines were to become a standard sculptural form of the Upper Paleolithic and followed a number of conventions. They had small heads, exaggerated breasts and vulva with wide hips and legs tapering to a point at the feet. The tradition of crafting Venus figurines was to continue from 40 to 11,000BP. The example found at Hohle Fels is one of the oldest undisputed depictions of a human being found anywhere. Even older still but of a comparable time frame is the lion-man sculpture also found in South West Germany and also carved from mammoth ivory. It has been reassembled from broken fragments and stands about 31cm high. This sculpture is of a man's body with a lion's head a form of artwork known as zoomorphic. This figurine was found in a chamber 30m from the entrance to the Stadel cave along with many other remarkable objects such as jewellery consisting of pendants, beads and perforated animals' teeth. A similar but smaller lion-headed sculpture was also found in the Vogelherd Cave. Older by far than any of these figurines is the very roughly carved Neanderthal figurine named the Berekhat Ram Venus from Israel, dated to around 250–280,000BP.

Other zoomorphic art has been found including cave paintings of part man part bison. The dual nature of these images is consistent with the idea that a Shaman's role of being a mediator between the world of people and the spirit world, offering a channel of communication between the two. The caves of Vogelherd and Hohel Fels could therefore have been the residences of Shaman during the Aurignacian period

Illustration 47 The adorant from Geissenklosterle
Credit: ICOMOS-IAU Thematic Study on Astronomical Heritage.

The mysterious sculpture of the Adorant from the cave at Geissenklosterle near the village of Weiler, close to Blaubeuren in the Ach Valley, measuring 14x4.5mm carved from mammoth ivory shows a figure of a man with his hands raised and is dated to around the middle of the Aurignacian Period. The name the Adorant or Worshipper comes from the fact that the figure has his arms raised as if in prayer. Curiously he seems to have a tail and may have been intended to be part man part lion reminiscent of the lion-Man of Hohlenstein, who came from a similar place and time. Intriguingly the arrays of dots and notches have been interpreted to have an astronomical significance by Working Group Chair Professor Clive Ruggles of ICOMOS:

Its archaeological context indicates a date within the Aurignacian, probably 35,000–32,000 BP. The artist cut, smoothed and carved one side (A) and finely notched the other side (B) and the edges. Side A contains the half-relief of an anthropoid figure, either human or a human-feline hybrid, known as the 'adorant' because its arms are raised as if in an act of worship. On side B together with the four edges is a series of notches that are clearly set in an intentional pattern. The edges contain a total of 39 notches in groups of 6, 13, 7 and 13. A further 49 notches on side B are arranged in four vertical lines of 13, 10, 12 and 13 respectively plus a further notch that could be in either of the middle two lines... Cultural and symbolic dimension: The grouping of the notches on the plate suggests a time related sequence. The total number of notches (88) not only coincides with the number of days in three lunations (88.5) but also approximately with the number of days when the star Betelgeuse (Orion) disappeared from view each year between its heliacal set (about 14 days before the spring equinox around 33,000 BP) and its heliacal rise (approximately 19 days before the summer solstice). (Ruggles & Cotte 30)

Ruggles and Cotte believe that even though each aspect of the Adorant piece, taken individually, may not provide conclusive evidence that there there is an astronomical association, all the characteristics taken together provide solid evidence that the small plate links religion and astronomy. The constellation of Orion has long proved a focus for religion. The star Sirius is part of Orion and the brightest star in the night sky after the moon. Orion was a hunter in Greek mythology, but written records of worship of Orion go back to the very earliest of writing, with the ancient Sumerians who saw Orion as the hunter fighting the Bull neighboring constellation of Taurus. Ancient Chinese astronomers also saw Orion as a hunter, called Shen. And of course the Ancient Egyptians associated Orion with their primary God Osiris, the God of rebirth and the afterlife.

They suggest that Orion was of great significance to the people of the Aurignacian, not just because of the brightness of Syrius, but because it is visible for 9 months of the year from German latitudes, which corresponds to the human gestation period. Thus linking Orion with human births. Furthermore Ruggles and Cotte believe that by timing conception with the heliacal rise in early summer, the baby would be born after the severe Ice Age winter, allowing it a better chance of survival before the onset of the next winter.

What's more they believe that the adorant figure bears a significant physical resemblance to the constellation of Orion. All these elements taken together do indeed provide a convincing argument that the Adorant piece had a religious and astronomical signifance, providing us with one of the earliest examples of humanity's fascination with the stars.

From the Aurignacian onwards we see an increase in the number of bone flutes, following in the tradition of Divje Babe 20,000 years earlier. A number of these bone flutes were found in caves in South West Germany such as Hohe Fels and have been dated to before 35,000BP. One of the best preserved was made from a griffon vulture radius bone measured 22cm long and 8mm wide, with five sound holes drilled into it.

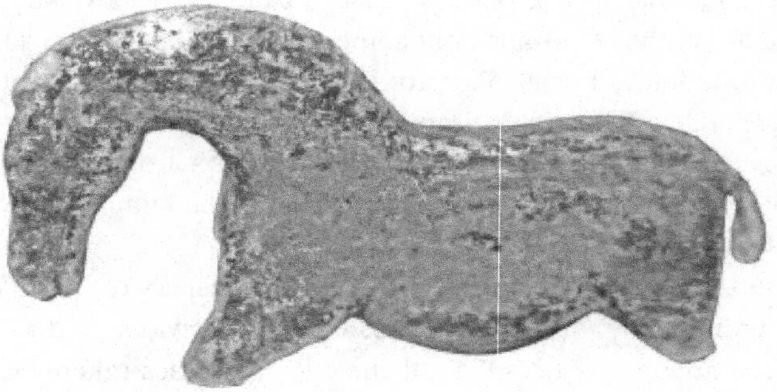

Illustration 48. Mammoth ivory horse figurine from Vogelherd

Another ground breaking find in Hohle Fels dating back to around 40,000BP was of a rope making tool carved from mammoth ivory. This is a curved piece of ivory with four holes drilled into it. Three of the holes (the 4th is on a break and not complete) have radial incisions carved in the form of a helix, which help to guide the strands of the rope while twisting them through the hole. This design is referred to by rope makers as a rope maker's top. The principal is to make rope a lot stronger by plying together yarn, or long plant fibers. The four fibers are passed through the four holes and attached to a stick or a ring, which is then twisted around. This twisting pulls the fibers through the rope maker's top and makes a 4-ply rope. The same tool could be used for a 3-ply rope if the intention was to produce a lighter weight rope. The strength of the rope depends on the regularity of the twist. The helical incisions help to guide the fibers through the holes imparting a twist as they pass through.

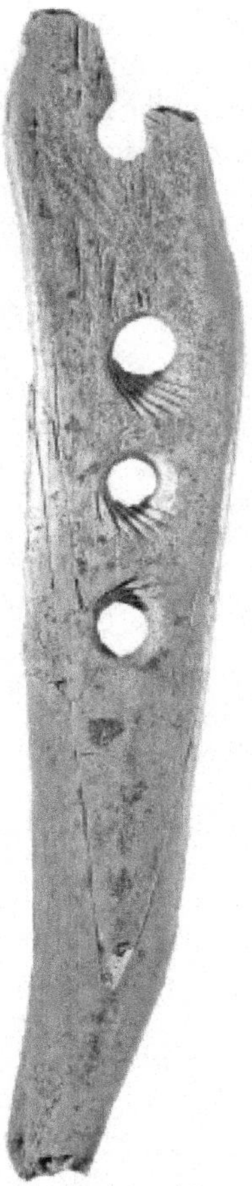
Illustration 49. Aurignacian rope maker's top from Hohle Fels

This find proves the existence of a mature rope manufacturing industry already thriving in the Aurignacian, which in turn implies that various forms of more primitive cord or single ply rope had been in existence much earlier. The photo below is of what may be the earliest example ever found of a rope maker's top dating to about 40,000BP the holes are approximately 8mm wide, making a 4-ply rope of approximately 2cm diameter. Hemp rope of 2cm diameter has a breaking strength of about three tons, even allowing for a less than perfect manufacturing process, the rope manufactured by this rope maker's top would be capable of taking forces in excess of 1 ton. This suggests that the people were doing some very heavy work with the aid of this rope. A length of 100m 2cm diameter hemp rope weighs about 30kg when dry, so anyone carrying such heavy-duty rope for any distance has chosen such a strong rope for a deliberate heavy-duty purpose. Among the many possible uses of such heavy-duty rope would be to create game fences using trees, so that hunters could herd their prey through a forest towards a pre-prepared rope trap which would stop their prey from fleeing to safety. Once the animals were trapped, the hunters could approach to within range of their weapons and could select the animal that they wished to kill. If they wounded it, it would still not be able to escape if the rope trap was closed once the animals had passed through. This form of rope hunting using rope traps is still in use in some remote parts of the People's Republic of the Congo to this day.

By making just one or two turns around intermediate trees any large animal charging the rope would have the impetus slowed by friction as the rope was pulled around the trunk, thus reducing the risk of a breakage and the herd escaping. Several strands of rope secured at appropriate heights would ensure that the game could not escape, in the same way that fences keep livestock in fields and paddocks. Such strong rope would revolutionise the ability of Europeans to trap and kill their prey, with a minimum of expenditure of energy and time compared to chasing a herd. The rope could then be used to drag large sections of carcass back to the camp for preparation, and potentially for preservation, as we have seen earlier with the Blackfeet tribe.

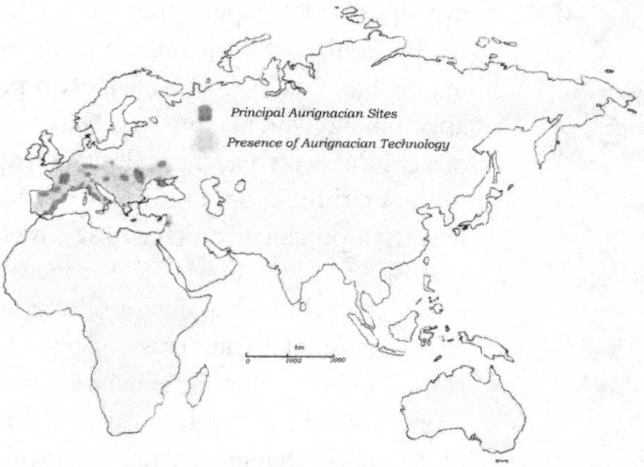

Illustration 50. Aurignacian presence in Europe

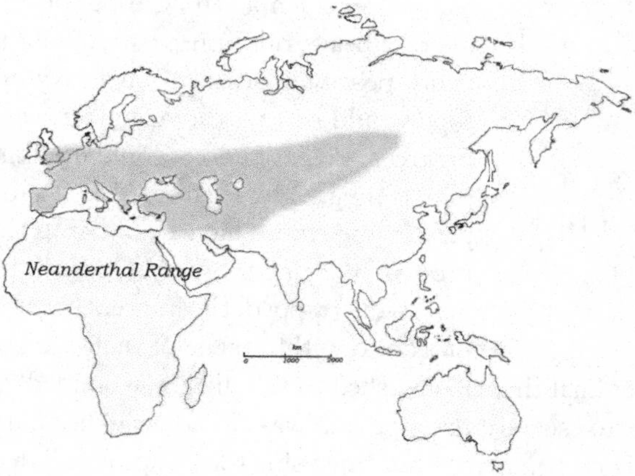

Illustration 51. Neanderthal presence in Europe

A look at the above maps with the known Neanderthal range and the known range of Aurignacian culture clearly showing that Aurignacian culture is centered on the Neanderthal heartland. The oldest figurines were found right in the center of this area, from where that art form appears to radiate outwards throughout the inhabitable parts of Europe where Neanderthals lived. There is no hard evidence that Aurignacian culture and technologies appeared for the first time anywhere apart from Europe or any convincing reason to believe that it was anything but part of the same revolution that created Chatelperronian and Uluzzian out of Mousterian.

Only in the most remotest parts of the continent isolated from the mainstream of movements of population and innovative ideas did the old technologies and classical Neanderthal appearance continue to persist for another 10 to 15,000 years, in such places such as Gibraltar and Western Portugal.

Neither Aurignacian, Chatelperronian nor Uluzzian are African technologies they are limited to Eurasia, specifically they are limited to the Neanderthal heartland

There are to date relatively few European human bones from the Aurignacian period. One notable exception is the Romanian cave Pestera cu Oase (cave of bones). The bones here date from around 37,800BP placing early within the Aurignacian time frame. Officially, these remains have been catalogued as modern human, but the details of each of the fossils reveals a more nuanced story. The Oase 1 cranium belonged to a male and has a significant proportion of classic Neanderthal DNA, the exact proportion depends on how Neanderthal DNA is defined. Unfortunately the reference for Neanderthal DNA is taken from an Altai fossil that lived right on the very edge of Neanderthal's range, in Denisovan territory, and as we have already seen, there was considerable mixing of different races in that area, resulting in localized dilution of Neanderthal heritage and DNA compared to European Neanderthals. Altai Neanderthal DNA is a very poor choice when selecting benchmark Neanderthal DNA, and can't be considered particularly representative. Nevertheless, comparing the non-Neanderthal alleles of Sudanese Dinke people of the same time frame, and Neanderthal alleles, and the commonality of these two with Oase 1, it has been found that Oase 1 contains 2.4 to 3.6 times more genetic contribution than from sub-Saharan Africa, making it abundantly clear that even in Eastern Europe Aurignacian peoples were predominantly Neanderthal.

Curiously, perhaps Oase1 shows a closer DNA association with East Asians and Native Americans than to modern Europeans and does not appear to have contributed much to later European populations in prehistory. Oase 2 was an adolescent with modern features such as projecting chin, slight brow ridge and a high forehead, while at the same time manifesting a large Neanderthal like face, large teeth which get larger towards the back and a Neanderthal bony ridge behind the ears.

More Aurignacian period bones were found at Kostenki above an ignimbrite eruption layer of volcanic material and have been dated to around 32,500BP. Unfortunately, they are not plentiful, just a tibia and fibula, no diagnostic crania were found on the site. DNA analysis suggests a mixed heritage of Neanderthal, North West Asian and Middle Eastern. So even as late as 32,500BP this individual had little or no African heritage.

One major catastrophic natural event had a massive impact on life during the Aurignacian period in Eurasia and that is the Campanian ignimbrite eruption which occurred in 39,280BP at the Phlegrean Fields Volcano 20km to the west of Mt Vesuvius. A huge volume, $300km^3$ of volcanic debris was projected out of the volcano covering an area of 3.7 million km^2. The eruption lasted between two and four days. A pyroclastic flow followed the collapse of the volcanoes caldera which flowed over mountain ranges 1,000m high and out into the sea covering an area of about $60{,}000km^2$. All life within this area was immediately extinguished. The region around the volcano was covered in a deposit up to 100m deep of ignimbrite tuff. The ash cloud drifted East North East as far as central Russia depositing up to 10cm of ash in its wake. Simulations estimate that around 450 million Kg of gaseous sulfur dioxide were discharged into the atmosphere causing changes to the climate, acid rains and was hazardous to life including damage to eyes, lungs and other organs.

Those humans living under the ash cloud probably died if not immediately then over a period of days due to poisoning from dangerously contaminated air and water, and settlements that showed long term occupation prior to the eruption remained unoccupied for a considerable time following the eruption.

Based on the estimations derived in the previous chapter 'The Neanderthal Way of Life' of 0.07 people/km^2 then even if people perished under just half the area covered by the ash cloud, then over a 100,000 people died in this massive volcanic eruption. By comparison, the Krakatoa eruption, of lesser power killed 36,000 people. The sulfate particles ejected into the upper atmosphere reflect sunlight and for very large eruptions cause global cooling. The Campanian Ignimbrite may well have made the Ice Age even colder. Indeed, the worst was yet to come.

According to the Volcanic Ash Fall Impacts Workgroup, ash fall of a depth greater than 10cm (see map below) results in a smothering of the soil preventing oxygen replenishment. This effectively renders the soil sterile. Everything that grows on it is rapidly killed off with the possible exception of mature trees, and as a result all the grazing animals in the area involved will starve, with the knock-on effect that many of the carnivores will also starve once the stock of dead herbivores has been exhausted.

The map below shows the area that was affected by this explosion. In all probability the flourishing Uluzzian culture and people were wiped out entirely from Greece and the Balkans and with probably few survivors in Northern Italy. Central Europe and Eastern Europe was devastated with probably few survivors. A great line of cleavage was made between people in Western Europe and all other peoples. North of the Alps Germany and France were mostly spared the worst effects of this cataclysmic eruption. From this huge no-man's land separating Eastern and Western Europe we can now see why the East European Neanderthals fleeing the ash cloud eastwards would have a closer DNA linkage with Central Asians. From the time of this Campanian Eruption we see the beginnings of a separation between Europe and Asia in terms of culture and technology.

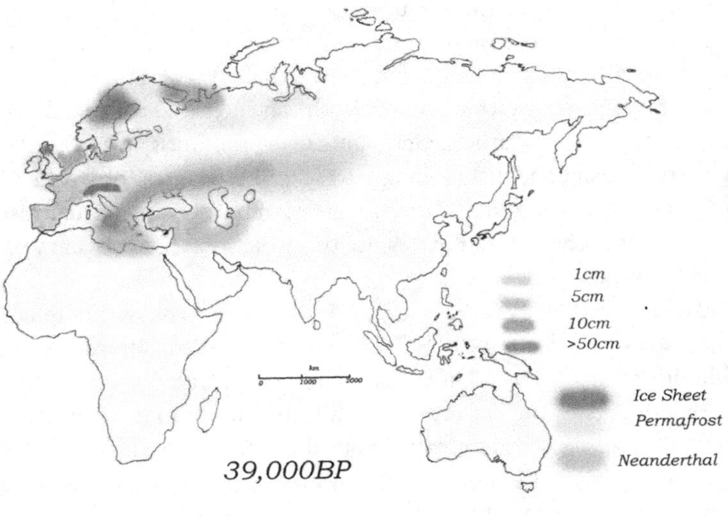

Illustration 52. Campanian ignimbrite eruption

The Campanian Ignimbrite Eruption and the layers of ash it deposited in red. In blue the extent of the European Ice Sheets at the time of the eruption and the regions in a state of permafrost. In green the areas of land presently below sea level but at the time above sea level.

The Weichselian Ice Age had now been going on for over 60,000 years and ice caps had developed in the Alps, over Scandinavia and the Baltic. Vast areas to the south of these ice caps were dominated by permafrost where only the hardiest of grasses could grow in the summer and conditions for life were similar to life in the polar circle today. Sea levels were lower than today and the British Isles were joined to continental Europe by Doggerland.

At the time of the Calabrian ignimbrite eruption 39,000 years ago life in Europe was dealt a massive blow. Neanderthals were caught between the periglacial conditions in the northern half of Europe and a sterile world of over 4 million km^2 to the east and south which was rendered uninhabitable by volcanic ash, acid rain and poisoned water sources and earth.

In just four days 39,000 years ago the Neanderthal world was cut in two following the Calabrian Eruption. The map shows how the Neanderthals in Western Europe to the North of the Alps and South of the permafrost and from the Alps westward to the Atlantic Ocean were isolated from those to the South and East. Some of the Aurignacian-like technology had already spread from Europe to the Levant by the time of the explosion, leaving a relatively small pocket of Aurignacian technology in the Levant, isolated from the rest of the south eastern Neanderthals by deserts to the East and the ash covered devastation to the North. The artistic spark in the form of figurines kindled in Southern Germany during the Aurignacian but because of the sterile ash zone it took longer to spread to the rest of world. For the first time since the arrival of *H. erectus* Western Europe was virtually isolated from the rest of the world. But despite this isolation, art and technical innovation thrived in Western Europe.

A wide swath of Southern and Eastern Europe rendered uninhabitable life unsustainable for hundreds if not many thousands of years, but slowly life did return firstly to areas that had been covered less deeply by the ash, then finally to the entirety of the affected area. On the southern fringes, around the Black Sea migrants from the South arrived, such as those of Pestera cu Oase with a mixed heritage of the remnants of the south eastern Neanderthals mixed with others including possibly some Africans. Meanwhile in Southern Germany and France the Aurignacian culture amongst the remaining Neanderthals with its innovations continued to flourish.

During the Aurignacian period the old Mousterian technology of shaping tools from a prepared flake continued linearly, but became more refined, partly thanks to the use of antlers as knapping tools. The use of ocher as decoration continued and other pigments were added to the color pallet such as manganese and other hues of ocher such as yellow ocher. Working of skins into leather, which was used as clothing, straps and cords for weapons such as spear throwers became more widespread. For the first time in humanity realistic three-dimensional figurines were made with great skill, firstly in South West Germany and then later in France. Tangible evidence of shamanism appeared, although it may have existed long before the first figurines we currently have in our possession were made. The use of shells for preparing hides (as scrapers) and storing pigments spread to them being used also as personal decorations along with other items such as pierced animals' teeth and beads. Weapons became more powerful, and man's dominance as the European apex hunter increased with them, which was some achievement given the formidable array of carnivorous megafauna which hunted the lands. (We'll take a closer look at the megafauna of the Ice Age in a later chapter). He learnt to kill at a safe distance and pluck birds from the sky with the use of slings and throwing sticks. As he became a more proficient hunter, he no longer had to spend all his waking hours in search of sustenance, which allowed him time for relaxation and the ability to express himself artistically.

The gradual process of physical change in Neanderthals which had been happening since the beginning of the Ice Age and which had gathered pace since the Chatelperronian had caused the people of Europe to appear more like modern Europeans than classic Neanderthals. To answer the vexed and perennial question 'How did the Neanderthals die off?' the answer is very simple, they didn't. Neanderthals evolved into modern humans by the normal (but in this case accelerated by tools) process of evolution, a process which has left so many Neanderthal traits visible in today's populations of ethnic Europeans and Caucasians, features which we looked at in the earlier chapter 'Neanderthals'. Because the Chatelperronian and Aurignacian cultural advances didn't occur simultaneously across Europe and Western Asia, the corresponding physical attributes of Neanderthals started to disappear in different places at different times. The last classic Neanderthal that we know of is a girl dating to around 26,000BP found in Portugal. Living right on the edge of Europe, isolated to a degree from the great Neanderthal migration routes, the new technologies and the consequential physical changes arrived later here than elsewhere.

On the sliding scale between classic Neanderthal and modern European, at the end of the Aurignacian the pointer was now closer to modern (albeit archaic) European than Neanderthal. It is thus a convenient point at which to stop referring to the name Neanderthal as the people of Europe. Other terms are frequently used for people of this period: Anatomically Modern humans or Archaic Modern humans or even Archaic Europeans, and from now on these terms will be used. Even though we change the term, these people were just modern Neanderthals who had by their own endeavors changed themselves.

We say farewell to Neanderthals who pass the baton on to archaic Europeans and bow out of this story with honor. They were by far the most advanced culture of their times. Thanks to their craft and their intelligence they bequeathed to the world innovations in the arts and the sciences which have proved invaluable to peoples all over the planet. We can still admire their craft in museums around Europe, and we can still see traces of their physical appearance in Europeans of today. Their determination, inventiveness, creativity and resilience in the face of such extreme conditions merit our respect, and certainly far more than modern historians have accorded them over the past 150 years.

By the end of the Aurignacian period around 28,000BP the Calabrian ignimbrite eruption was long forgotten, Italy and the Balkans were repopulated from the rest of Western Europe.

For the time being the peoples of Western Europe and Eastern Europe together with Western Asia shared a similar culture and were genetically very similar. Central Asia populated by people with mixed heritage, some transitional Neanderthal, some African and some indigenous peoples evolved from *H. erectus*. Some of these latter people moved into the vacuum that followed the fallout from the Calabrian eruption and crossed into Western Europe.

A broad-brush picture was starting to emerge of racial boundaries which we could broadly recognize today. Most of Europe had a predominantly Neanderthal heritage. Neanderthal genetic heritage in the Levant became diminished with new waves of migrants from Africa who were funneled along a thin fertile coastal strip between deserts and the Mediterranean. A partial vacuum in the Neanderthal population following the Calabrian eruption, followed by a slow repopulation of Asia Minor meant that there was little migration in the reverse direction towards Africa. This slowed the spread of Neanderthal Aurignacian technology to Africa. In South East Asia indigenous peoples blocked the spread of the migrants coming out of Africa into their regions although some mixing of genes did occur. Many of these migrants were diverted North and East and some of whom managed to cross the Bering Strait into North America and from there they succeeded in populating both the Northern and Southern continents with humans for the first time in history, taking with them some of the Aurignacian derived technology that they had acquired along the way.

The Gravettian

The Gravettian followed the Aurignacian culture in Europe. The first signs of it appeared around 33,000BP and the last traces of it disappeared by around 17,000BP. The exact dates of the culture are debated and some give the dates as between 27 and 16,000BP. The diagnostic relics of this culture are small, fine stone blades with one sharp edge and one blunt back to allow finger pressure (inherited from the Aurignacian), these are known as Gravettian Points.

In a now familiar pattern we see almost seamless continuity with the Aurignacian. Venus figurines abound in Gravettian sites although executed with increasing care and a formulaic style. Spear throwers made from antler resemble those found in the Aurignacian as well. Pierced shells and pebbles are frequently found. Other tools such as scrapers seem almost undistinguishable from those found in Aurignacian layers.

One very significant technological advance was the appearance for the first time of ceramics, the first of which in the world were found in sites along the middle Danube, where there developed a sub-culture somewhat different from Western Europe (due in part no doubt to the Calabrian ignimbrite eruption), which has been termed Pavlovian. Evidence on the surface of these fired ceramics shows the imprint of textiles, the earliest proof that some form of weaving was now taking place and probably had been doing for some considerable time.

In short, all the technological innovations created during the Aurignacian are still present, but many are more refined in the quality of their finishing. The one distinguishing element between the two classifications of technology being the Gravettian point. Whether ceramics are an Aurignacian or Gravettian innovation remains to be ascertained. Venus Figurines are one of the characteristic art forms frequently found at Aurignacian sites in Europe and Western Asia.

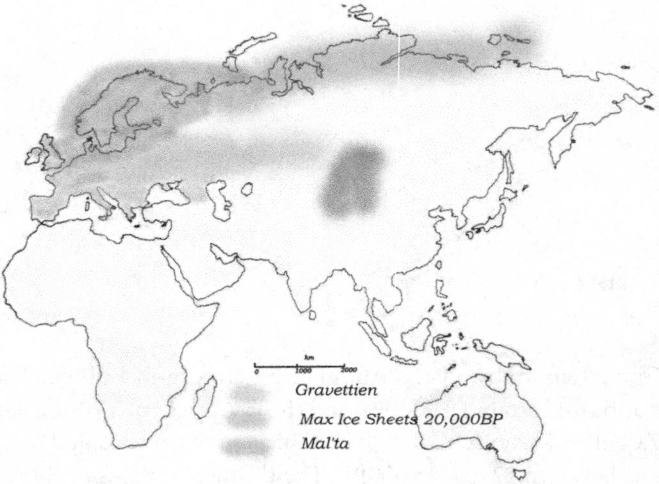

Illustration 53. Gravettian range

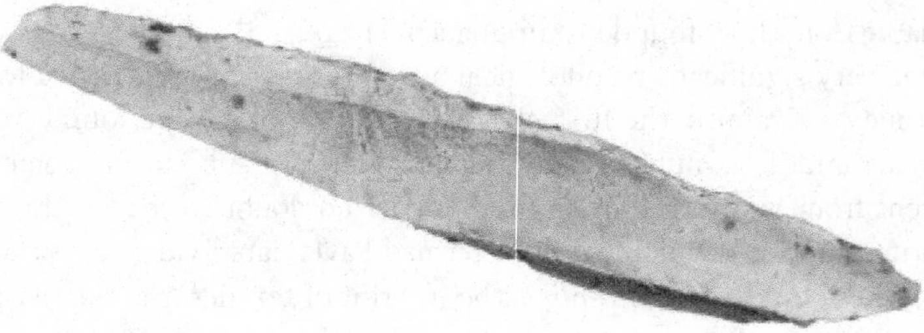

Illustration 54. Gravettian point

Differences in the nature of the finds exist between the Gravettian cave sites in Western Europe and open settlements in Central and Eastern Europe with buildings. Italy and the Balkans were now fully resettled following the Calabrian eruption with also their share of Gravettian sites.

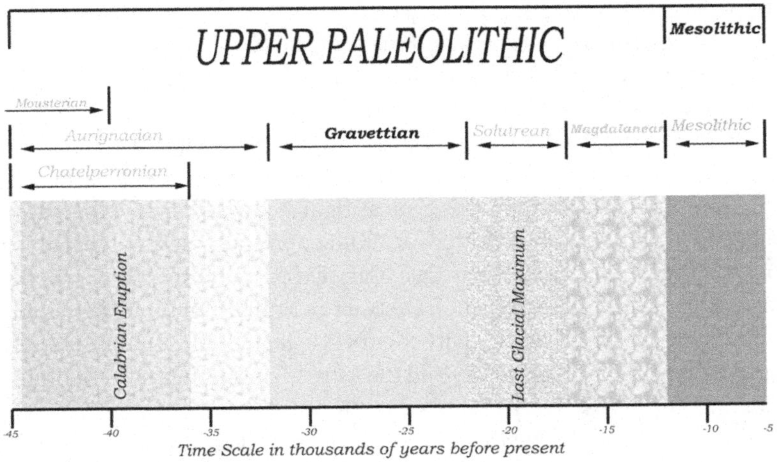

Illustration 55. Gravettian period

There was no tangible difference between the Gravettian people and the Aurignacian people with the exception that the slow process of the modernization of physical appearance away from the classic Neanderthal features continued. The jaw continues to become finer, teeth smaller and a chin continues to develop.

In Italy one of the most important Gravettian sites is the Arene Candide cave in Liguria, located 90m above present sea level. Exceptionally dry conditions helped to preserve the remains that dated from the Paleolithic and continued through to the Byzantine era. Inside the cave were found 19 burial pits with well preserved remains, the most famous of which is known as the young prince, a 15-year-old boy dated to 23,500BP. The body lay on a bed of ocher 7m below the floor of the cave accompanied by a rich collection of burial goods. He wore a creel-like cap covered with hundreds of sea shells and pierced red deer teeth and was accompanied by a large number of ornaments made from shells, deer antler and bone. In his grave were also found four spear throwers and a large flint knife. He was killed by a blow to the chin which was tidied up with yellow ochre before the burial. Isotope analysis of his teeth reveal that ¼ of his diet was sea-food.

At the Grotte de Pape (Pope's Cave) in the village of Brassempouy, SW France was found the head section of a famous ivory Venus figurine noteworthy because of the realistic depiction of a female face and a detailed head cap or elaborate hair net. Dated to 25,000BP it is one of the earliest realistic sculptures of facial features in the world.

Amongst many other Gravettian sculptures in France, the Venus of Laussel stands out. Partly because it is a beautifully executed bas-relied with considerable attention paid to proportions and also because she is sitting down. In her right hand she is holding a bison horn with the large end towards her in a posture of drinking in profile, revealing that she has long hair. This sculpture differs from the typical figurines which are 3-dimensional sculptures with the subject simply standing upright. This bas-relief appears to show the woman drinking from a horn. Drinking horns made from bovid horns are still in use today and have been prominent without interruption throughout European history with plenty of evidence and references stretching back into classical antiquity and the Iron Age in Germany. In Georgia the drinking horn is used in ritual toasting. In antiquity there are many Scythian stellae from the 6th century BC which feature warriors holding drinking horns. Scythian warrior burials usually include their drinking horns and historians associate the drinking horn with Scythian kingship or high warrior status. Scythia was the name given during classical times to a vast area of Central Eurasia, which also happened to be peopled by Neanderthals and their descendants. The ancient Greeks referred to them as nomadic peoples. Vikings, Scots, Germans and Georgians all consider the drinking horn as an object of importance and associated with people of high status. In Switzerland a drinking horn with an oak leaf wreath is the traditional prize for the winner of a Hornussen tournament which involves hitting a puk at speeds of up to 300 kph. We will never know for sure the true significance of the Venus of Laussel and her horn, but given the particular status of the drinking horn in European culture, it is quite likely that she was someone of high status who warranted a portrait of her engraved on the wall of the Laussel shelter and who offers us an insight into drinking practices which evolved with the Neanderthals and continued through to modern times.

Close to Lake Baikal in far distant Siberia, 30 ivory Venus figurines known as the Venus Figurines of Mal'ta have also been discovered dating to the Gravettian period. Like the Venus of Brassempouy they have detailed faces and are either slender in form or like most Gravettian Venus's generously endowed.

Sungir

Probably the most well-known of Russian Gravettian sites is at Sungir, 200km to the East of Moscow close to the river Klyazma dating from around 34-30,000 BP. The main focus of attention at the excavation was four burials, dug into the permafrost at the time (which helped with the preservation), and containing very revealing grave goods with graves 1 & 2 being described as the most spectacular of European Gravettian graves. Grave 1 contained an adult male and grave 2 contained two adolescent children placed head to head one of whom was holding an adult femur filled with ochre. All three wore elaborate grave goods when buried which included ivory beaded jewellery, clothing and spears. More than 13,000 beads were found in these two graves. The man was adorned with 2,936 beads, in strands covering most of his body. He wore a head cap which too was covered in beads and fox teeth. It is estimated that each ivory bead would have needed about an hour of work to produce, creating clothing of almost incalculable value. He wore 25 mammoth ivory bracelets on his arms just above the elbows, some of which still showed signs of black paint. Around his neck he wore a flat schist pendant, painted with red ochre but with a black dot on it.

The small boy wore strands of 4,903 beads, which were roughly 2/3 the size of the man's beads but carved in an identical way. He also wore a cap of beads adorned with fox teeth, and a belt adorned with 250 polar fox canine teeth, an astonishing quantity. Under his left shoulder was a large ivory figurine of a woolly mammoth. At his left side lay a part of a very large human femur packed with red ochre. At his right side and continuing along to the side of the girl lay a very large straightened ivory lance 2.4m long and weighing 20Kg. Close to the lance and lying upright in the soil was a beautifully crafted pierced ivory wheel which appears to have been mounted on a now disintegrated wooden lance.

The girl was covered with 5,274 ivory beads, as with the boy about 2/3rds the size of the man's beads. She also wore a beaded cap with an ivory pin at her throat, possibly as a clasp for a cloak. But she had no fox teeth whatsoever. But she was accompanied by several small ivory lances, more appropriate to her size. She also had three small ivory disks each with a central hole and decorated with carved latticework. There were two further, larger and perforated disks one of which was inserted over one of the smaller lances. A line of stone microflakes was found alongside the small spears, suggesting to the excavators that they were used as barbs on the point of the lance.

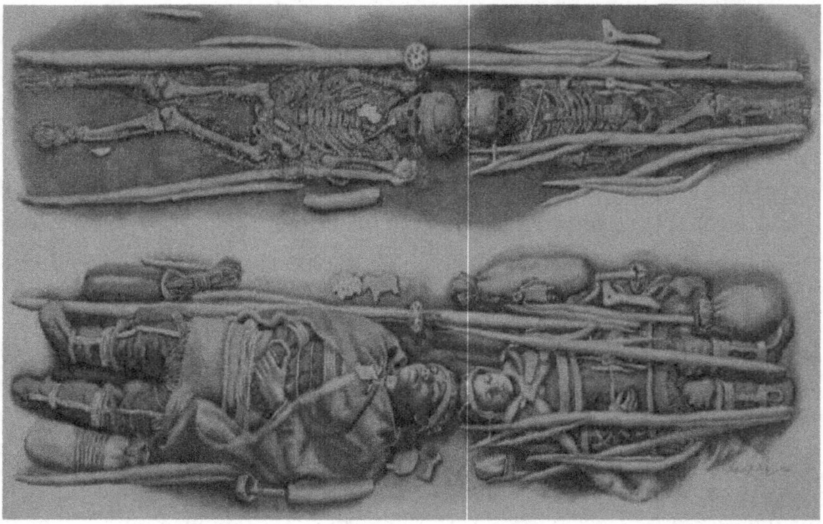

Illustration 56. Reconstructuon of Singir burials

Credit: Sungir Burial reconstruction credit Libor Balák

The pierced, decorated disc on the girl's lance bears an unmistakable resemblance to the discs found on Native American spirit sticks. A Native American spirit stick is a stick used by a Native American shaman to invoke spirits and healing spirits. It is also called a healing stick. They are used to banish evil spirits occupying the settlement, or to bless an animal before it is used by the settlement. As a precursor to the bishop's rood, it was also used to bless warriors prior to their departure on a hunting trip or prior to war. The wheel ornament on the stick represents the earth.

Modern shaman equipment from the Hmong people from the Yangtze River region in China, (substantial numbers of them still live throughout South East Asia) includes a ring with a collection of discs with a central hole in them. This important item is a shaman's cymbal. It is used for making a rattling form of music performed by the shaman during his rituals. The ring in modern times is made from metal, but in the Gravettian it was probably made from a piece of wood bent into a large ring on which the ivory discs were inserted, the two ends of the piece of wood having completed the circle were then made into a handle. The wood of the shaman's cymbal has long since rotted away. Hmong shamanism still exists and shaman can be men or women, the chance of someone becoming a shaman is increased if an elder relative was also a shaman. If shamanistic powers are recognized in someone then they are expected to seek out a practicing shaman for formal education into shamanistic practices. Shamanistic tendencies manifest unusual human behavior and in modern times it has been found that such people are also inclined to manifest clinical disorders such as bipolar disorder or multiple personalities or schizophrenia.

Curiously whereas today such disorders are considered to be medical problems that require treatment, among Shamanic peoples these disorders are thought to be related to special powers, setting Shaman apart from ordinary people.

The burial is still an extremely important time for Hmong people and whose protocol is strictly controlled in order to protect both the living and the dead from evil spirits which gather when there is a death. As part of the burial regalia that is still required are a crossbow and a knife that must be placed next to the dead body, similar to the case with the Sungir burial, and interestingly similar to meteorite iron knife of Tutankhamen.

Shamanism

It is quite probable given her high status, rich adornments, spirit stick and shaman's cymbal, the zoomorphological figurines, the association of animal figurines in graves that are often found in Gravettian culture that the girl was a female shaman. The boy with the mammoth by his shoulder and the fox teeth who also had rich clothing may have been a young shaman too.

Another prominent Gravettian site is at Dolni Vestonice in the Czech Republic, to whom the Sungir people in Russia were genetically related. One of the more interesting graves is considered to be that of a female shaman. The female skeleton is buried ritualistically beneath a couple of mammoth scapulae leaning one against the other forming a sort of protection. A flint spearhead is placed close to the skull and the right hand holds the body of a fox. The whole body was covered with ochre, probably as a symbolic link to the earth.

15,000 years later Israeli archaeologists discovered the burial of a female shaman belonging to the Natufian culture. Her body is surrounded by animal parts; a wild boar humerus on her shoulder, 50 tortoise shells by her stomach, an aurochs tail by her legs, marten skulls in her hands and eagle wing bones by her arms (implying presumably that she could fly like an eagle).

The word 'shaman' is of Russian origin stemming from 'Shamanka' of the Tungus people and Siberia is currently considered to be the birthplace of shamanism. If the Gravattian culture was based around a shamanistic world view, which seems very likely given the symbols, figurines and close links that they had with animals, then the religion managed to survive for nearly 40,000 years in central Asia and was only extinguished as a major world religion when Russians conquered the shamanistic Khanate of Kazan in 1552. Amongst other places around the world, Manchu Shamanism was one of the official religions of the Chinese Qing dynasty and parts of the Imperial Palace in Beijing are still maintained for shamanistic rituals.

The central Asian Nganasan people practiced shamanism through to modern times and some of their rituals have been captured on film. The last shaman of the Oroqen people of Mongolia died in the year 2000. Shaman in Central Asia wore animal skins and underwent transformations into animals during spiritual journeys. Animals served as human guides and rescuers and sacrificial victims, themes which recur frequently in the Ancient Egyptian religion where the C1 haplogroup (originating from Northern Asia and parts of Europe) was also found in Ancient Egyptian DNA.

As a religion rooted in nature, shamanism held a special reverence for the relations between earth, sky and water and belief in the mystical nature of mountains and trees. In Central Asia shamanism places a strong emphasis on the extreme contrasts of summer and winter. Because of the extreme weather changes between summer and winter, Central Asian peoples often lived nomadic life styles following herds of mammoth or reindeer as they moved north to summer pastures and south to escape the snow and extreme cold. Naturally, these nomadic peoples followed shamanistic beliefs. The link between hunting, nomadism and shamanism created the great warrior tribes of central Asia that culminated in the huge armies of the Golden Horde.

Female shamans have existed throughout history, not just throughout Asia but in Africa, Polynesia and elsewhere. The Chinese Wu were priestesses who danced until they achieved a state of trance receiving shen spirits into their bodies which enabled them to heal and pronounce prophesies. The priestess of Ukok (from a shamanistic burial discovered in Central Asia) was buried with a 1-meter tall headdress representing the Tree of Life with gilded felines and birds in its branches. Similar burials have been found in Kazakhstan and the Ukraine with the Tree of Life remaining a recurrent theme. Codices made by the Aztecs show shaman women presiding over the sweat lodge ceremony. As part of the Catholic Church's attempt to convert Latin America to Catholicism priests branded female shamans as evil. But the information that has come down to us of their work has been that they acted purely for the good of the communities that they served. The Jesuit priest Acosta proselytising in Peru referred to the female shaman there as witches. The Spanish Inquisition in Peru forbade women 'witches' to consume achuma, chamico and coca and also to produce illusions and predictions.

Circumpolar shamanism unites the Inuit and Yupik cultures and is still remembered today. As we shall see later there are very strong links between these people today and the descendants of the Gravettian peoples. Circumpolar shamanism may thus shed some light on the beliefs of the long gone

Gravettians. Shamanism assumes links between living people, the souls of dead people and of hunted animals. In this belief system the soul has a dualistic nature; part human and part animal. Despite considerable cultural differences between modern Inuit and Yupik cultures around the globe there appear to be commonalities in shamanistic practices and the language used specifically by shamans.

Various ivory figurines were found at Sungir in common with other Gravettian sites, including two ivory horses used as pendants, with a hole drilled in a rear foot so that they could be suspended around the neck.

All three bodies were laid on their backs with their hands folded across their pelvises. Everything was covered with red ochre. DNA analysis shows that all three bodies tested together with other partial remains found on the site belonged to the Y-DNA Haplogroup C1a2 and possessed DNA closely related to DNA found in skeletal remains at Kostenki. Y-DNA haplogroup C1a2 also known as Haplogroup C-V20 is DNA which first occurred in Europe, the earliest find of which is from Belgium dating to about 35,000BP, it has also been found in the Czech Republic around 30,000BP, the age of the Sungir people from Russia lies comfortably between these two dates. These Gravettian people from Europe and Western Asia were related. Starting in Europe later derivations of this Y-DNA have spread to North Africa and as far afield as Nepal. It is also present in Europe to this day. Geneticists believe that it first evolved in Europe around 40,00BP during the great transitional phase when physical characteristics of Neanderthal people changed so much and so fast. The grandparent of this Haplogroup (i.e., the Haplogroup from which C1a2 evolved) is C1. C1 has two primary branches, the oldest of which is C1a, and the oldest examples of this group originates from Paleolithic Neanderthals around 48,400BP. In other words, DNA analysis, confirming all that we have seen so far on Neanderthal heritage, demonstrates that the haplogroup of the Gravettians originated with Neanderthals. Thus, the Gravettian peoples were descended directly from Neanderthals.

At another Gravettian site not far from Sungir, called Gagarino an ivory figurine portrays an identical burial of the boy and the girl, lying on their backs and attached at the heads. This confirms if it isn't already obvious that their positioning in the grave was highly symbolic. It has been suggested that the symbolism intended is the concept of mystical polarity.

A forensic reconstruction of a young man buried at Sungir reveals a massive protruding jaw, similar to Neanderthal but with a high forehead and no supra-orbital ridge of modern humans, thus showing the mixture of features from both Neanderthal and modern, typical of these transitional peoples.

Pavlovian

Pavlovian culture groups a number of open settlements along the middle Danube basin and dates to between 30 and 25,000BP. Typically these are settlements of no less than 100m in diameter comprising of clusters of huts.

The increasing number of settlements comprising of clusters of huts, with some of them of considerable size, shows the increasing tendency of these peoples to live in communities of increasing size who couldn't comfortably be housed in caves with fixed and limited space. Settlements such as these enable communities to grow and benefit from economies of scale and allocation of specific tasks. They demonstrate a greater form of social organization necessary for larger numbers of people together. The shamans would have fulfilled a vital role of teaching, organizing and leading such communities. These economies of scale enable time to be freed up for tasks not directly linked to survival, such as creating artwork, and decorating clothing.

Quite a few intentional burials have been found on these sites, where bodies have been covered at least partially in ochre and buried with personal decoration such as pierced animal's teeth, and in several cases harking back to the zoomorphological figures in SW Germany of the Aurignacian, have been buried alongside animals. In quite a few cases burials were protected by mammoth shoulder blades. There are also ivory Venus figurines found at Pavlovian sites some of which reveal the hairstyles worn by women there; these include long hair attached in a bun style on top of the head.

At Predmosti 1 site in the same region, a burial area was used outside of the settlement and clustered around a large, prominent rock. In other words, an intentional graveyard had been selected for the careful burial of members of the community. In some cases, it would seem that foxes dug their dens close to the graves and gnawed at the bodies for some considerable time after the burial.

Willendorfian-Kostenkian

A second phase of the Gravettian culture in Central Europe is the Willendorfian-Kostenkian which lasted approximately from 25-20,000BP. This phase shows a different settlement pattern to the Pavlovian phase. The geographical area covered by these types of settlements increases considerably.

The Willendorf site itself is worth looking at in detail as one of the two case sites for this period. Willendorf is a village on the west bank of the Danube in Austria and contains at least 8 locations close together in the upper half of a 20m deep loess accumulation, a stone's throw from the river. The west bank appears to have been chosen because of its sheltered location from the dominant west wind which tends to blow down the Danube Valley. The four lower excavations date from the Aurignacian period and the four upper ones from the eponymous Willendorfian in the Gravettian period. The location is interesting as it is midway between the famous Aurignacian sites on the Upper Danube and Pavlovian sites further downstream. Thus emphasising the importance of the Danube as an important axis for settlements in the period from 40-20,000BP.

The most important and iconic find here was the Willendorf Venus 1 (see below) dating from roughly 25-23,000BP although given the uncertainty about the layer during the excavations and the fact that it is carved from mineral oolitic limestone, there is a degree of uncertainty about the exact age. Ollitic limestone has small characteristic 'egg-like' crystals in it, enabling the determination of where the stone originated from, which was about 130km from Willendorf, close to the town of Brno.

This Venus displays some interesting features. Like the older Hohle Fels Venus found further upstream and from the Aurignacian; she has generous breasts, with her arms folded over them. She is very fat with large thighs which taper down to very fine ankles and no feet. Stylistically she is very similar indeed to the earlier Hohle Fels Venus. However, her head is covered by what appears to be a form of cap or hair net that covers all the features of her face. The experts seem to all be in agreement that this is an intentional part of the design, to hide the face. Considerable care is taken over the detail of the cap which appears to be of woven material and is the only garment that she wears. This is another example of the existence of woven fabrics from the period. The vulva is shown in graphic detail. Questions have arisen given the generous dimension of these Venus figurines about obesity during the Aurignacian and Gravettian periods. Various theories have been put forward concerning the obesity of these figurines and that they are all female. It would seem that the most likely suggestion is that because of the generally energy intensive lifestyle of the period most people were lean. Someone who was fat was fed by the hard work of others and thus someone with considerable status and authority in the community. If that is the case then the figurines may be symbols of authority in a matriarchal society, justifying the consideration given to them in these many figurines.

Other such Venus figurines have been found in the Gravettian to add to the collection already dated to the Aurignacian, all of which show very similar features. Some however wear jewellery and beads some have bangles on their arms. Some differ in that they were more abstract, with less attention to realism. Some of these were found buried in pits within the dwellings, which recalls the Roman practice of burying family treasure under their houses during times of invasion and political instability.

The Venus was apparently carved with sharp flint tools using a regular technique with strong vertical chiseling to achieve the outline and smoothed off with lighter horizontal strokes to achieve the smooth finish. Some of the traces of these strokes can be seen on the buttocks when examined closely.

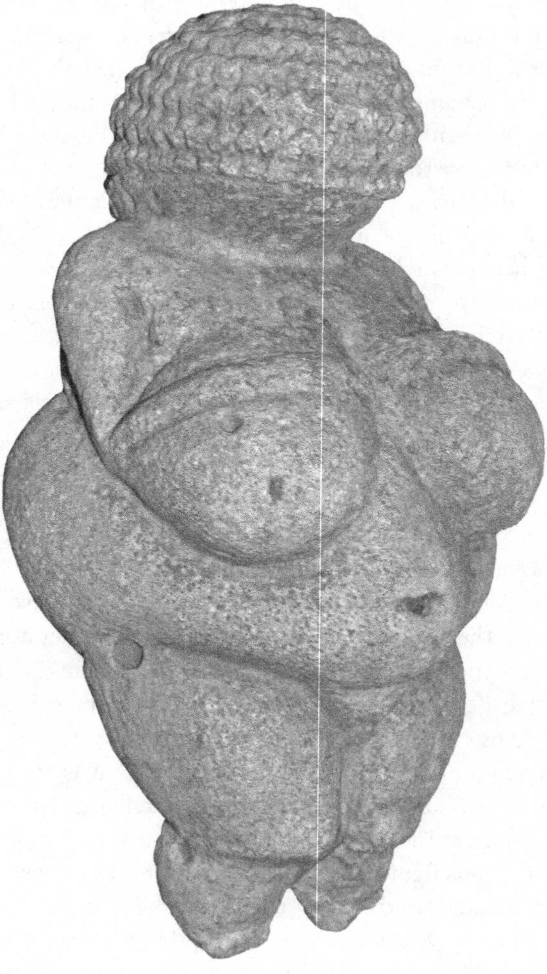

Illustration 57. Venus of Willendorf

The discovery of this Willendorf Venus was a fortuitous combination of determination and chance. Already by the 1870s the area was known to have been a Paleolithic site with stone tools having been discovered by chance by, amongst other people, the owner of a local brick factory, Frederick Brun who recognized some bones during the digging of a new clay pit at the end of the 1880s. Further digging for clay in 1904 revealed what appeared to be human skeletons. In 1908 systematic excavations were started with the aim of discovering more Paleolithic remains. Sites were chosen in the village and the road that traversed it, that didn't interfere too much with gardens belonging to the locals and houses. But it was the arrival of the railway with considerable excavation work for the line that gave the digs a great helping hand. The archaeologists were working against the railways tight time schedule so were limited in the scope of their work. The area was dug out to a considerable depth which offered the excavators access to layers that they wouldn't normally be able to access, but these were industrial diggings and many artifacts and bones might have been missed in the process. Nevertheless, the Venus of Willendorf amongst other important finds were saved.

This anecdote reveals just how much depends on luck when trying to find evidence of our Paleolithic past and how much remains to be found in the future as well as just how easy it would be without the interest of educated people like Frederick Brun and his colleagues to overlook important Paleolithic remains.

Many other items were recovered from the site as well, including scrapers, typical thin Gravettian blades and chisels. It is considered that most of the scrapers found were used for wood and hide working as in the Aurignacian period. Other scrapers include side scrapers where the blade is located along the long side of the tool. Also scrapers with a notch knapped in on either side, to facilitate attaching them to a bone or wood handle. From now on hafting of blades into handles, spears, arrows etcetera becomes increasingly more frequent. Impressive piles of flint tools have been uncovered on the site and which are on display at the Vienna Natural History Museum.

Most animal bones belonged to either ibex or reindeer indicative of the cold climate north of the Alps and south of the Periglacial conditions prevailing in Northern Europe. But there were plenty of others animal bones too including eagles, cave bears, cave lions, mammoth, horses and red deer.

Pierced sea shells were also found having been transported for thousands of kilometers from the sea and used as personal decoration. Carefully prepared, profiled and smoothed bone points dating from the Aurignacian were also found having been used as spear tips.

Other objects of interest and presumably of some rarity and thus intrinsic value include shark's teeth and Moldavite a greenish mineral formed by the impact of meteorites and found in the Danube watershed close to the Austrian border.

Five superimposed camps were located at Willendorf spanning a period of nearly 20,000 years, testament to the longevity and stability of the cultures occupying the middle Danube during this period.

Up until the start of the Willendorfian period the raw materials for tools had been sourced locally from the Danube, but after that period a majority of them were sourced from the moraines of the great Northern Ice Sheet hundreds of kilometers to the north. This raises questions of whether such significant journeys were made purely for obtaining ideal flints, whether there was a form of trade with peoples to the north or whether they were simply recovered when following herds of animals northwards in the summer.

Still more precious material has been discovered in the Willendorf village, some of which still remains to be analyzed and catalogued. How many more sites such as these remain to be discovered along the Danube and its tributaries remains to be seen?

Kostenki

Kostenki (sometimes written as Kostyonki) is an important group of Paleolithic sites of various settlements in Russia, 6 of which have several layers belonging to the Gravettian culture, and fit into the expected date range from 30–20,000BP. Kostenki is located on the banks of the River Don, about half way between Moscow and the Black Sea. The Campanian ignimbrite eruption which we looked at earlier deposited a thick layer of ash here, under which earlier classical Neanderthal settlements were found. The archaeological remains go down to 20m below the current land level, requiring very deep pits in the small areas chosen for excavation.

All of these Gravettian excavations contain backed bladelets. One of the unusual features of Kostenki is the presence of what have been called bone shovels. These are long bone handles with carefully carved small spatulate ends which look more like large spoons than shovels. But digging was becoming an increasingly frequent activity, not just for graves but for pits with various uses. The Kostenki sites located at various heights above the River Don were settlements with structures rather than rock shelters and so share some common features with the Willendorf settlement on the Danube. At Kostenki 8, there is evidence of about 8 small circular structures and a much larger one. There is a wide range of animal remains with a majority belonging to hares and wolves, but also include: aurochs, mammoth, rhinoceros, red deer, cave bear, arctic fox, as well as various birds and fish. In just one layer of just one part of the overall Kostenki site there were found 22-23,000 worked stone pieces of which 2,100 were retouched and 900 of those were backed. The majority of the stone tools were made of flint which was imported from elsewhere because there was no local source of natural flint and most of the blades were retouched to exhaustion in order to avoid wastage. Many of the 900 backed bladelets discovered there were broken and presumably discarded once they could no longer be of use.

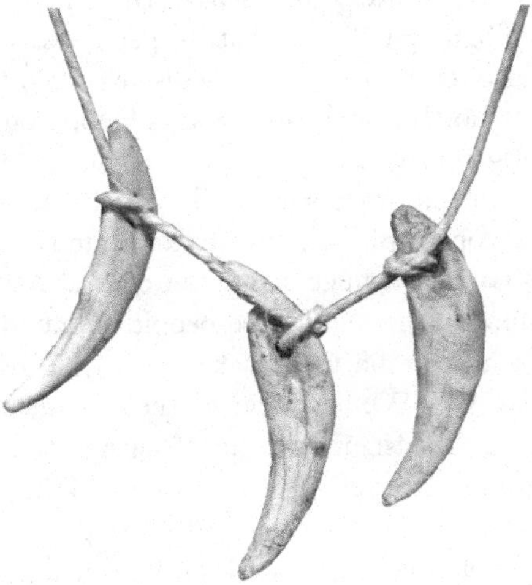

Illustration 58. Fox canine necklace

At one of the other Kostenki excavations, Kostenki 4, where two of the layers were Gravettian the settlement took on a different aspect with two lines of hearths surrounded by collections of finds, in what is considered to be a longhouse arrangement. The layer above this, i.e., more recent in time, contains just small two round structures. The lower layer contained about 16,000 stone tools of which 1,700 were retouched and 400 of those were backed bladelets. On the layer above, about 60,000 stone tools were found including 7,000 retouched pieces of which 2,600 are backed pieces. Tellingly animal figurines were found here, similar in style to another Kostenki excavation, Kostenki 11. Also, other sculptures found here were Venus figurines very similar in style to those found in France; pendulous breasted naked female figures with cords circling the body above the breasts and at the waist. Some of the Venus figurines show women's hair cut in a bob style above the shoulders.

Among the ornaments found were bone sewing needles necessary for the creation of well insulated clothing as protection from the bitterly cold climate prevailing in central Russia.

At Kostenki 14 (the main site in the Kostenki complex) a male burial was found dated to between 40 and 35,000BP. In 2014, Eske Willeslev extracted 12 bone samples from the body's left arm and analyzed the DNA. It was found that it belonged to Y-DNA haplogroup C1b, and that the person was closely related to Neanderthals, and also related to the people discovered at the site of Mal'ta (which we'll look at shortly). Interestingly this haplogroup is an ancestor of about 40% of aboriginal Australian males. This important DNA evidence tells us that the transitional process from Neanderthal to modern humans that we have seen in Europe applies equally in Russia and that these descendants of Neanderthals covered a huge swathe of central Asia to at least as far as Lake Baikal. More surprisingly these people migrated down through South East Asia to reach Australia, presumably leaving Neanderthal descendants also in South East Asia. We have seen in the Ice Age chapter that human migration throughout the islands of South East Asia during the Ice Age was made easier by the low sea levels which transformed the present islands into a larger land mass.

At Kostenki 12 DNA analysis of a male burial with the body in a crouched position and as usual covered with red ochre, revealed that the person belonged to the Y-DNA haplogroup C1, and was thus related genetically to the people of Sungir 500km to the north. This man lived around 30,000BP.

Avdeevo

The Avdeevo site on Rogozna River in the proximity of Kursk has close links to the Kostenki site from which it is little more than 100km distant. The excavation has revealed occupation during the period 23-22,000 BP in the form of two oval structures accompanied by semi-subterranean living areas and 8 storage pits. The main building seems to be huge; 45m long by 20m wide containing a substantial communal living area, and necessitating considerable building skills and cooperation between a significant number of builders. The small semi-subterranean pit houses are 4-8m^2, occupied possibly by individual families. Beyond these structures there are few human related finds. At an adjacent site another very large building has been discovered 28m long by 15m wide. As with its sister site the main building is fringed with pit houses and storage pits. A staggering 33,000 pieces of knapped flint were found at the two sites. About 600 pieces of worked bone were found here, including tusk, antler and bone. The so-called shovels were made of mammoth ribs, and wear patterns suggest that they were used as mattocks, a tool similar to a pick axe, which may have been used for the substantial digging that was done at the site. The handles of these were decorated with various cross-hatching patterns.

A number of items that are considered to be long needles were found here, ranging from 12 to 36cm long and made from waterfowl bones, again the shafts were decorated with cross-hatching patterns.

Also, mammoth bone spoons were found with short handles, but with clearly recognizable concave cups in which there was more cross-hatch decoration. Other carefully made bone implements include what seem to be handled spatulas and a top-hatted tool handle. Zoomorphic bone points have a hole drilled in at the wide end, possibly for hanging around the neck, when working skins and leather, ensuring that it is constantly to hand and to hang from the wall when not in use. In addition, there was a mammoth ivory armband with engravings similar in design to a tyre tread.

The artifacts at Avdeevo are similar to Kostenki including the so-called bone spades, but with other typical Gravettian artifacts such as bone awls, beads, diadems and bracelets as well of course as Venus figurines. One Venus figurine is a variant on the dual man-woman one found at Kostenki. At Avdeevo the dual ivory figurine is of two women attached back to back and head to toe. This may be a symbolic representation of the shaman's tendency to be schizophrenic, passing from one personality to a different one.

Most of the other Venus figurines represent women including several of women in various stages of pregnancy and compared to other sites are fairly roughly finished. One seemingly unfinished Venus is still attached to the unworked segment of mammoth tusk. There are rarely any facial features on any of the figurines. As with Venus figurines elsewhere of this period there is a sort of cord girdle above the breasts.

Among many other figurines found at Avdeevo was one that was found at the bottom of a pit next to an ivory wand similar to the shamanic wand at Sungir, a carved wolf in ivory, two ivory 'shovels' and a large flint blade. The excavators believe that the pit was used for ritual purposes.

Not all the figurines were sculpted from ivory, some were made from chalk and marl and these tend to be small and incomplete rather than entire bodies, fracture lines suggest that this may be due to the lack of strength of the base material rather than due to intentional design. One of these figurines shows a head cap in detail, very similar to the one in France at Brassempouy which once again confirms the trans-continental shared culture.

Another figurine that stands out from the rest is known as the 'woman in labor'. Rather than being upright with straight legs – the traditional stance for these figurines, she is shown in a sort of kneeling position with the lower legs drawn back and pressed against the buttocks. The legs are wide apart at the hips and the genitalia are shown in considerable detail. The researchers on site believe that this is a figurine showing the process of childbirth.

Consistent with the shamanistic symbols found at many Gravettian locations there are zoomorphological figurines many of which represent combinations of women and animals. Red ochre is abundant in the occupied layer. The animal remains here are similar to Kostenki including mammoth, hare, rhinoceros, reindeer, wolf, bison, cave lion, brown bear, arctic fox and marmot, together with plenty of bird bones including: swan, steppe eagle, crane, geese, raven and other species of eagle.

There are also a good number of animal figurines including mammoths and horses. One ivory spear thrower is sculpted in the shape of a horse.

One particularly well-made article appears to be an ivory handle with the head of an owl sculpted into it.

Mal'ta

Groups of settlements dating from 24-15,000BP have been found in the region to the West of Lake Baikal just North of Mongolia in Eastern Russia. During excavations, most of the buildings there were found to be semi-subterranean as in Avdeevo. The walls were built with large animal bones similar in principal to some settlements found in the Ukraine, with reindeer antlers and hides forming the roofs. Far to the East of other Gravettian sites, tool manufacture here seems to be less sophisticated. The flint tools do not appear to have been made through pressure flaking and there don't appear to be any side scrapers. No composite tools have yet been found in association with the Mal'ta settlements nor have chisels, this apparent lack of sophistication as well as its remote location sets Mal'ta apart to an extent from other Gravettian sites, making it seem like a kind of frontier community, detached from the main-stream of Gravettian culture by its considerable remoteness from Europe and Western Asia.

But there are many common features too. Around 30 Venus figurines carved from mammoth ivory have been found in Mal'ta settlements. In common with other Gravettian Venus figurines the breasts and buttocks are of generous proportions, although some of them show slender bodies. Often facial details are recorded on the figurines. Some of them are nude whereas others appear to be clothed in furs.

So, who were these early East Asian peoples with some common cultural features with the Europeans and Central Asians and some fairly unique tool manufacturing techniques for the period?

We have already seen that they share a close genetic relationship to the people of Kostenki and that they had a culture based on the Gravettian.

One of the burials uncovered was of a 24,000-year-old boy, MA-1. Analysis of his DNA has shown curious affinities. His Y-DNA belongs to Haplogroup R, which is considered to have originated around 3,000 years earlier in the same general region as MA-1, but MA-1 is currently the oldest example of his haplogroup analyzed. What is of considerable interest is that the people to whom that boy belonged spread their DNA far and wide, including to North America, throughout South and Central Asia, Europe and some parts of Africa. Haplogroup R is the 2nd most common haplogroup amongst Native Americans.

In short, people closely related to this somewhat mysterious population of Mal'ta migrated from Eastern Russia across the Bering Strait and populated the Americas. They also spread out over central Asia. It is clear that the Mal'ta people shared strong cultural associations with the widespread populations of the Gravettian culture, who populated all of Europe and Western Asia. Shamanism is still a popular cultural and religious phenomenon amongst the people around Lake Baikal today a cultural inheritance stretching way back into pre-history.

Summary

In summary the Gravettian culture was a pan European and Central Asian culture lasting from around 33,000BP to in places 19,000BP, which succeeded smoothly from the Aurignacian culture which emerged north of the Alps, which in turn emerged from the Neanderthal Chatelperronian culture. Of considerable global importance, the Gravettian culture helped to shape human culture around much of the planet, it extended over much of the classic Neanderthal regions of occupation with the exception of the Levant and the Near East. The Gravettian was a culture whose artistic expression was closely linked with its shamanistic religion. Venus figurines, mainly of women carved from ivory are found throughout the Gravettian range. Some of the figurines, as with Aurignacian, are part animal and part human. Sophisticated working of ivory and bone are amongst the defining features of Gravettian culture. Leather working, sewing and weaving techniques enabled the Gravettian people to create well-made garments that protected them from the intense cold of the Ice Age, thus allowing them to populate regions colder than had ever previously been possible and to penetrate deep into Siberia. Parallel improvements in the design of buildings, allowed them to live permanently in cold regions where there were no caves or rock shelters. Off-shoots of the Gravettian shamanistic culture spread throughout South East Asia brought probably by the descendants of the Mal'ta people. This shamanistic culture along with Gravettian tools crossed from Asia into North America, then down to South America, transforming shamanism into a religion which covered most of the populated world with the exception of parts of Africa. Also, a form of shamanism along with some descendants of these Gravettian peoples descended into Egypt and contributed to the formation of the great Ancient Egyptian animalistic religion.

From the start of the Gravettian period onwards the climate over Europe and Asia became colder, with the colder climate the great ice sheets of the north expanded, crossing the Baltic and occupying the northern parts of Germany and Poland as well as vast swathes of northern Siberia, as we have seen in the chapter on the Ice Age. Periglacial conditions prevailed over vast areas south of the ice sheets making the lives of humans increasingly more challenging. As the ice sheets advanced sea levels descended significantly exposing greater amounts of land, particularly around Doggerland the Western Coasts of France and Portugal, and the Northern Adriatic. This process of lowering temperatures and expanding ice sheets continued until the Last Glacial Maximum roughly 20,000BP when the process halted and started to reverse. Around this time the Gravettian culture started to change again, gradually and not evenly over the whole vast range. The last great flowering of the Stone Age was on the way.

A Note On Ochre

Neanderthals and other European burials in the Paleolithic are almost always accompanied by ochre, either covering the bodies or covering certain precious figurines or filling deliberately hollowed bones. It comes in colors ranging from yellow to deep orange or brown; all of these colors were used by ancient Europeans. A variant of ochre containing hematite has a reddish color, also used by ancient Europeans. In many caves where Neanderthals lived, the floor of the cave is so densely covered in ochre that it sometimes seems that the floor is made of ochre.

Ochre has been used throughout the prehistoric world from South Africa to Australasia. The first European encounters with North American Indians in Newfoundland who painted themselves with red ochre caused the colonists to refer to them as 'Red Indians'. Ironically, as each side discovered each other; neither group realized that they were in fact distantly related.

One of the reasons why ochre was used around the world in Paleolithic cultures is that it was extracted from many different minerals, such as mica rich shale, snuffbox shale, iron oxide, dolerite, sandstone, siltstone, mudstone, yellow clay any of which found in prehistoric excavations and outside of their mineral context would be classed as pieces of ochre. Sometimes these pieces show signs of ochre extraction, which depending on the actual mineral could be done with standard tools like flint points or scrapers. For example, snuffbox shale contains pockets of powdery ochre which can be easily removed with a shale point from the surrounding 'snuffbox'. Once ground into ochre powder, ochre can change color, and even single pieces of ochre can contain ochre of different colors, so the Paleolithic person would have to grind his ochre onto some form of sheet, possible a leather skin, and sift the colors manually. Evidence from the south of Spain has shown that the containers that sea shells were used as vessels for storing ochre. Also, various burials contain hollowed long bones, with the marrow removed, and are filled with ochre. This strongly suggests that these bones were also used to contain and safely transport ochre, by blocking up each end, as a sort of primitive bottle. Once leather working had become discovered, then leather pouches could have been used for carrying ochre also.

Among the different colors of ochre used, bright red ochre is often the color of choice for prehistoric peoples. Different forms of ochre tend to produce different grain sizes, and these grain sizes can affect their usage. So, a very fine almost clayey grain size would be used for body paint, general cosmetics and protection from both insects and the sun. The role of ochre as an insect repellent would allow ancient Europeans to inhabit waterside locations with all the benefits that they offer (fresh water, fish, transport, washing...), while allowing them protection from mosquitoes and other nuisance insects which could otherwise have rendered their lives a misery. The large number of unused pieces of ochre found throughout ancient European settlements, caves and shelters is accounted for by the explanation that once many pieces of ochre were brought back to the settlement for preparation and powder extraction, some pieces would render a grain size too large for practical purposes and so would have been discarded. This suggests that the tasks of gathering the pieces and the process of extraction were specialized roles undertaken by different members of the community and by extension that hunters would collect ochre on their travels, offer them up on returning home and the women, elderly and young who remained at home would be tasked with ochre extraction. The presence of unused pieces of ochre being found in excavation sites is therefore best explained not by the carelessness of the members of the group as some have suggested, but by the fact that it was simply waste material, discarded because properties such as grain size were considered unusable. Also, small pieces of ochre below about 1.5cm would have proved tricky to handle, so that once a piece of raw ochre was ground down to that kind of size then it would likely be discarded as being too small to handle effectively, especially if larger pieces were readily available.

Ochre had other practical uses such as being a component in adhesives, such as attaching bone points, so important in the Gravettian period, to their shafts. Mixed grain sizes of ochre, as in concrete act as an effective aggregate in conjunction with, for example, pine resin glue.

Ochre was also used in hide tanning, a process that we have looked at in a previous chapter and it would seem that ideally pieces of medium hardness were preferred for this process. Possibly linked to the use of ochre in tanning either as a consequence or a fortunate coincidence, ochre was also used for coloring clothing. Clothes no longer needed to be the color of their native material, but could be bright red. Old clothing could be reinvigorated with a fresh coloration of ochre. And given the various hues available from Neanderthals onwards some people would have worn very colorful clothing. Natural furs would have been preferred for hunting as a form of camouflage. Whereas back at home where camouflage was unnecessary women and others remaining in the community could have been brightly dressed. Thus, a tendency emerged for women to wear more decorative clothing while the hunters wore more natural skins, a tradition which reaches down to the modern era where women's fashion is often considerably more varied and colorful than men's generally drab suits.

Ochre is often found in prehistoric hearths; the explanation for this is that heat can change the hue of the native piece of ochre, this deliberate baking process can occur at temperatures as low as 250C. The final color of the ochre is influenced by the temperature of the fire. In general, the higher the temperature the more bright red or brown streaks are found within the ochre. As bright red was generally the most coveted color for use as a cosmetic, then it is no surprise to find pieces of ochre remaining in prehistoric hearths.

The End of the Ice Age

The turning point of the last great Ice Age is marked by a stage known as the Last Glacial Maximum, which occurred around 21,000 BP. Europe was barely recognizable. The ice sheets of Scandinavia, Northern Britain and North Western Siberia had all united and spread south. The South of Britain and the North of Europe became a polar desert. In the Alps, glaciers covered all but the highest summits and in places the ice was over 2,000m deep, with glaciers spreading out like rivers of ice into the surrounding lands, so that the Rhone Glacier stretched virtually to Lyon. The atmosphere was dusty and dry. The sea level had descended to about 125m below today's levels extending Europe's coastline by considerable distances in all directions, but the deep channel cut by the outflowing waters of the Mediterranean ensured that no land bridge existed between Gibraltar and North Africa thus restricting cultural and genetic exchanges between Europe and North Africa to the mostly the Levant corridor.

In Western Russia the glacial maximum was somewhat delayed compared to the rest of the world, as it continued to expand south and east for another 4,000 years beyond the maximum elsewhere in Europe. As the glaciers slowly made their way down the North West Russian planes they literally wiped all traces of human occupation off the face of the earth, grinding all surface matter encountered into dust, which was to become glacial loess. Thus, we have no evidence of other settlements such as Sungir further to the North. An arctic desert preceded the advancing glaciers rendering life in Northern Russia unsustainable and forcing the people there to abandon their settlements and move either south or east. Escape to the west and south west being already blocked by advancing glaciers. Sungir itself was probably abandoned around 30,000 BP ahead of the advancing glaciers, because of the prevailing tundra like conditions that began to dominate the region around Moscow, rendering life in the tundra unsustainable.

The abandonment of North Western Russia by the Gravettian people of Sungir and many other similar settlements started a mass migration to the south and east, causing Gravettian influence to spread further and further eastwards from 30,000BP onwards, a general movement which would influence East Asian cultures such as the Mal'ta and as we have already seen even further afield.

In Central Asia the Tibetan plateau was also covered in an Ice Sheet. The lowered sea level had exposed land bridges extending from the mainland of South East Asia southwards, linking thousands of islands and creating a new land called Sundaland, taking in islands as far East as Bali and Borneo were linked to the mainland. Just about all the Philippine islands were linked together in a single great island, only just separated from the mainland by a narrow strait of sea. Australia, New Guinea and Tasmania were all linked together in a landmass called Sahul. The sea gaps between all these were dramatically reduced thus favoring the movement of migrating humans in a generally southward direction in the direction of new unpopulated lands.

In North America an ice cap covered just about all of Canada and a great area of land rose above the ocean, called Berengeia, linking Asia and the Americas. Even on Hawaii glaciers formed on the mountains. Despite this land bridge being in place, it is thought that there were no human migrations across it until 16,000BP at the earliest. Amongst these migrants were descendants of the Mal'ta people taking with them their epiGravettian like culture and shamanic beliefs and practices.

In South America glaciers linked up along the length of the Andes and pushed out East and West covering substantial areas of the continent in ice.

For the 10,000 years or so following the last glacial maximum, the ice that had been accumulating all over the northern hemisphere melted, returning water to the oceans, which rose as a consequence and continued to do so until historical times. Communities that had established themselves close to the sea shore were forced to retreat inland and the remains of their settlements disappeared under the waves. Some of these underwater settlements have been found, although the majority probably haven't been as yet. Low lying land such as the great expanse of Doggerland disappeared entirely beneath the waves, but thanks to the work of trawlers some of the human and other animal remains from the Ice Age have been brought to the surface.

The migration of peoples and land animals around the planet which had been facilitated by the linking of islands and creating land bridges reduced. Some communities of humans such as in the archipelagos of South East Asia became isolated from cultural innovations and genetic exchanges, until historical times, and evolved independently from their relatives on the mainland. The end of the Ice Age marked a period of the beginnings of speciation for remote communities where they adapted to specific local conditions and the adaptations were not diluted by a regular exchange of DNA due to the movement of migrating people.

In the same way the peoples of the Americas became separated from their Asian relatives and evolved in a different direction.

Epigravettian

The name means on top of the Gravettian and is simply a continuation of the Gravettian after the Last Glacial Maximum, with general improvements in workmanship and artistic expression over the Gravettian range. A plethora of other named and slightly varying cultures have been identified across Europe as the climate warmed and the glaciers retreated. It isn't particularly illuminating to dwell on all of them, but it is worth taking a look at some of them to see how the grains of artistic talent were starting to flower into the high points of the Stone Age. The Aurignacian and the Gravettian had seen the basic arts of music, painting, sculpture in three dimensions and bas-relief, clothes making and make-up all appear. The tendency across Europe and Western Russia was for all these art forms to improve markedly. All these considerable achievements continued to develop sometimes with notable local variations from the general European trend.

Solutrean

The Solutrean is considered to date from roughly 22 to 17,000BP and is limited the Western fringe of Europe; England, France and Spain where it is believed to have originated, named after a rocky hillside overlooking the River Saone in East central France which provided a rich source of beautifully made tools unrivalled in their quality to date.

Curiously the Solutrean site itself isn't even a settlement. It is a huge killing field of horses with skeleton remains sometimes piled up 4meters deep, forming what is known as a bone magma. In amongst the bones are weapons and tools, but there doesn't appear to be a settlement on the site. Or possibly the settlement just hasn't been found yet. The hunting of horses was concentrated in a relatively compact area at the top of a dry valley below a prominent limestone outcrop above the River Saone seems to have gone on intensively on this site for many thousands of years. Possibly horses migrating north and south along the Saone valley were herded up this dry valley and tired from the climb were easier targets at the top, where large, fallen boulders from the outcrop offered places for hunters to lie hidden in ambush.

The distinguishing features of Solutrean culture are the appearance of pressure flaking flints to produce tools of finer finish, with less of a reliance on percussion knapping. The flints may have been heat treated before the final working to improve the efficiency of the pressure flaking. The result was delicate slivers of flint ideal for tanged arrow heads and fine shaping tools.

Illustration 59. Solutrean spear tip with laurel leaf flint tip

Pressure flaking is a pain staking method of producing a very fine sharp edge with considerable control. Long gone are the days when finished tools are produced by a great whack of a hammer stone on a blank. Using pressure flaking methods, a blank is produced by the previous Aurignacian methods, once the general shape has been achieved. An animal skin is used to absorb the impacts and protect the worked. The blank is held in one hand while a hard, fine pointed flaking tool is held in the other. The fine point is then applied to the unprepared edge about half way down its depth. Then applying pressure with both hands, the point breaks away a tiny flake from the unprepared edge leaving a cut away. Then the point is moved along slightly to the end of the tiny cutaway and the process is repeated. The blank is then flipped over and the process repeated in order to chip away flakes from the other side. This long process is repeated to the end of the blade, leaving probably a bluntish edge with a noticeable thickness. The whole process is repeated but this time achieving a sharper edge and removing even finer chips this time. Expert pressure flakers vary the angle of pressure, not only downwards but to the sides, to create the best and sharpest blades. When done carefully by skilled hands the results are astonishingly fine. A damaged blade can be repaired by further pressure flaking making it smaller than previously but saving a lot of time on the initial shaping.

Large, fine spear heads, scrapers with the scraping edge on the end of the tool and saws can all be made with surprising precision. Fine, bone fish hooks were also manufactured, identical in form to today's modern fishhooks except the base material is different. The shaft of the fishhook had a small tag at the end which was used just as spade end hooks are today to attach a line. A fine thread would also have been necessary to attach the Solutrean bone hook, and such a thread had become available through improvements in Gravettian sewing technology.

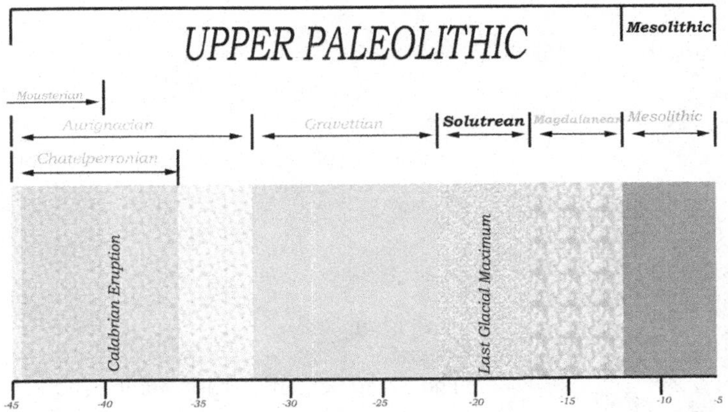

Illustration 60. Solutrean period

Illustration 61. Gravettian point

Sewing needles with eyes at the end, also made from bone were used, and pulled a fine thread.

Animal remains in Solutrean communities include cave lion, horse reindeer, mammoth, rhinoceros, bear and aurochs.

In short, the Solutrean culture with the aid of pressure flaking produced finer tools than previously available in Western Europe. These fine flint tools in turn allowed the manufacture of finer bone tools, in form identical to some basic tools that we still use today.

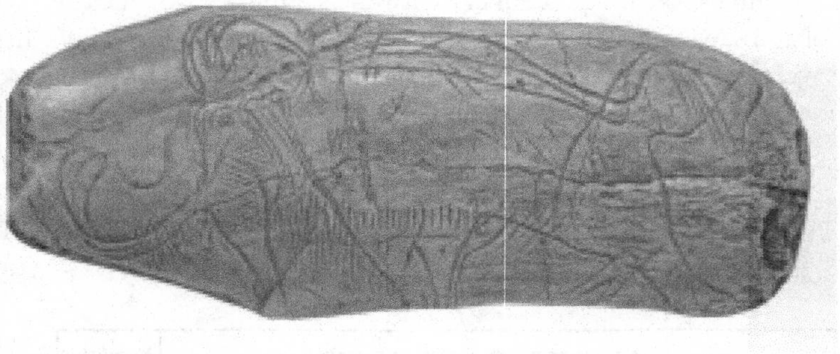

Illustration 62. Woolly mammoth engraving on mammoth ivory

Illustration 63. Solutrean harpoon head with hole for line to help recover the fish

Magdalenian

The Magdalenian culture superseded Solutrean in the Western fringes of Europe and spread to cover central Europe and Italy. It lasted from 17 to 12,000 BP. This period is dominated by bone tools throughout the tool kit prepared with greater finesse and quality of finish than ever existed before. Art both mobile and static improved in quality during the Magdalenian period. There are considerable collections of Magdalenian products around Europe today, preserved in part due to the relatively young age of the articles. In paintings not only do single animals appear as they did way back in the Aurignacian period but now compositions start to appear in some cases telling stories; such as a snake biting a man's leg, a landscape with trees, aurochs and horses. Herds of horses galloping together and hunting scenes emerge.

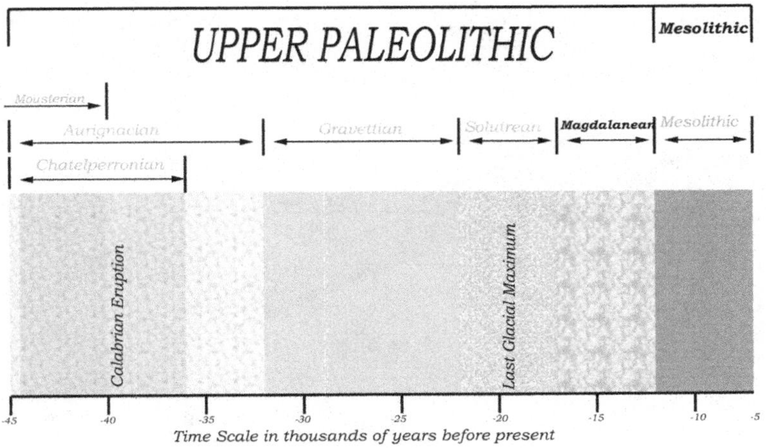

Illustration 64. Magdalenian period

In Europe the last glacial maximum was 3,000 years in the past; the climate was warming and with it the composition of the animals started to change. Indeed, towards the end of the period much of the mega fauna present throughout Europe and the Last Ice Age became either totally extinct or about to become extinct by the end of the Magdalenian. The woolly mammoth on whom Neanderthals and early Europeans so much depended became extinct along with the woolly rhinoceros the saber-toothed tiger, the cave lion, the European hyena, the giant deer, and others. Meanwhile the ever-present reindeer remained, but with time slowly followed the retreating ice caps northwards alongside arctic foxes and arctic hares. But before that happened new species such as tigers arrived fleetingly from the south.

Analysis of European's physiognomy of the time shows remnants of the traditional Neanderthal features such as low, retreating foreheads and pronounced brow ridges alongside more modern features such as chins and less robust jaws, as would be expected as the process of modernization towards modern humans continued.

As the Glaciers retreated northwards with time and the climate warmed, grasses started to appear in place of the ice, and herbivores soon arrived to graze the grasses. European hunters were not far behind them. Research has revealed that these hunters made seasonal forays north, before returning to warmer quarters in the winter further south.

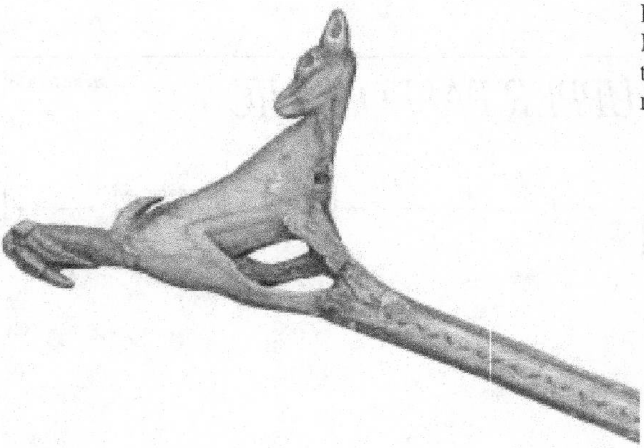

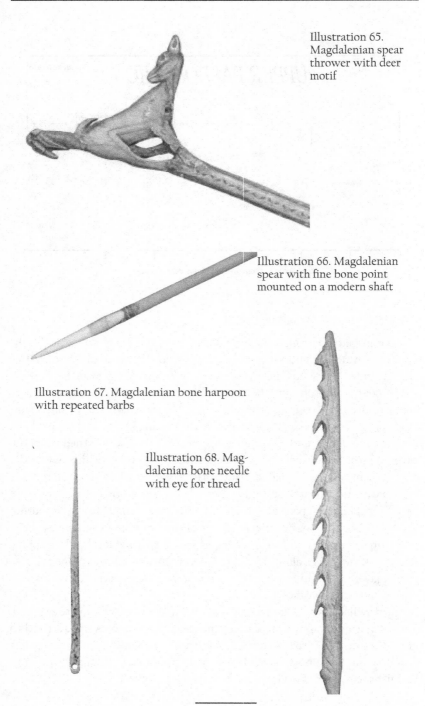

Illustration 65. Magdalenian spear thrower with deer motif

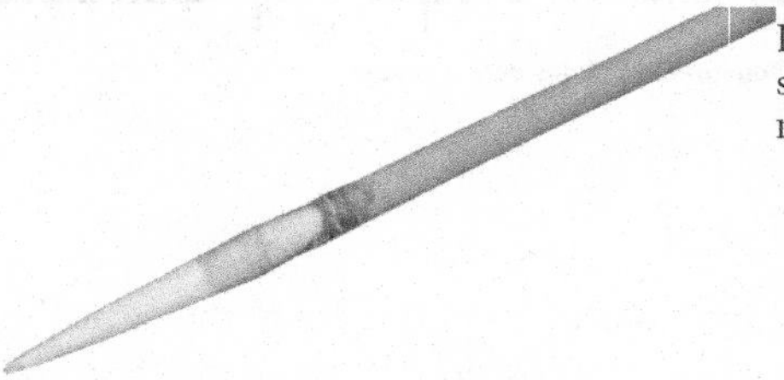

Illustration 66. Magdalenian spear with fine bone point mounted on a modern shaft

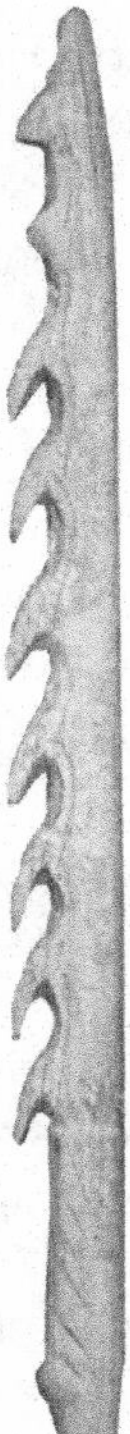

Illustration 67. Magdalenian bone harpoon with repeated barbs

Illustration 68. Magdalenian bone needle with eye for thread

Illustration 69. Magdalenian bone figurine of a bison licking an insect bite

Above is a magnificent carved section from reindeer antler and formed part of a spear thrower, dating from the Magdalenian period and found at the eponymous rock shelter of the Madeleine. The animal represented is considered to be a steppe wisent (Bison priscus), which once roamed throughout the northern regions of the northern hemisphere. Though now extinct in the wild two entire mummified specimens have been found preserved in the permafrost, one in Alaska and one in Siberia. The scientists preserving the Alaska specimen cut out a chunk of meat stewed it and ate it. Although the mummified steppe wisent lack hair both this carving and an excellent cave painting in Altamira indicate that there was a prominent ruff on the animal's hump, a separate mane on top of its neck and long beard like hair underneath the neck. A closely related species the European wisent (bison Bonasus), in modern times the largest land mammal in Europe (weighing up to a ton) also nearly became extinct, but a few animals survived in Bialowieza Forest on the border of Poland and Belarusse and have since been reintroduced into various countries in Eastern Europe.

Some of the greatest artistic accomplishments of the Stone Age appear during this period with cave paintings becoming realistic, multi-colored and of executed with considerable imagination.

Altamira Cave

The Altamira cave close to Spain's North West coast is a fine example of Magdalenian art, and one of 18 such caves in the region. It is 270m long with cave paintings throughout, but apparently was only permanently inhabited close to the entrance. Between the Solutrean and Magdalenian periods it was inhabited by animals. The best quality cave paintings date from both occupations with possibly the finest in The Great Hall of Polychromes. The entire collection of artwork in the cave spans an impressive 20,000 years and was apparently first started by classic Neanderthals during the Aurignacian roughly 36,500BP.

When the cave was first discovered in the 19th century the initial discoverer, Marcelino Sanz de Sautuola, was accused of forgery such was the disdain for prehistoric skills and artistry at the time, an attitude that prevailed for a long time. While Snr de Sautuola was digging for tools in the cave floor, it was his 8 year old daughter Maria Justina who looked up at the ceiling and declared 'look Daddy, painted oxen'. Tellingly two French experts at the time led the charge of forgery. Sadly, by the time the accusers recognized and publicly admitted their mistakes, Snr de Sautuola was long dead.

The cave contains three principal areas of cave art. The Great Hall contains most of the cave's paintings and is located not far from the entrance, it includes polychrome compositions with a dense mass of about 100 well painted animals without spatial cohesion, including a herd of steppe wisent, horses, deer and a wild boar. Also, importantly this chamber shows anthropomorphic figures, demonstrating the cultural and religious links with the earlier Gravettian period and a continuing practice of shamanism. This chamber is roughly 18m long, 10m wide but has a ceiling of just 1.3m high and it is the ceiling, well within the occupants reach that is the most decorated.

The colors used include red, yellow, black and violet produced from carbon and ochre. Some of the skill comes from dilutions of various pigments to achieve shading effects and chiaroscuro (the use of shading to achieve a natural 3D effect) which was supposedly invented during the renaissance, but nonetheless practiced 18,000 years ago. The natural relief of the cave walls was also exploited to achieve 3-dimensional effects. As the pigments are of mineral origin rather than biological they have not decayed. To achieve the subtle shading effects, animal blood and saliva were also mixed with the pigments. The large number of visitors in the previous century caused mold to colonize some of the paintings, which has caused the cave to be permanently sealed from the public. Faithful copies of the artworks can be seen in other caves nearby.

Experts believe that they have understood the painting method used for these artworks. Instead of using brushes they used spray paint techniques employing hollowed out bones. They believe that a system analogous to the modern spray gun was used with two bones. One bone emerges vertically from a container with a mixture of pigment and water, while another one is put to the painter's mouth. The painter blows air through the bone in his mouth which passes over the top of the vertical bone. The drop in air pressure sucks an aerosol of paint out of the container and deposits it on the rock. Differing diameters of bone and distances from the rock vary the intensity of the paint. A bird's leg bone has been found with ochre pigment inside it, which tends to support the theory. Whereas in Lascaux where manganese was used to draw the outlines, here in Altamira it was charcoal.

Over the 20,000 years that the cave was painted the animals were executed in distinct stages. Firstly, a herd of horses was painted, followed later by female deer, later still the anthropomorphic figures and finally by the bison. Finally, charcoal sketches of bison were made just before the entrance to the cave collapsed sealing it off until Snr de Sautuola rediscovered it in the 19th century. The anthropomorphical figures include what is described as part bird, part man figures, although to me the figure resembles more part bear part rabbit part bird, but it is unmistakably male.

Solutrean and Magdalenian tools were found as were harpoons for fishing similar in design to the ones shown above. Some of these had holes to attach a cord or line so that when the shaft broke away the fish could be hauled in; in a similar way to modern whaling fishermen harpoon whales. Flint awls for drilling, and fine flint spear heads with regular, fine pressure knapped edges were found there. There were fine bone points with beveled shafts to facilitate attachment to spear shafts.

Works of sculptural art without obvious functional use were also found, such as a well executed deer's head engraved on what looks like a large scapula, cut to shape.

Other objects were found which look like they formed some useful purpose but no explanation has so far achieved universal acceptance. These include rectangular plates made from horse's hyoid bones. These have been pierced at one end probably to be suspended from a necklace but also all the edges have been notched at regular intervals. Some researchers believe that they were used for some method of counting. I counted 35 notches on one and 45 on another, and 25 on yet another. Others think that they might have been used as bullroarers for hunting or communicating

An area of the cave close to the entrance, known as the kitchen, permanently sealed under thick flowstone deposited since the prehistoric occupation, revealed a sample of what the occupants of Altamira relied on for food. The bulk of the remains are limpets and periwinkle shells, also the remains from 14 red deer, bison, horse, bear, fox, wolf and salmon.

The Chamber of the basin includes black painted animal figures and engravings. Finally, a 50m long, 1m high narrow passage contains a large number of symbols including tectiforms, which are assumed to represent dwellings such as tents. Many of the other symbols appear abstract, but probably are not and remain to be interpreted. The latter are also found in cave art in France. Also, as in Lascaux Cave in France the artwork falls into three categories: colored paintings, black paintings and engravings. What makes Altamira exceptional is the respect for proportions and the subtle shading effects achieved by these expert painters. The finesse of Altamira's work in the eyes of many objective experts makes it a collection superior in quality to the excellent cave art that we shall look at in Lascaux.

Magdalenian In Britain

As the ice sheets retreated northwards after the Last Glacial Maximum and periglacial conditions gave way to cold steppes with summer grasses and birch woods, animals followed in their wake.

A mere few thousand years after the Northern Ice Cap that had covered the northern half of Britain had started to retreat, people following the Ice Age mammals were back again, bringing with them their technology from France, the Low Countries and Germany. They brought with them their knowledge for making ivory and bone tools such as harpoons, awls and needles, as well as their techniques for producing bladelets and backed flint knives. Also, a unique tool was produced known as a cheddar point, a large flint chisel which harks back to the Aurignacian, significantly different from the usual Magdalenian toolkit. 28 sites have so far been found corresponding to this period of between 15 and 11,000BP in England and Wales, while none have been found in Ireland or Scotland to date. No doubt many more lie under the waters of the English Channel and the North Sea. Conspicuously absent from the items found at these sites are Venus figurines.

These Britons fed on the usual selection of Ice Age mammals and fishes, including woolly mammoth, red deer, wild horse, arctic fox, reindeer, hare and wolf.

Dorothy Garrod who studied these Magdalenian finds in the 1920s proposed tentatively to call the culture Creswellian, believing that it was sufficiently different from the mainstream Magdalenian culture to merit its own classification, while noting that the cave at Creswell Crags offered the greatest number and variety of human related finds associated with the period.

Paleoanthropology is littered with a bewildering number of names of cultural and technological classifications, often coined because of trivial local variations from broader more useful classifications. In some cases, these new cultural classifications have been created by archaeologists hoping to achieve lasting scientific renown with their finds. So, it is worth being a little skeptical when yet another classification appears, and tries to distance itself from the surrounding well-established cultural backdrop.

If we take a closer look at Creswell Crags caves, what do we find? One of the most elegant pieces of art is a well executed horse's head found engraved on a segment of rib and dated to about 12,500BP. It is also a very rare item, as one of the few pieces of mobile art in Britain from the Magdalenian period. The undoubted skill of the artist suggests that he or she was accomplished in his or her work and would have produced other pieces. If the artist was local, so far no other similar work has come to light. Some have suggested quite reasonably that the piece may well have originated in France where such pieces are more commonplace. But the chemical profile of the bone is similar to other bones found at the site, indicating that it is probably of local origin. Another interesting aspect of this engraving is a series of vertical lines which have been carved over the original engraving of the horse. It has been suggested that this represents a form of palisade demonstrating the capture of a live horse. Is this elegant engraving a clue to the domestication of the horse, which is supposed to have occurred 10,000 years later in roughly 3,500BP? If so, it is not the only one. Contemporary engravings of horses from the South of France appear to show harnesses around the horse's necks. These corroborating engravings surely are first hand evidence of the domestication of the horse 12,000 years ago.

Another piece of mobile art found at the site, in a nearby but different cave is pinhole man, found in Pinhole Cave engraved on a segment of woolly rhinoceros rib and dated to about 12,000BP. The engraving is of a man, sporting a prominent penis, with his arms stretched out from his body. There is some debate about his head, whether he is wearing an animal mask, whether he has a peculiarly protruding nose and jaw or whether it is a zoomorphological figure. It appears that he has a crooked back.

Cave art has also been found at Creswell, with the image of a stag and bison engraved on the roof of Church Hole Cave. Also, crucially there appear to be anthropomorphological figures of women and birds. As some of these engravings have been partially covered by flowstone deposits, the minimum age of these engravings is given at 12,800BP and may be as old as 15,000BP.

Once again, we come across evidence of shamanism in Magdalenian Europe. This site represents the most northerly location of Magdalenian art.

Artistic finds in prehistoric Britain are not limited to Derbyshire. An engraving of a reindeer has been found on the Gower Peninsula in Wales which may be as old as 14,500BP.

A finely worked leaf point has also been found at Creswell, showing evidence of pressure knapping on the sharp edges and consistent with Magdalenian production techniques.

Other interesting British locations with evidence of human occupation during the Magdalenian period have been found in the South West, notably at Gough Cave at Cheddar Gorge near to Bristol. Here, discarded animal and human bones have been found mixed together, all showing signs of having been butchered. This has sparked controversy over whether these ancient Britons were cannibals, with some suggestions of ritual cannibalism being made, sparking amongst other things some far-fetched television documentaries based on these findings. The idea of ritual cannibalism stems from the discovery of crania that appear to have been cut deliberately to form drinking vessels, the one at Gough's Cave was dated to 14,700BP. Skull cups are items which have been made by humans around the world and are frequently found on the Eurasian Steppe. In historical times, the Scythians who we have come across before in this book routinely made skull cups from the heads of their enemies. The Celts also made skull cups. In relatively recent history, the Emperor Krum of Bulgaria made a skull cup from the Byzantine Emperor Nicephorus' head to which he added jewels. The Lombard King Alboid defeated the Gepids, killed the King Cunimund and made a skull cup from his head, while marrying King Cunimund's daughter, a rather irreverent treatment of his father-in-law in the circumstances.

In later history the writer Byron made a drinking cup from a skull his gardener dug up at Newstead Abbey, considering the practice to be typically Gothic.

In China and South East Asia there is an abundance of evidence of the use of skull cups, particularly once again, using skulls of defeated enemies. In Tibet the Kapala is a skull cup, but there is no suggestion that the skull should belong to an enemy, rather it is used as in India, during religious ceremonies. In South East Asia, skull cups were often filled with blood; a gory drink with distant echoes possibly of the Christian mass.

Whether or not the Magdalenian inhabitants of Gough's cave were routinely cannibalistic or whether, as was common elsewhere, the broken limbs and skull cup were the result of a conflict in which the defeated were carved up, and a skull cup made to mark the event, we shall probably never know.

But given the cultural links across the Eurasian world that Magdalenian Britain so obviously displays it would seem more likely that the remains of Gough's Cave are the result of a territorial dispute over the ownership and use of the cave.

The usefulness of attributing British Magdalenian culture to a different category from the rest of Western Europe seems to be fairly pointless. Britain was simply another location to which Magdalenian culture spread by the peoples of Western Europe, with a few rather insignificant adaptations.

Lascaux Cave

Lascaux is justifiably one of the most famous cave groups for prehistoric art in the world and together with Altamira represents a high point in the late Paleolithic with some of the most sophisticated and inspiring art ever produced in the world up to that date. It is to be found close to the small picturesque town of Montignac in the South West of France, in a region which we have already looked at quite closely in connection with evidence of dense Neanderthal occupation. In an area which is the densest in Europe for cave paintings, there are 37 of them in the environs.

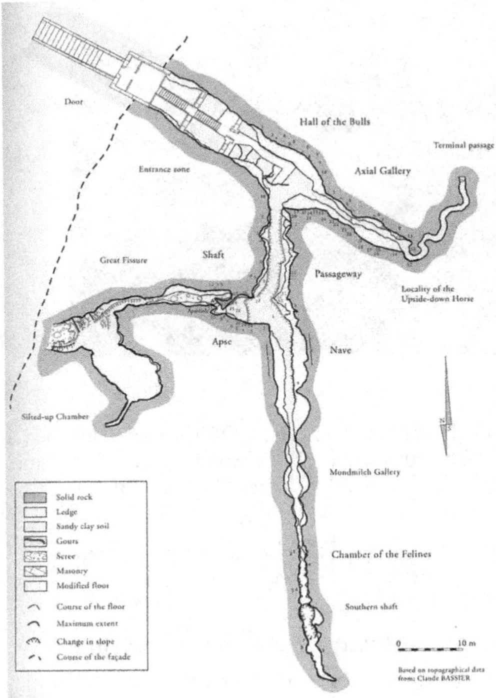

Illustration 70. Plan of Lascaux cave

Credit: Map of Lascaux : Photo and text: © Norbert Aujoulat, CNP, Ministere Source: http://www.american-buddha.com/lascaux-.3.htm

There are over 6,000 figures depicted in Lascaux, with subjects divided between animals, humans and abstract. Most of these have been executed in colors by mixing manganese and hues of ochre (see the chapter on 'A Note on Ochre'). In some paintings the colors have been suspended in animal fat, or clay rich groundwater from the cave, and either blotted on with the aid of shaped moss, or sprayed on using the technique that we noted at Altamira. Some of the images have been engraved into the stone and painted over.

Of the 900 or so paintings of animals 605 have been identified in terms of species. The majority, 364, are of horses, 90 of stags, there are also aurochs and bison as well as 7 large felines, a rhinoceros, and a bear. Oddly, considering that the staple diet was reindeer, there are no images of reindeer.

The most famous section of the cave is the Hall of Bulls where among the 36 animals depicted four aurochs in motion are the dominant subjects, one of which is over 5m long the largest single painting in prehistoric art.

Some of the paintings of dense herds of horses convey a scene of a herd in flight, with a convincing sense of great movement.

Illustration 71 Lascaux cave

Credit : Aujoulat N., Perazio G., Faverge D., Peral F., 2005: Contribution De La Saisie Tridimensionnelle A L'etude De L'art Parietal Et De Son Contexte Physique, Bulletin De La Societe Prehistorique Française. 2005, Tome 102, N. 1. Pp. 189-197

In another chamber, named 'The Nave', there is an image of two bison, which gives the impression of perspective, and is one of the earliest examples of that technique to exist.

Considerable work has been done to interpret the paintings including on their symbolic importance. There are noticeable groupings of certain animals.

Two main groupings exist; one which includes a bison, horse, lion group and the other aurochs, horse, deer, bear group. However, bison, aurochs and ibex are never portrayed in close proximity. The suggested interpretation is that these groupings reflect which animals that may have been found together in the wild. Certain symbols can be found mostly in connection with dangerous animals, and might have been used to display wounds associated with these animals given and or received.

Another chamber known as the Apse for its semi-spherical form is covered in thousands of entangled paintings covering the walls and roof which ranges from 1.6 to 2.7m high. Some researchers believe that scaffolding was constructed to paint the ceiling. There are holes drilled into the floor in places which could have held scaffolding stanchions, particularly in the axial cave, and pieces of prehistoric oak have been found in the cave to offer some support to the theory.

Illustration 72. Lascaux herd of horses

Credit: David Purdy/ Flikr

Where the Apse joins the Nave there's an interesting engraving of the structure of a teepee like hut with the vertical poles meeting at the apex, where they all taper to a point, and tied together with what looks like rope, just below the apex. Unlike the American Indian teepee design, the poles don't cross below their ends. In the same place is a faded painting of an aurochs. But also, there are peculiar disembodied eyes and what appears to be a bird's head at the top of the teepee.

The Passage gallery connects the Hall of the Bulls to the Nave and the Apse. There are 385 figures mostly engraved, but some painted. Identified animals include horse, bison, ibex, aurochs and deer, but there are also plenty of symbols. One of the engravings is of a large horse with what appears to be a sort of goatee beard.

There is a 6-meter-deep shaft dropping off from the end of the Apse. A door protects access to the shaft, and beyond a ladder leads down to the bottom of the shaft. In this inaccessible place, there is a very intriguing painted scene. A bison is standing with its bowels hanging out in a series of great loops, its tail up, and its head lowered, in front of him is a tall thin man, seemingly naked and with a large erection, apparently lying on the ground, with a bird's head. A tall spear lies across the bison and what appears to be a short broken spear lies on the ground. Another spear or staff is stuck in the ground has a small bird mounted on the top of it.

Not surprisingly, this mysterious ensemble has sparked a lot of discussion. But what is the painting telling us? The bison although mortally wounded appears to still be standing up with its tail lifted. The spear used to wound it appears to be next to the bison. The tall, thin man lying on the ground, right in front of the bison would appear to have been one of the warriors to have hurled the spear, which mortally wounded the bison. Although wounded, the bison appears to have killed the warrior who has a bird's head. That much is immediately apparent from the scene. The presence of the bird's head and the bird on the shaft however add another dimension. The anthropological figure of a bird's head on a human body is familiar to us by now as being related to shamanism. But this shamanic figure is portrayed in a hunting scene, which indicates that the shaman was taking part in the hunt for game.

Birds play a very particular role in the shamanic world; they have a symbolic as well as a literal role. Symbolically the presence of a bird evokes the shaman being in a trance-like state during which the spirit leaves the body and flies through the spirit realm with the ease of a bird in flight. Literally bird spirits work as helping spirits with shaman, like the ancient Egyptian ben-ben bird. The bird may be a guardian spirit, a guide or the form into which the shaman transforms to enter the altered state.

According to shamanic tradition, the first shaman was a teacher, who taught people how to survive; in particular he taught people how to hunt, search for specific plants, to heal and how to conduct rituals.

Here, it would seem that we have both a literal bird, as well as the symbolic bird in place of the man's head, who was obviously a shaman. Could it be that the shaman was present to teach the hunters in the process of hunting and that he was killed by the wounded and dangerous bison? As a result of which the shamanic bird appeared to guide the shaman's spirit through the spirit world.

Still in the shaft to the left of the shamanic scene is a large outline of a woolly rhinoceros, which appears to be executed in a different style with considerably thicker lines. All the images in the shaft were drawn with black manganese dioxide.

Given, its distance from the entrance and its inaccessibility, artificial light was absolutely essential to perform these paintings. Conveniently embedded in the floor of the shaft is a superbly made oil lamp carved from sandstone in the form of a large spoon with a wide shaft as a handle, beautifully smoothed on both sides. Apparently, it used deer fat for burning. One can easily imagine the artist; lamp held in one hand, painting equipment in the other, accidentally dropping the lamp which fell plunging the cave into darkness, followed by prehistoric expletives echoing down the corridors, the precious lamp never to be found for another 17,000 years. Decoration on the shaft of the spoon consists of a longitudinal groove down its length with on either side a series of chevrons abutting each other. When the lamp was found, it contained a fine; sooty dust which when subsequently analyzed revealed that it contained a wick of juniper. The technique with these lamps was to cut a piece of fat from an animal and place a long burning wick beneath it. The heat from the wick would melt the fat and burn it, some of which would melt and accumulate around the wick. The lamp would be replenished with additional pieces of fat and an additional wick when necessary. More light could be produced by one lamp by simply adding more wicks. Scorch marks on these lamps indicate that the wicks were positioned away from the handles, to avoid burning the fingers of the holder. Could it be that the wick slipped in the painter's hand, momentarily burning his fingers causing him to let go of the lamp?

In the Nave, there's a scene of stags swimming a river, possibly the River Vezere which runs close to the cave. The presence of the antlers and the number of stags together suggest that this is a winter scene. These stags appear to have about 10 points making them probably young adults, which tend to gather in winter after the fall rut. In March they lose their antlers.

Even though the main animal featured in the nave is the horse with over 27 of them painted, two bison painted charging out of a deep recess attract the attention, not only by the composition and the use of the recess to help the impression of depth to the painting, but in the skillful portrayal of the legs on the far side of the animals. In these two cases there is no doubt which legs are on which side of the animal. The artist has taken this little trick a step further by crossing the rear ends of the two animals; one is in front of the other, giving yet more depth and reality to the scene. Some commentators claim that this attempt at perspective wasn't used again until the renaissance; however, the Romans were well accustomed to this artistic technique (see the mosaic of the Emperor Justinian in Ravenna). This painting is referred to as the crossed bison.

Beneath the great black female aurochs, painted over a previous group of horses, there are two curious multicolor squares consisting of smaller squares and rectangles of different colors. In each group there are 7 different quadrilaterals of varying colors, black, red, orange and yellow. They don't appear to relate directly to the surrounding animals, and may have simply represented a form of prehistoric pantone chart.

The chamber of Felines contains more than 80 figures, 51 of which are animals, and 29 of those are horses. There are 6 felines; more than elsewhere in the cave. Of particular interest in this cave is an unusual engraving of a horse realistically portrayed, head on to the viewer. There are however even more symbols in this cave than figures of animals.

The paintings on the cave walls have not been dated scientifically, but antler, charcoal and wood remains from the floors all indicate a period of roughly 19-15,000BP, spanning the Solutrean and Magdalenian periods. Considering the vast number of over paintings, it wouldn't be too surprising to learn that some of the oldest date to before 30,000 BP, but access to the cave now is strictly limited and any requests for taking samples from the walls is likely to be promptly refused.

Other objects were found in the cave including blocks of manganese dioxide and hematite, both exploited for their pigments. 350 flint tools were found there in the form of blades, backed bladelets, scrapers and flakes. Some of the flint points have wear marks consistent with engraving on the walls of the cave. There was also a collection of bone spear points, like the one shown earlier in this chapter. Two pieces of clay show the imprint of textiles.

Interestingly the cave entrance is aligned with sunset at the summer solstice at which time it shines down the axis of the cave for just a few hours, providing the early Europeans a glorious and fleeting natural illumination of their amazing cave.

Ice Age Megafauna

Europe was a very dangerous place for humans to live during the last Ice Age and for the hundreds of thousands of years before it. The animals, particularly the mammals that dominated Europe during that period were very different from the animals that we're familiar with today and thrived for most of the last 100,000 years, only disappearing very recently indeed in geological terms. During the last Ice Age, early Europeans forged an extremely close relationship with just about all these animals, on which they relied to survive and thrive in the most difficult of conditions imaginable for human survival.

Woolly Mammoth

Perhaps the most iconic of all Ice Age mammals on the Eurasian continent was the woolly mammoth, a huge animal similar in size to today's African elephant, but in fact more closely related to the Asian elephant. Indeed, Asian elephants are more closely related to woolly mammoths than to the African elephant. But their build was different, while modern elephants have generally level backs from shoulder to hindquarters, the mammoth was taller at the massive shoulder and the back sloped down to the lower hind quarters. Wherever the woolly mammoth roamed early Europeans were not far away. The height of males was between 2.7m and 3.4m at the shoulder and they weighed up to 6 tons, females being considerably lighter, weighing up to 4 tons. The woolly mammoth was the last surviving species of the mammoth genus which had been around for about 5 million years, since the early days of bipedal man. The woolly mammoth evolved from an African species of mammoth which migrated out of Africa 1 million years before *H. erectus* followed him out of Africa, like *H. erectus* the mammoth adapted to the cooler, then colder climate to become a separate species. Other species of mammoth were even larger, some as tall as 4m and weighing as much as an awesome 12 tons, twice the size of the largest African elephants today.

Their range extended over the mammoth steppe, vast plains covering Europe, Asia and continental ice-free North America. They were a cold weather adapted species with small tail and ears to reduce heat loss and reduce the risk of frostbite. They were covered in a thick insulating coat of long guard hairs and a short undercoat. Their size alone offered a form of protection against the bitter cold of the Ice Age. Like Neanderthal and many other megafauna of Eurasia of the period this animal too adapted to Ice Age conditions. Its ears became very small to reduce heat loss, although being of similar mass to an African elephant the woolly mammoth's ears were far smaller. The same goes for the tail, which was shorter. The woolly mammoth was famous for its woolly coat, another adaptation to the Ice Age, which grew up to a meter long under the body, and 30cm long on the upper body. Their diet was based on grasses and sedge.

Mammoths survived predations by man until quite recently with the last survivors being stranded on Wrangel Island and St Paul Island. On St Paul, an island now far distant from the Russian and North American mainland, the most recent remains date to about 6,000 years ago. The current theory is that they died out there because of lack of water, although predations by humans can't be excluded.

Wrangel Island lies 140km north of the Russian mainland. Currently with an area of 3,700km^2, the island was able to support a substantial mammoth population; indeed, it was the very last outpost of the once great mammoth population, which finally died out 3,700 years ago, long after the first Egyptian pyramids and roughly concurrent with Stonehenge. On Wrangel Island there is substantial evidence of early human populations who no doubt hunted the mammoth and contributed to its demise. A theory exists that the diminishing population also suffered from genetic meltdown, a phenomenon where deleterious mutations cause an increase of the death rate exceeding that of the birth rate, leading to inevitable extinction. The disappearance of the mammoth and the people who survived by hunting them is remembered today by tribal stories of the Chukchi people, who relate that a chief called Krachai fled with his people across the ice to the island. Amazingly reindeer migrated annually across the frozen sea from Russia to reach the island where they grazed during the summer months. A prehistoric settlement called Chertov Ovrag has been discovered on the island at which stone and ivory tools have been found.

Mammoths are among the most studied of prehistoric animals, partly because some of them have been found preserved in the permafrost in relatively good condition, some so well preserved that they've provided mammoth steaks for hunters and archaeologists. There is still an active ivory industry in Russia where mammoth tusks are regularly found and their ivory harvested and sold. 60 tons of mammoth ivory are exported from Russia to China annually. mammoth skulls are routinely found simply lying on the ground in Eastern Russia, or found protruding from river banks. human interest in mammoth ivory is the continuation of a passion for mammoth ivory which stretches back over 100,000 years. High quality mammoth tusks can be bought for $95,000 whereas complete tusks of a lesser quality can be bought for just $600 with individual segments for as little as $50.

We also know about mammoths from many cave paintings and from sculptures showing us eye witness accounts of the color and form of the mammoths. We know what they ate from the contents of their stomachs, which in some cases are still recognizable, and that they had considerable fat reserves to help with energy storage and thermal insulation.

Mammoths provided the Europeans of the Ice Age with food from the meat, with structural materials for buildings, particularly from the larger bones such as shoulder blades and leg bones, the tusks framed doorways and the great skins forming water proof roofs. Mammoth ribs were often used for leather smoothers or as a support for engravings thanks to their smooth, flat surfaces. Mammoth ivory was used in great quantities throughout the Ice Age for tools and ornamentation. It was straightened to form spears, and cut and smoothed to form a great variety of tools and weapons. The fat was eaten or collected and used in lamps.

During the Ice Age in Europe mammoth herds migrated north in the summer to graze on grasses poking through the tundra. As they moved they were followed by nomadic groups of humans who lived in temporary tent like shelters, designs of which have been drawn on caves in Spain and France. Before the onset of winter, the mammoth herds and their human followers would return to warmer conditions in the south. The mammoth migratory routes became also the human migratory routes.

A mammoth carcass could keep a human group alive for up to several weeks, so there was no need for the whole group to follow the mammoths every day. Nevertheless, for great numbers of Ice Age Europeans their daily lives revolved around the life of the woolly mammoth, so not surprisingly the mammoth was the 3rd most represented animal for Stone Age European art after the horse and the bison.

Cave Bear

One of the most dangerous threats to Ice Age Europeans was the cave bear, not only because it was easily capable of killing and eating humans but also because the cave bear competed with humans for the occupation of the caves after which the cave bear was named (*Ursus spelaeus*). So prolific were cave bears during the last Ice Age that during the 1st world war when phosphates for explosives were scarce, in caves where cave bear bones were found, the dung was mined for the phosphate content and the bones discarded as waste. In one cave alone in Romania 140 complete cave bear skeletons were found. Some scientists believe that given the amount of cave bear remains that there must have been vast herds of them. In the Drachenloch Cave in Eastern Switzerland, a staggering 30,000 cave bear skeletons have been discovered. Also, in the cave was a stone chest containing a number of bear skulls, as well as a bear skull with a femur embedded in it. In the Regourdou Cave in Southern France a stone lined pit also contained the remains of at least 20 cave bears and was sealed with a stone lid. A Neanderthal skeleton was found in a nearby pit which included a cave bear humerus and a variety of stone tools, including a scraper. This latter burial reminds us of the various shamanistic burials found during the Gravettian period which usually contained parts of animals and or sculptures of animals.

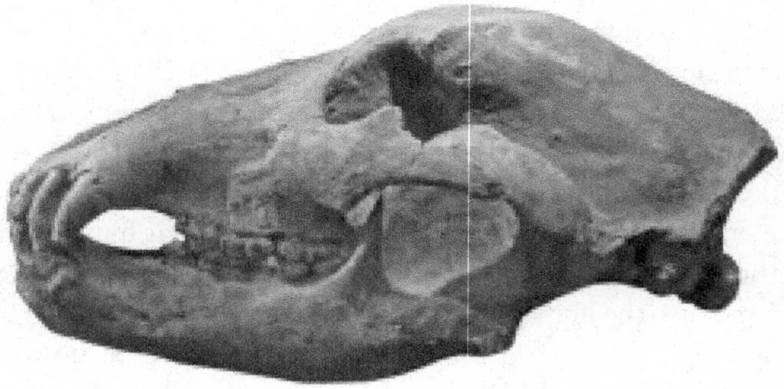

Illustration 73. Cave bear skull

Ice Age man was in direct competition with cave bears for the use of caves, both were capable of killing the other, but it was Ice Age man who emerged the victor by the end of the Ice Age. The cave bear was similar in size to the largest of today's polar bears, with males weighing up to 1 ton, and females to just 300Kg. Their size tended to vary according to the climate. Consistent with the size of the polar bear, the cave bears becoming larger during the colder periods of the Ice Age, and smaller during the warmer interstadials. This climatically dependent variation in size is considered to be due to the advantages of a larger body mass being more thermally efficient with sufficient extra fat reserves to enable the bear to hibernate through longer periods, when plentiful food was harder to come by. This increase in size with a colder climate is a standard mammalian adaptation.

Close examination of the cave bear's teeth indicate that it was probably an omnivore. During the colder phases of the Ice Age when the growing season would be shorter and grasses and herbivorous animals that the cave bear would feed on would be scarce, a cave bear would need to hibernate for longer to avoid wasting precious energy awake and active when there was no food available. Many cave bears appear to have died during their hibernation, possibly because they had insufficient energy reserves to see them through the longest of winters but also due to various ailments including bone tumours, osteomyelitis, kidney stones and rickets, possibly as a result of an impoverished diet. Their natural predators appear to be wolves, cave hyenas, cave lions and man. Some disarticulated cave bear remains found in caves would seem to be the work of cave hyenas. One complete skeleton of a cave lion found deep in a cave where cave bear remains were found suggest that potentially cave lions preyed on cave bears in their caves, possibly while the cave bear was still hibernating.

Of the various now extinct Ice Age mammals the cave bear was the first to disappear. The number of finds post 35,000BP dropped dramatically and by 27,000BP it was probably extinct; more than 20,000 years earlier than the mammoth. Early explanations for this decline include the changing climate, but as the cave bear had successfully survived many previous climatic cycles this explanation seems inadequate. A more probable explanation is that the cave bear relied mainly on caves for hibernation and inevitably this brought them into direct conflict with humans who also required the use of the caves. Caves as a refuge from the bitter cold, and from wild animals were vital for the survival of Ice Age humans and a hibernating cave bear would have been a relatively easy kill for stealthy well-armed men. In the competition for use of Caves it was well armed, well organized humans who won and the cave bear became the first species that we know of to be made extinct by the actions of humans.

A close relation of the cave bear which appears to have existed during the Ice Age was *Ursus maritimus tyrranus*. Only one bone has been found belonging to this bear, and that is an ulna (forearm bone), which was discovered in gravel beds in the Thames near to Kew. Estimations of its size from this one bone give the animal a weight of 1.2 tons and standing 1.8m high at the shoulder. Very little is known of this creature, even whether it was actually a giant polar bear or whether it was a giant brown bear. But it is considered to be one of the largest mammalian carnivores ever to have existed.

Cave Lion

The cave lion was another dangerous species that inhabited caves during the Ice Age in Europe and Asia. In size it was about 10% larger than a large modern African lion, being about 1.2m high at the shoulder and over 2m long excluding the tail. DNA analysis reveals that it had similar colored hair to African lion's although probably somewhat lighter in shade. Being adapted to Ice Age conditions it had a very dense insulating under coat of closed and compressed light colored hairs, with a darker coat of guard hairs. Thanks to various representations of the cave lion in Ice Age art and sculpture, we know that it had small rounded ears (a probable adaptation to a cold climate), a tufted tail, possibly faint tiger-like stripes and a mane around their necks, although some males, possibly immature ones were depicted without manes. It ranged across Europe, Northern Asia, over the Bering Land Bridge and North America. A sister species which it is thought became isolated from the main cave lion population in South America became the American lion, the two species diverging, it is thought around 340,000 years ago.

Analysis of the bone collagen of cave lions reveals that they fed mostly on cave bears, or cave bear cubs and reindeer, as well as other cervid species and young woolly mammoth. It is likely that it competed in the same ecological niche as the European Ice Age Leopard. As it is highly unlikely that the cave lion hibernated, it wasn't as vulnerable as the cave bear to human predations, and survived far longer. Cave lion remains dating to later than 12,000 years ago have been found in Fairbanks Alaska, but it is believed that it died out in Europe 2,000 years earlier. Two well preserved cave lion cubs were found in a den, which appears to have been blocked by a landslide, where they were entombed and preserved in Yakutia, Russia. Another Russian cave lion has been found with clumps of preserved hair still remaining.

Ice Age humans obviously held the cave lion in some regard as zoomorphological figurines from the Gravettian show human bodies with lion heads. We will probably never know for sure what Ice Age man saw in the cave lion, but it is easy to imagine that he held this large, powerful and fast carnivore in high regard, and quite possibly admired his courage and strength, qualities that some hunters probably aspired to.

The Saber-Toothed Cats

If the cave lion and the cave bear weren't sufficient to terrorize Ice Age man, there were even more ferocious carnivores to contend with not least the well-known saber-toothed cat or homotherium. Of about the same size as the cave lion, homotherium was one of a very large group of saber-toothed cats sometimes mistakenly referred to as saber-toothed tigers, but in no way related to the tiger. Some of the saber toothed cats are more closely related to marsupials than to tigers. Homotherium occupied a vast range from Africa to Eurasia to both North and South America. As its name implies it had very long saber like canines which were clearly visible when the mouth was closed, but unlike some other saber-toothed cats these long sharp canines didn't project beyond the lower jaw, which itself projected well downwards of the teeth, making for a very powerful jaw. In size it was similar to a modern African lion weighing about 190Kg, but in form it had the look more of a hyena with hindquarters sloping down from the shoulder. It possessed only a stumpy tail comprising about 13 vertebrae about half the number of most long-tailed felines (another adaptation to a cold climate). Large nasal openings allowed for rapid intake of oxygen like a cheetah, suggesting that it was a very fast runner. At Friesenhahn Cave in Texas, which contained a substantial number of homotherium bones, sufficient evidence has been found to provide researchers with indications of its lifestyle. The cave also contained the remains of 400 juvenile mammoths which showed tell-tale indications of homotherium teeth marks. It would seem that homotherium targeted young mammoths using its powerful canines to puncture the thick mammoth hide and possibly sever arteries in the neck. It is thought that homotherium was far more effective at killing young mammoths than African lions are at killing elephants. Once dead, homotherium dismembered the mammoth at the kill site, and dragged the parts back to the cave. It would also seem that homotherium lived in groups as do modern lions, had a strong social bond within the group and lived in dens or caves. As with cave lions and cave bears, Ice Age man would have had to contest ownership of caves with homotherium. Also, as prides of homotherium hunted mammoths then, both homotherium and humans would have been in the same vicinity, making hunting mammoths even more of a perilous activity. Purely for reasons of self-preservation Ice Age man would have wanted to eliminate as many homotherium as he was safely able to. For this reason, homotherium was exterminated in Europe by

28,000BP thus removing one of the most formidable predators on the continent. He may well have survived for considerably longer in the vast plains of Asia, but there too his fate was sealed by competition with man; and homotherium for all his prowess as an organized hunter over a very wide range, joined the list of extinct Ice Age species.

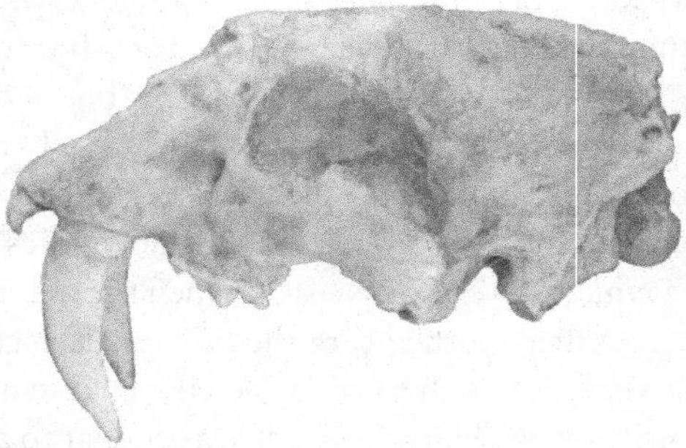

Illustration 74. Homotherium cranium

Cave Hyenas

In what may seem like an almost endless list of highly dangerous predators which inhabited Europe and lived in caves, the cave hyena was one of the biggest threats to Ice Age man. Just like homotherium the cave hyena was a highly social and well organized hunter. The cave hyena occupied the Eurasian continent from the Iberian Peninsula to Eastern Siberia in considerable numbers. It was considerably larger than the modern African hyena, the increased size probably an adaptation to a very cold climate, but in common with its African relative, females were larger than males weighing more than 100Kg. Cave paintings reveal that like the African hyena he had a pelt which was spotted over the front half of his body.

He was an active and highly successful predator, killing large mammals, mainly wild horses, steppe bison and as a testament to his prowess the formidable woolly rhinoceros. Secondary prey species included red deer, giant deer, reindeer, wild ass, chamois and ibex. Unlike homotherium he seems to have avoided hunting mammoth, possibly because the mammoths thick hide was a sufficient protection. cave hyenas lacked the enormous canines of homotherium. Competing with cave bears and cave lions for suitable caves, cave hyenas also killed and ate these species, gaining food and shelter simultaneously. However, a lack of cave hyena remains in a human context reveal that it wasn't customarily hunted for meat, although that did happen on occasion. Possibly because of the taste and possibly because Ice Age man steered clear of cave hyena packs wherever possible.

Very many cave hyena dens have been found containing vast quantities of bones, including in Great Britain. Together with caves they lived in sink holes, clay pits. Bone remains have shown that cave hyenas were also brave enough to approach Neanderthal groups and steal their kills.

Remains of cave hyenas start to diminish around 20,000BP and disappear altogether around 11,000BP. The reasons for their disappearance can't be attributed to either climate change or to lack of prey species, as horses, ibex and chamois were still plentiful. Once again, competition with man proved the cave hyena's downfall. With more powerful and long-distance weapons, including latterly the bow and arrow, cave hyenas which would have been at best a nuisance and at worst a very real threat to the survival of Ice Age man, like the other dangerous predators and would have been eliminated where possible and their caves liberated for use by man. That said, one of the reasons considered for the late expansion of man into North America is the concentration of cave hyenas in Easter Siberia rendering the passage of the Bering Straits too perilous.

Woolly Rhinoceros

The woolly rhinoceros was the largest of the European land animals after the woolly mammoth, and with its two sharp and prominent horns was a dangerous animal to hunt, nevertheless, Ice Age man, homotherium and others did indeed actively hunt it successfully. It measured nearly 4m in length and weighed nearly 3 tons and was slightly larger than today's white rhinoceros, although the woolly rhinoceros is more closely related to today's rhinoceros. The front horn measured up to 60cm in length although cave paintings show specimens with horns of nearly 2m in length. Several intact and well-preserved woolly rhinoceros have been discovered including one in Poland and several in Siberia. The woolly rhinoceros fed on large quantities of cellulose rich, protein poor periglacial steppe grasses. Thanks to its thick coat and bulk, the woolly rhinoceros was well adapted for the Ice Age climate and was found in the same areas as woolly mammoth.

Possibly thanks to its tough hide, speed, bulk and pointed horn, it was one of the last great Ice Age mammals to become extinct, once again probably due to over hunting mainly by man. The last woolly rhinoceros seem to have disappeared from Siberia around 8,000BP

The woolly rhinoceros was not the only rhinoceros to live in Europe during the Ice Age. An even larger one comparable in bulk to a woolly mammoth also thrived during the Ice Age, given the unwieldy name elasmotherium (derived from the layered structure of the teeth). Three subspecies of this rhinoceros existed in Eurasia. The largest was over 5m in length and weighed up to 4.5 tons. The white rhinoceros at half the weight has been clocked at

30Km/hour with all legs off the ground while running, twice per cycle. Given that elasmotherium had fairly rigid legs with little flexibility in the ankle a feature which enables fast running, it is thought that elasmotherium had a similar gait and quite similar top speed to the white rhino. Encountering a 4.5-ton animal galloping at 30km/hr, considerably faster than man was able to, but armed with a large pointed horn, must have been a very alarming sight indeed for Ice Age man.

Not much is known of elasmotherium, whether he possessed a horn or not is debated as are his habits. Remains of a skull found in Russia in the 19th century indicate the likely seat of the horn, which with a circumference at the base of 91cm and very large blood vessels, is thought to have been enormous. But to date no such horn has been found, being made of keratin like hair, it degrades considerably faster than bone and so the actual dimensions remain uncertain. Like the woolly rhinoceros he ingested large amounts of poor quality food to maintain his bulk and lived in the Eurasian Steppe. Elasmotherium may not have been as well adapted to extreme cold as the woolly rhinoceros and it is maybe for this reason that he died out earlier. The latest specimens recovered date to around 37,000BP in Siberia.

Imposing, frightening even, as elasmotherium may have been at 4.5 tons and an enormous horn, he wasn't the largest of the rhinoceros family. That honor goes to the long extinct Paraceratherium one of the largest land mammals to have ever existed and who also lived on the Eurasian continent, although long before the arrival of humans. Its weight has been estimated at up to 20 tons, with a height at the shoulder of nearly 5m but with a reach of considerably more thanks to a 2m long neck, and a body length of nearly 5m. Elasmotherium's 20-ton mass is considered to be the upper limit in terms of size for a land mammal. By comparison, the weight of one animal was the equivalent of about 10 family saloon cars or two large buses. The skull alone is a gigantic structure. No traces of the root of a horn have been found on the skull, but then with that size a horn was probably a superfluous weapon on an animal which probably required no extra help in looking after itself.

The Reindeer

The reindeer (also known as the Caribou in North America) was one of the most important animals to Ice Age man even more so than the woolly mammoth, as it still is to many present day inhabitants of Polar regions. As we have already seen the reindeer provided nourishing meat, highly insulated skins for clothing, antlers for various tools including precision hammers from the Aurignacian period onwards, and in addition bone for tools and sculpture. In addition, Ice Age man learned to use the reindeer for transport, not only for pulling sledges over the snow but also to ride in the same way as a horse. The reindeer is a species of cold adapted deer evolved to a life in polar and sub-polar climates. It is accustomed to life in large herds. Even today there is a Russian herd containing between 400,000 and 1 million individuals. During the Ice Age, as they do now, reindeer migrated, moving northwards to high latitude summer grazing and southwards again during the Northern Winter for overwinter stays. Some modern herds migrate an astonishing 5,000km in one year the most of any land mammal and travelling up to 55km in a single day. Such was the importance of the reindeer to Ice Age man that many communities evolved to rely entirely on the animal for their own survival, due in part to the large numbers of animals available to hunt and the great variety of products that a reindeer provided to serve man. This dependence continues for certain polar peoples such as the Inupiat, Northern Tutchone and Han peoples amongst other present-day tribes.

The reliance on reindeer is also remembered in folk tales such as the animals which pull Santa Claus' sled during his annual round of delivery presents in the middle of winter when life in the high north is harshest. Even today the reindeer provides the Inuit with a host of tools including snow knives, snow shovels, drying racks and seal hunting tools, handles, for sculptured artworks and weapons.

There are about 15 sub-species of reindeer with localized variations and adaptations across the North of the globe, but only two occur in Europe: the Eurasian Tundra reindeer and the Eurasian Forest reindeer. During the Ice Age their range stretched from the Mediterranean to just south of the great glaciers and everywhere in between.

Reindeer are effective swimmers, helped in part because of the buoyancy provided by air trapped in their fur. Conservation of energy is critical when surviving in the far north and reindeer have evolved a number of specific energy saving survival strategies. They are energy efficient in part because of the quality of their fur which has been described in a previous chapter, but also because there is a heat exchange in blood circulating to the legs where heat loss would naturally be greater. Blood moving from the torso to the legs passes close to the returning blood, so that the oxygen rich blood flowing to the legs is cooled by the returning blood, thus conserving heat in the torso and reducing heat loss in the legs. Equally, heat is recycled in the nose. The temperature gradient across the nasal mucosa is controlled; incoming cold air is warmed by body heat before passing to the lungs where it would otherwise chill the center of the torso. Condensation from moist air being exhaled is recovered and recycled in the body. Nasal turbinate bones as with other cold adapted mammals greatly increases the surface area that the air comes into contact with before reaching the lungs thus allowing for greater heat efficiency.

Reindeer have four toes of which two are crescent shaped and help not only to spread their weight on snow and marshy ground, but also serve as snow shovels to help them clear the snow from the lichen on which they feed. As a further adaptation, their hooves change with the season. In the summer the foot pads become soft and spongy providing extra traction on soft ground. In the winter the pads contract and harden exposing the hard edge of the rim used for cutting into the ice like crampons, providing a firm grip, this also lessens contact with the soft, warm part of the hoof thus reducing heat loss through the hooves.

Reindeer eyes also adapt with the seasons from gold through to blue, allowing them to adapt to varying degrees of visibility from the stark dazzle of the Arctic summer to the near darkness of the Arctic winter. They are sensitive to wavelengths as low as 320nm; well below the human threshold of 400nm, enabling them to distinguish colors in the ultra violet range.

Reindeer have a four-chambered stomach and are unique among large mammals in being able to digest lichens, thus allowing them unrivalled access to a niche food source that no other large animals can utilize. They can also eat their own fallen antlers, sedges and grasses and when very hungry have been known to eat rodents, fish, bird eggs and mushrooms. All these polar specific adaptations allowed reindeer to thrive without competition from other herbivores in periglacial and arctic conditions.

Another adaptation to life in the arctic is the loss of circadian rhythms, meaning that their body clocks are not synchronized over a 24-hour period so that their sleep cycles are not necessarily calibrated to night time.

Current reindeer herds living in a much-reduced environmental space give an indication of just how many reindeer may have existed over the vast area of Ice Age Eurasia. The Porcupine herd numbers 169,000 and until recently counted over a million heads. The Western Arctic Caribou Herd numbers about 300,000. The Central Arctic herd numbers about 100,000 head. The Ahiak herd numbers 250,000. In Southern Norway 23 herds contain about 35,000 individuals. In Russia the Chukotka herd is around 70,000 and the Taimyr herd around 700,000. All these herds have shrunk enormously in size from far greater numbers within living memory, with several of these herds having contained more than a million animals per herd.

Hardly surprisingly, given the abundance of reindeer during the Ice Age all the large European predators including, including man, hunted them. In addition, wolverines and eagles preyed on the calves. Reindeer calves were not defenseless for long, even at just a day old they can outpace an Olympic sprinter. Some wolf packs and bears followed the great reindeer herds on their migration year round, living off them as they travelled as did groups of Ice Age humans, once again concentrating humans and other top predators in a relatively confined geographical space.

The Wild Horse

The Ice Age ancestor to the domesticated horse is called the tarpan or Eurasian Wild horse. It had two slightly different sub-species the forest tarpan and the steppe tarpan. DNA analysis reveals various different coat colors including bay, black, dun and spotted on a white background. There is debate about whether the tarpan had a standing mane or a hanging mane. There is evidence for both. A mummified specimen from Siberia had a hanging mane whereas various cave paintings appear to show a standing mane. It has been postulated that the hanging mane is a result of domestication. Evidence from recent sightings of tarpan and from certain cave paintings indicate that there were probably stripes also, on the back, shoulders and legs. The tarpan had a continuous range from Western Europe to Alaska with the two sub-species occupying the Steppe and the boreal forest.

Certain settlements from the Gravettian period onwards in central and Eastern Europe had large amounts of tarpan bones either in pits or close to the settlement indicating that the tarpan formed a major part of their diet, as we have already seen at Solutrea. There are many cave paintings of tarpan in France and Spain. The tarpans main form of defense was its ability to outrun its attackers, but with the advent of the spear thrower and the bow and arrow humans could kill at a distance without necessarily getting close; in addition, tarpan could be caught in rope traps in the forest or pit traps.

According to DNA analysis domestication of the tarpan began in Eastern Europe around 6,000 years ago, although in isolated communities it may have begun long before that date. Indeed, evidence from carvings as we have seen strongly suggest that it was already being domesticated around 20,000BP, although there is no direct evidence of horse riding until much later. Despite some herds being domesticated, the tarpan continued to thrive in its wild state into historical times. In classical times, Herodotus described light colored wild herds in parts of modern Ukraine. It would seem that herds of tarpan continued to exist in Central and Eastern Europe into the 18th century. Eye witness descriptions vary to a degree, but common features are of a black eel stripe, a frizzy mane, extremely shy and potentially aggressive. There is doubt to just how pure these tarpan herds were, because it is assumed that feral horses escaped from captivity or from battles joined the wild herds thus diluting the wild DNA. There are numerous examples of farmers complaining that tarpan stallions would sometimes impregnate domestic mares producing foals that were unmanageable. Nevertheless, tarpan survived into the 20th century the last one dying in a Russian zoo in 1909. Their close descendants however live on in the form of the domesticated horse.

Megaloceros

The Ice Age was full of giant versions of species that we are quite familiar with today such as a giant deer known as megaloceros otherwise known as the Irish elk or the giant elk. It was in fact related to the European fallow deer rather than the red deer, but measured over 2m high at the shoulder with a huge set of antlers which measured a breathtaking 3.65m wide, the largest of any known cervid species. This giant weighed up to 700Kg.

A superb painting of megaloceros can be seen in the French cave of Lascaux. And a life size model of a megaloceros is on display at the Prehistory Museum at Les Eyzies in France.

Illustration 75. Megaloceros

The megaloceros seems to have died out less than 8,000 years ago in Siberia, probably around 2,000 years after its extinction in Europe. Despite having disappeared about 10,000 years ago, memories of the megaloceros appear to be preserved in folklore; another reminder that events of our distant prehistoric past have come down to us through the generations. Mention of megaloceros is thought to be made in the Niebelungen folk tale in the form of Schelch (an early version of 'elk'). Also, the Middle Irish word 'segh' is thought to refer to the megaloceros and in County Clare the word Fiaghmore is thought to refer to the megaloceros.

It may also have been a megaloceros that attacked and killed the Byzantine emperor Basil in a well-documented hunting incident. During the attack the antlers became caught up in the emperor's clothing and carried him a long distance, before the other members of the hunt managed to catch up with it and when they did so they killed it with their spears, finally liberating the emperor who died several days later in 886AD. All the hunters attested to never having seen such a huge deer in their lives before.

These and many more tendrils, often considered to be fairy tales of no consequence offer us glimpses of the thoughts of Ancient Europeans long before history was ever recorded in writing and possibly even some sightings in recorded history.

The Aurochs

The Eurasian aurochs (from which we derive the name Ox), ancestor of domesticated cattle, was just one of a number of bovid like large grazers to be found in Europe and Asia during the Ice Age, including the European bison and the wissent. During the Ice Age northern aurochs, like many other cold adapted species could grow very large, with bulls reaching 1,500Kg whereas to the South of Europe they only reached about half that size. Both males and females were equipped with large forward pointing, slightly curved horns which they used to defend themselves. There is some evidence that Ice Age Man hunted aurochs, but less so than the mammoth and the reindeer. The aurochs reached Europe from India long after Neanderthal, in about 270,000BP, leaving behind a subspecies, the Indian aurochs with its high shoulder hump and which was later domesticated to become the Indian Zebu.

The aurochs was fast and powerful and when provoked extremely dangerous. Julius Caesar wrote about them during his campaign in Gaul.

'These [aurochs] are a little below the elephant in size, and of the appearance, color, and shape of a bull. Their strength and speed are extraordinary; they spare neither man nor wild beast which they have espied. These the Germans take with much pains in pits and kill them. The young men harden themselves with this exercise, and practice themselves in this sort of hunting, and those who have slain the greatest number of them, having produced the horns in public, to serve as evidence, receive great praise. But not even when taken very young can they be rendered familiar to men and tamed. The size, shape, and appearance of their horns differ much from the horns of our oxen. These they anxiously seek after, and bind at the tips with silver, and use as cups at their most sumptuous entertainments.'

[credit: Julius Caesar : The Gallic Wars]

Schneeburger a 17th century German writer, described aurochs as not being afraid of the approach of man, but if provoked would become highly aggressive, tossing him in the air with his horns.

It is believed that, like modern cattle, the aurochs lived in open grassland, helping to maintain it, and deter forest growth. They lived in small herds of frequently single sex groups of 30 or so individuals. Both sexes fought amongst one another in an attempt to achieve dominant status. The bulls fighting for breeding rights over the cows would often fight to the death. This characteristic of fighting amongst themselves is maintained in certain modern breeds such as the Herens breed of Switzerland the females of which in spring and fall fight amongst themselves to become the dominant cow which leads the herd up to and down from the summer pastures.

It is currently believed that the first aurochs were domesticated twice from different sub-species after 10,000BP on the Indian subcontinent and also in the Near East creating two principal sub-species, *Bos indicus* and *Bos taurus* respectively. Bos Indicus becoming the traditional hump backed cattle still seen today on the Indian subcontinent. *Bos taurus* or Taurine cattle gave rise to the cattle which evolved in Europe and elsewhere.

By historical times aurochs had started to disappear from around Europe. But they remained prevalent north of the Alps. By the 16th century they were limited to forests in Poland, the last one died in 1627 in the Jaktorow Forest.

The importance of the aurochs to Ice Age man is demonstrated by cave paintings in France and Spain as well as the use of drinking horns portrayed in Magdalenian sculptures. In many early cultures the aurochs had considerable religious importance. It was worshipped by the Ancient Greeks and Minoans. In ancient Middle Eastern cultures, it was worshipped as the Lunar Bull and became important to the cult of Mithras. It is still revered by Hindus as an animal that should never be harmed.

But perhaps the biggest contribution that the Ice Age aurochs made to man was in its domesticated form as cattle. Its strength was used to till fields and pull wagons. Its milk is used as the basis for the cheese industry around the world and its meat remains the basis for farm produced meat around the world. With the domestication of aurochs livestock farming was born.

The Wolf

There are various contenders for the ancestor of the modern dog, including the Eurasian wolf, the Paleolithic dog (*Canis c.f. familiaris* – c.f. indicating uncertainty), the Pleistocene wolf, the eastern wolf and the western wolf. To add to the uncertainty, it would seem that interbreeding at various stages between the various contenders has further muddied the waters.

What is becoming clearer however is the general process of domestication. At some point probably after 50,000 BP wolves which had been shadowing Neanderthal camps, scavenging for discarded remains, became familiar, just as some garden birds do when regularly provided with food. This was probably a widespread process over time. Some researchers believe that the earliest dogs date back as far as 130,000BP.

Familiarity over generations would have led to a form of symbiosis where in exchange for food the wolves performed certain useful services such as guarding the camp from other predators, particularly while the Neanderthals were sleeping, and eventually in helping with the actually process of hunting.

Experiments in Russia by geneticist Dmitry Belyaev looking into the process of domestication of wild foxes by natural selection shed considerable light on the question of domestication, and the results are surprising. Certain wild foxes trapped and kept in cages were found to be naturally less hostile to human presence than others. Certain foxes remained openly aggressive when humans approached the cages whereas others slowly became accustomed to human presence. When those that showed less hostility to humans were used as breeding pairs, the offspring also showed a tendency to accept the presence of humans. Offspring, however of those foxes which showed aggressivity towards humans despite never having been raised in the wild maintained the same degree of hostility as their parents. This general trend continued, with the more easy-going foxes becoming even more tolerant of humans even accepting to be held and petted, whereas the aggressive ones showed no inclination to accept human presence at all.

By the 4th generation of the experiment, the tamer foxes started to behave like dogs, wagging their tails when familiar humans approached, eagerly sought out their presence and licked the hands of the researchers. After 20 years of breeding tame foxes, they followed human cues and responded correctly to human gestures and glances.

What may be even more surprising is that those foxes which had become friendly towards humans also began to show physical traits very different from the rest of their species. These changing traits included floppy ears (which also occur in other domestic breeds), curlier tails and changes in fur color. The vocalizations that they made were different from wild foxes. Skeletal changes also started to occur, with shorter legs and jaws and widened skull, changes described by the researchers as more cute-looking.

This experiment succeeded in creating the first domesticated breed of fox, a new sub-species.

This experiment shows what can happen over just a few generations when humans come into contact with some wild animals. Some wild animals will probably retain their natural independence whereas some others may tend to tolerate and eventually appreciate human presence, particularly if they are rewarded for that close proximity.

As an interesting aside, one of Belyaev's conclusions was that the domesticated foxes produced more serotonin, which is a mediator in aggressive behavior, and which also influences growth in the early years, causing the physical changes that he produced in his domestic population. Projecting this to human development he posited that presence with other humans has the same result and that as we evolved we domesticated ourselves, and in the process became less aggressive. Less aggressive particularly, noted Dr Belyaev than our closest relatives the chimpanzee. Furthermore he suggested that human evolution selected in favor of tolerance, cooperation and gentleness.

As with the foxes in the Russian experiment the friendly wolves which had become accustomed to living in the proximity of humans gradually changed their physical appearance, and slowly the races of Paleolithic wolves and eventually early forms of dogs emerged. As with Belyaev's foxes the Paleolithic wolf's jaws were shorter than that of the wild wolf. It would seem that in yet another example of convergent evolution, the ancestors of modern dogs in Asia and in Europe do not share the same ancestors, suggesting that this gradual process of accommodation and finally domestication occurred separately in Europe and Asia, where conditions and needs were identical, but the species of original wolf was different, leading to different species of dogs, from which later domesticated breeds emerged, each one adapting to specific needs from a slightly different base DNA.

From 36,000BP onwards it was the Paleolithic dog bones that were most frequently found close to human habitations. The new species of the domesticated dog had been created, and man had found his closest and most reliable ally in the animal kingdom, a close and lasting partnership which endures to this day. By this time the Paleolithic dog had diverged significantly from the wolf, becoming smaller (average 36Kg compared to 42Kg) with a shorter snout, reduction in number and size of teeth and wider head. It would appear that the closest modern dog to the Paleolithic dog is the Central Asian Shepherd. A cave painting whose date is estimated at 19,000 BP from Font-de-Gaume in France shows what the Paleolithic dog looked like, with erect ears, and a fur free face and lower legs, but with thick fur covering the rest of the body from the ears and neck backwards.

Affection that human ancestors had for their dogs has come down to us from the distant past, thanks to a dog burial from Predmosti in Moravia, where a dog was buried with an animal bone placed carefully in its mouth, and which was dated to somewhere around 32,000BP. At this site, dogs were touchingly buried with humans, quite possibly their owners.

Analysis of bone collagen from a camp in the Czech Republic indicated that the Paleolithic dogs had a different diet compared to the people in their camp. Whereas the humans had a diet of uniquely mammoth meat, the dogs fed on musk ox and reindeer. The reason for this different diet isn't clear, but certain peoples living in the Arctic today give their dogs different meat to the meat that they eat themselves.

The origins of wolves are somewhat complicated by their many ancestors and rapid extinctions. The modern gray wolf is not the ancestor of the modern dog, but considered to be a sister taxon with a now extinct common ancestor. Amongst the possible common ancestors possible are the eastern and western wolf, and from each of these two separate domesticated dog populations evolved. But there has been so much mixing of genes across Europe and Asia since the first association of wolves and humans that geneticists are unable to disentangle a clear line of descent.

Looking over the wonderful variety of mammals that existed during the last Ice Age in Europe and the number which are now extinct, a pattern emerges. Those predators that came into conflict with humans and represented a very really threat to human survival were gradually exterminated either by deliberate killing or incidentally by depriving them of their prey or a combination of the two, or additionally by depriving them of their shelters in the form of caves. Of the predators that did survive the Ice Age, the most successful was the wolf, although numbers in Europe are low. Of the great herbivores, the mammoth, woolly rhinoceros and giant deer were hunted out of existence. Other species survived in effect by submitting to human will and becoming domesticated such as the horse, the cow, goat, pig, dog, cat, and the reindeer. It was of greater interest to humans to find a use for these animals alive than dead. Thus, humans protected them and, in the process, changed them dramatically with species such as the Pekinese and other lapdogs being selectively bred for their companionship, or charming attributes. Some of the Ice Age mammals survived the Ice Age because they lived in habitats where man found survival difficult such as in high mountains, their inaccessibility to humans saving them from extinction. These include the ibex and the chamois.

The Great Extinction

By today's standards, Ice Age Europe was a continent of extremes. Since the arrival of man's ancestors 1.8 million years previously it had never been so inhospitable and dangerous. The Ice Age began with tropical species like Hippopotamus inhabiting the River Rhine and at the Last Glacial Maximum, only 20,000 years ago, the whole of the North of the continent was engulfed in a truly enormous ice cap which had grown, purely by means of snow fall, from covering the coldest parts of Scandinavia to entirely covering the Baltic and beyond that southwards to extend into Germany and Poland and covering the majority of the British and the North Sea. South of this great continental ice cap was a huge expanse of Arctic wasteland of permafrost where nothing grew in the frozen ground. Similarly, a great ice cap covered the Alps with glaciers flowing out onto the plains in all directions.

This land was inhabited by a vast array of giant and deadly predators from bears weighing well over 1 ton, one of the largest mammalian carnivores to ever prowl the earth, to groups of saber-tooth cats, lions, families of well organized large hunting hyenas, to packs of dire wolves, cave bears and cave lions. Herbivores also evolved into giants such as megaloceros, the woolly mammoth, the well armed and dangerous woolly rhinoceros the irascible 1.5-ton aurochs using horns, tusks and foul tempers as defenses against the large, powerful predators that preyed on them. In the thick of all these dangers man had managed to survive. As he developed new and more effective ways of hunting and protecting himself, not only was he capable of holding his own but through resistance and resourcefulness he was asserting himself over even the deadliest of his enemies.

The last Ice Age (110,000–12,00BP) saved the worst for last; a showdown was fast approaching. The last glacial maximum made everything many times worse. Whereas for the previous 80,000 years of the Ice Age the great mammoth herds had vast plains to roam and feed and the dangerous predators were spread over equally large areas, the ice sheets which had expanded over so much of the continent and the tundra over yet more of the continent compressed the available space for all these animals into much less than half of the original area. For the previous 80,000 years of the Ice Age a form of natural equilibrium had prevailed, vast quantities of herbivores supported a vast number of predators.

The great grassy plains were much reduced, bringing the woolly mammoth herds, the woolly rhinoceros herds, the European bison, the aurochs, the herds of wild horses, the herds of wissent, great herds of reindeer, herds of red deer and megaloceros closer together and gathered around them great numbers of the Ice Age's predators.

Ice Age Europeans whose weapons were now by far the deadliest that had ever been made, could deliver death for the first time in the history of the planet at a safe distance of over 100m from his prey, was undergoing a population explosion, but like every other mammal in Europe during the Last Glacial Maximum was being concentrated into a smaller and smaller living space, which he was forced to share with all the other great Ice Age fauna, herbivores and predators alike.

The Last Glacial Maximum became a survival of the fittest scenario on steroids. Only the very fittest would survive. A mass extinction event occurred; great herbivores and great predators alike disappeared from Europe for ever, leaving one apex predator dominant over all the others, humankind.

Cave lions, cave hyenas, woolly mammoth, woolly rhinoceros, dire wolves, megaloceros, saber-toothed cats, Ice Age leopards and many other species all became extinct in Europe. Some of these species survived still in the near empty fastnesses of central and eastern Asia in much diminished numbers for thousands of years beyond the Last Glacial Maximum where man was not present in such great numbers.

When the glaciers started to retreat rapidly from 19,000BP onwards, the grasslands grew back, and the numbers of animals could once again increase. But there were no longer the once great herds of woolly mammoth and bison herds to hunt. They were gone from Europe for ever. For the first time in human history but not for the last time, an expanding population was confronted with a continental wide food shortage. The ever increasingly efficient hunting practices that had been honed for hundreds of thousands of years focusing on a seemingly unending cornucopia of animals were becoming self-defeating. In a world where nature had provided a seemingly endless supply of wild animals to hunt, something had changed forever. That supply was disappearing fast.

Necessity is the mother of invention, and once again, as so many times in the past, Europe's most intelligent animal found a solution. If nature couldn't provide wild animals in sufficient numbers, man would have to step in and do it himself. He would look after the remaining animals that he had, he would own them, look after them, and when he wanted, he would eat them. Livestock farming was born.

Europeans captured certain wild animals and kept them in confined areas. With the help of his faithful friend the dog and with ropes he protected them from other predators. In time animals such as the aurochs, the wild boar, the wild horse, the wild sheep and wild goat would become accustomed to the presence of man. Domestication on a large scale began and with it the seeds of a farming revolution. Now man could ensure that he had enough meat to eat, because he had learned to control the meat supply. By eliminating one by one the other predators, he managed to steward these precious resources for himself alone.

But to keep these domesticated animals he needed land and that land needed to be protected from all forms of predation that posed a threat to his food supply. This not only applied to wild predators such as wolves, but also to opportunistic humans who considered that wild animals belonged to no one and were free game. Conflict was inevitable. Large communities protecting their animals also protected their land and the notion of land ownership was created. Foreign hunters on that land would be repelled. Man, for so long pitted against wild animals was now pitted against his fellow men. Small scale conflicts over land rights were inevitable. As settlements found mutual causes for cooperation amongst themselves alliances were formed to pool resources, and the scale of local disputes escalated. Tribal warfare ensued. The seeds of modern civilization were sewn.

Meanwhile the Neanderthal hunting and nomadic traditions honed over hundreds of thousands of years did not disappear entirely. As the glaciers retreated north leaving tundra and periglacial conditions behind, the great arctic adapted reindeer herds followed, and following them in Europe were humans, dogs and wolves. The shamanic traditions of the Neanderthals were preserved as was the way of life, the technology, the tool and weapon making. These people had learnt over tens of thousands of years to thrive in the most extreme of cold conditions and this they continued to do and in a modified way still do to this day.

The great changes forced on Europeans by the mass extinctions that they had themselves caused ended the long Paleolithic age and ushered in a new one, the Mesolithic.

Mesolithic

The Mesolithic epoch marks transitional time from the Paleolithic to the Neolithic epoch, a time of great changes when the old hunting traditions perfected over hundreds of thousands of years start to disappear to be replaced by established farms and eventually the Neolithic permanent settlements consisting of permanent buildings. As its name suggests the Mesolithic is still a stone-based culture and not yet the last. That honor goes to the Neolithic (or new lithic) culture, after which stone tools finally give way to the earliest metal tools, copper, bronze then iron.

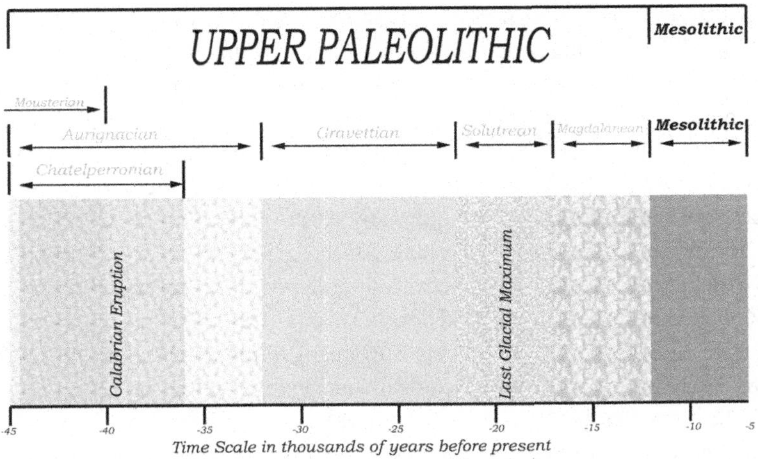

Illustration 76. Mesolithic period

But what brought about these great changes? In two words, 'mass extinctions'. The transition from hunting to farming was a gradual one, taking place as the great extinctions of the traditional herds of megafauna left Mesolithic man searching for new ways to feed himself. A combination of the Last Glacial Maximum and man's increasingly efficient methods of hunting together with his increasing numbers drove the mammoth and other great species to extinction, first in Europe then later in Asia. As man was forced to find new ways of feeding himself, so his way of life changed dramatically. But this didn't occur at the same time across Europe and Asia, in places the old way of life carried on, so the change from the Paleolithic to the Mesolithic occurred over thousands of years depending on the location. Partly for this reason and partly because people were settling, different cultures sprang up simultaneously across the continent. Previously the nomadic nature of Neanderthal life ensured the exchange of new ideas over vast areas, resulting in remarkable homogeneous cultures across Europe and much of Asia. With the end of nomadic traditions, this exchange of culture ended also.

Only in the far north of the continent did the old hunting nomadic traditions prevail and that was thanks to one animal, the reindeer. Here, the people who had evolved and learnt over hundreds of thousands of years the techniques for survival in this inhospitable world maintained their old nomadic traditions and as they did so they maintained a remarkably homogeneous circumpolar culture.

The reindeer with its unique adaptations to life in a permanently bitterly cold world inhabiting an icy environment where humans were never numerous enough to hunt them to extinction, managed to thrive. These peoples had no need to change, their main source of food was still plentiful (unlike their southern relatives), and their methods of hunting the reindeer were well adapted to the Arctic way of life. These arctic peoples, the direct ancestors of the Inuit, Esquimos and many others carried on as they had done for hundreds of thousands of years. As the glaciers retreated northwards leaving behind them newly uncovered lands, so the cold adapted reindeer also moved north leaving behind Southern and Middle Europe until the next Ice Age. The last of the Paleolithic Europeans followed these great reindeer herds, which probably numbered over a million individuals.

Mesolithic archeological sites around Europe are plentiful. In Southern Germany and Switzerland alone 1,500 are known; in Austria and Central Europe over 2,000 and in France over 400.

In general, Mesolithic cultures improved the principals of Magdalenian technology to produce as standard, composite tools. Thus, arrows had wooden shafts with fine flint points, harpoons had wooden shafts with fine barbed bone points, sickles with wooden and antler handles. As tools improved they became more specialized.

Also, in general during the Mesolithic, the fine figurative art techniques perfected during the Magdalenian gave way to rough schematic sometimes abstract art in what appears to be a retrograde step.

Within the Mesolithic period, individual cultures sprang up replacing the Magdalenian over different parts of Europe. Indeed, as Europeans no longer travelled following the migrating herds, they began to settle down permanently in favorable areas, each with its own reliable source of food and water. Inevitably as Europeans travelled less; ideas, tools and cultures became more localized. The great pan-continental homogeneous cultures of the past like Mousterian were forgotten. A confusing patchwork of relatively localized cultures appeared. There's no great need to detail each one, but it's worth looking at some of the main ones, bearing in mind that local traditions developed upon local needs, people became specialized in just certain skills according to local requirements. Local specialization resulted in local identities evolving. These identities were the grain that was to grow over time into the city state.

Hamburgian Culture

An immediate successor to Magdalenian on the northern fringes of Europe, almost on the fringes of the great retreating Scandinavian glaciers Hamburgian culture lasted from 15,500 to 13,100BP. This culture was centered on the hunting of reindeer which occupied the periglacial steppes recently uncovered by the retreating glaciers. This culture covered the Northern borders of Europe from Northern France, Northern Germany, Denmark and Poland. It also provided for the very first repopulation of Scandinavia during the process of deglaciation as the great Scandinavian Ice Cap retreated northwards. The Gulf Stream warmed the Norwegian coastline which became ice free, allowing the Hamburgian peoples to migrate northwards along the coast line between the ice cap and the sea, hunting and fishing as they went. The sea level was rising as the great ice caps around the globe melted but it was still 50m lower than today. Norwegian river valleys slicing through high mountains close to the sea became invaded by the sea, producing the fjord landscape for which the Norwegian coast is famous.

The Hamburgian culture was characterized by what are called shouldered flint points and zinken tools. Shouldered points if made from stainless steel would be recognizable in form to many modern knives. A straight, sharp blade, with a blunt back, the tip of the blade ending in a fine point, whereas at the other end a cut away (or shoulder) allowed the blade to be socketed into a handle made of bone, wood or antler.

The Hamburgians were still nomadic; the remains they left indicate small and apparently temporary settlements as they followed the reindeer herds. Rings of stones have been found which would appear to be the bases for their teepees, where the skins were anchored down to the ground to protect against the wind.

Federmesser Culture

As the Hamburgian peoples moved slowly northwards towards Scandinavia following the reindeer herds another culture arose in its place in the Northern Plains of France, Germany, Poland and Britain. The Federmesser culture lasted from 14,000 to 12,800 BP. Following on from Hamburgian small sharp knives, the Federmesser used small, sharp precisely worked flint knives and arrow heads. The name originates from the German for penknife or bird quill knife (feder being german for feather). As with the Hamburgian culture the main food source was medium to small animals and the main weapon was the bow and arrow. There were many similarities with the Cresswellian culture in Britain as well as the Azilian culture in Southern France and Northern Spain.

Ahrensburg Culture

In North Western Europe, including England, the vestiges of the disappearing Doggerland, Germany, Denmark and Poland the Ahrensburg culture prevailed. Now there were no more mammoths to hunt, the use of spears with powerful spear throwers were less effective against smaller animals, amongst others, reindeer and they disappear from the architectural record. Instead the bow and arrow became the weapon of choice as the principal method of hunting smaller animals. Small arrows were of little use against the mammoth, but the bow and arrow were very effective at killing reindeer, red deer and ibex which became the principal sources of food for the people of the Ahrensburg culture. Fine lithic points were made, often with tangs to help in attaching the arrow to the shaft. Fishing was another form of diversification, with bone hooks being associated with many Ahrensburg sites. The Mesolithic was a period of rapid change; the Ahrensburg lasted from around 12,900 to 11,700BP and consequently was short lived.

Maglemosian

Maglemosian (9,000–6,000) at the end of the Mesolithic, covers a variety of similar lithic industries across Northern Europe extending from Britain (including the now ice-free Northern Britain) across Doggerland, Holland to the German plain Poland and parts of central Europe. The characteristic tools are stone axes and obliquely blunted points and the typical Mesolithic microliths. Most Maglemosian sites are found on lakesides during the summer and fall months. Remains reveal a combination of hunting forest species such as the aurochs and deer together with increasing reliance on fishing. Considerable fishing remains testify to the importance now accorded to fish in the daily diet of these Northern Europeans, including fish nets, net weights, net floats, fish hooks, canoes and paddles and bone harpoons. Sea-side Maglemosian settlements include the remains of shellfish and seals. In contrast to other previous cultures where caves were the primary choice for the location of settlements, Maglemosian sites were often open air; the choice of location being dictated by the proximity of a lake or seaside. Buildings could be built wherever they were required. The need for security from dangerous carnivores had now receded with the extinction of the megafauna and Europeans were now free to populate open areas wherever there was ready access to food.

Swiderian Culture

Following on from the Federmesser and Ahrensburg cultures and centered initially in Poland, the Swiderian culture flourished between 11,000 and 9,000 BP. As with the Ahrensburg Culture the Swiderian was characterized by small flint tanged blades with a blunted back for finger pressure. The glaciers that had only quite recently covered northern Poland had left behind dunes of fine dust and sand; the product of the relentless grinding of the glaciers. It was on these dunes that the Swiderian Culture took root.

It is believed that the Swiderian peoples were newcomers, as there appears to be a gap of about 300 years in the archaeological record, immediately prior to their arrival. The first of the Swiderian settlements found to date is the Silesian site of Chwalim. This 300 year gap separating the previous Paleolithic peoples of Poland and the new Mesolithic peoples who arrived, bringing Ahrensburg cultural advances from the West is taken as proof that the Mesolithic spread through Europe generally from West to East, and that the Mesolithic first came about in Western Europe.

The Swiderians were the first to repopulate Estonia following the retreat of the glaciers from the Eastern Baltic.

This general eastward advance of the latest developments brought about by the Mesolithic and adapted locally in Poland by the Swiderian peoples continued eastwards. The subsequent cultures of the Ukraine, Eastern Europe and Russia are all considered to be derived from Swiderian. The result of this Eastward spreading influence was an expanding region around the Southern Baltic, Eastern Europe and Central Russian of a relatively homogeneous and largely separate culture to the one developing in Western and Southern Europe. A separation that later would crystallize into the division of Western and Eastern Europe.

Kunda Culture

The Kunda Culture is considered to have evolved from the Swiderian between 10 and 7,000BP. It appears to have originated around the Southern Baltic shore, and spread eastwards into Russia. As the reindeer migrated further northwards the Kunda people relied more on fishing, seal and red deer for their food. Most Kunda settlements are found close to rivers, marshes and lakes. As the animals that they hunted changed so did their weapons and tools. Fine bone tanged harpoon points were worked from bone and antler. Barbs appeared on harpoons and the tanged fine flint Swiderian blades were retained.

While in the North of Europe people followed the reindeer northwards and modified their behavior to adapt to the disappearance of the mammoth to the West and South of the continent developments were going in a slightly different direction.

Azilian

Whereas the great glaciers in the North of Europe caused considerable discontinuity in the cultures, particularly south of the Baltic with the Swiderian culture, life carried on in the Southern half of Europe. In France, Germany, Spain and Switzerland the Azilian evolved directly out of the Magdalenian and Federmesser cultures and was named after the Mas d'Azil cave in Southern France around 12,000BP, part of the same watershed as the great Magdalenian caves such as Lascaux, but further upstream in the Pyrenean headwaters. The typical stone tool of the Azilian was the Azilian point; microliths with rounded, retouched backs. A close variant of Azilian developed in Southern Spain and Portugal known by the cumbersome term Iberian microlaminar lithism. The surprising Mas d'Azil cave which is so large that today a road, a small river and a path run right through it. In addition, it also houses various prehistoric displays, has given up some amazing finds from the Magdalenian and Azilian layers. One of the most curious items is the carving of an ibex on the tooth of a Sperm Whale. The assumption is that the whale was washed up on the Atlantic coast and the tooth transported and possibly traded from there to the Mas d'Azil people. Other new items include geometric (consistent with Mesolithic abstract art found elsewhere) and abstract ochre paintings on flattened pebbles; over 1,300 of which were found in the cave. Similarly, decorated pebbles are found also at Azilian sites in Switzerland, Spain and Italy.

Amongst the vast horde of finds recovered from the Mas d'Azil cave are very many engravings of animals, many of the smaller animals that were now the mainstay of Azilian peoples such as horses, ibex and bison. For the first time (not forgetting the putative Creswell horse already mentioned) what appear to be halters appear on some of the engravings of horses' heads revealing that horses were now beginning to be domesticated, whether for transport or for food is not clear. There are no known images of horses being ridden this early in pre-history. This pushes back the generally accepted date of horse domestication by 8 or 9,000 years.

One very interesting pair of engravings on a disc is of a confrontation between a man and a bear. The man, with what appears to be a bear's head appears to be reaching out to a bear standing on its hind legs. The bear seems to be making a swipe at the man with its claws clearly visible. On the reverse side of the disc the man is lying supine, presumably dead next to the bear. This is clearly reminiscent of the shamanic scene in the Lascaux well area, where a zoomorphological figure in that case with a bird's head has been killed by an eviscerated bison. A number of these engraved discs were found in the cave some with very skillfully executed images of animals on them, and perforated in their centers, suggesting that they were hung around the neck on a chord. The base material was often cut from the shoulder blades of animals, indeed one such shoulder blade has been found with three circular holes in it where the discs were cut from.

Engravings of fish are also plentiful, with sufficient detail to identify them as salmonids from the adipose fins, which is quite possible as salmon still run in the Dordogne and Gironde river systems. Also, very small barbed harpoons were found in the cave, which could have been fitted to the tips of arrows.

A growing prominence of images of fishes and small single-sided barbed harpoon points, with holes for cord attachment attest to the Azilian Culture and other contemporary cultures developing new and far more efficient methods of fishing as they sought new sources of food. Dug-out canoes fashioned from tree trunks with paddles have been found at Mesolithic sites, as have fishing nets. Weirs were constructed to channel migrating fish into narrow channels where they could be speared with ease. With the arrival of dug-out canoes came boating, and navigation, a skill allowing Mesolithic peoples to populate otherwise inaccessible islands and fish in large lakes and even the sea. Europeans were no longer confined to getting about on his two legs. Narrow to medium sized seas were no longer an obstruction to migration.

Nearby and contemporary with Mas d'Azil is the Bedeilhac Cave, higher up the valley. A huge cave with a massive opening, it contains some beautiful wall paintings of horses and bison. One feature there is unusual, engravings of animals made in large slabs of clay, which were then attached to the rock walls with slip, creating a sort of prehistoric version of plaster moldings.

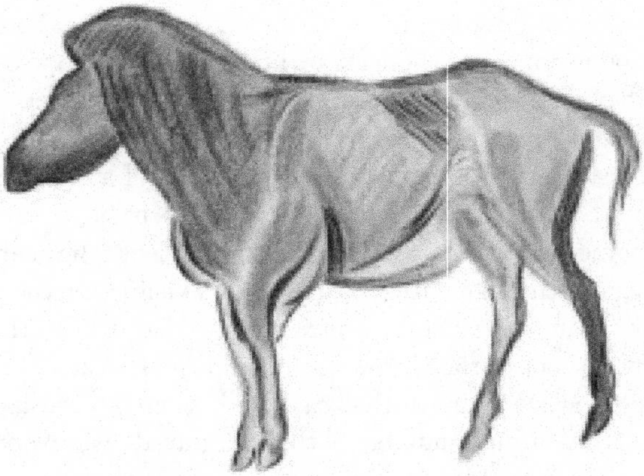

Illustration 77. Painting of a horse from Bedeilhac cave

Sauveterrian

Another French culture in the Mesolithic dating from 9-8,000BP, the Sauveterrian is identified by narrow blades and small triangular points probably used as arrow tips. It seems to have first appeared in South Western France and spread out across Western Europe reaching Britain and also Central Europe.

Mesolithic in Italy

On the Italian peninsula the Mesolithic period shows regional variations which appear to have emerged from the late Gravettian period.

In Apulia and other parts of Southern Italy from about 11,000BP schematic cave art starts to replace naturalistic cave art as with Mesolithic art elsewhere in Europe. The schematic design for example makes rectangular blocks out of humans. One engraved block from the Romanelli cave shows a naturalistic aurochs on one side, while on the other a schematic deer. In the Addaura Cave some schematic bovids have been drawn over the top of a large naturalistic scene. In addition, from this time numerous blocks, slabs and bones are thickly engraved with geometric designs in the same way as the nearby and contemporary Azilian culture. The culture which produced this form of schematic and geometric art in Italy is referred to as Epiromanellian, and lasts until about 8,200BP

In an area of North Eastern Italy and Slovenia just north of the Adriatic are a series of caves which were inhabited from the Mesolithic through to the Roman times. In the Edera Cave, the Mesolithic layers reveal broken pottery, wild and domesticated animal bones. The flint tools show trapezoidal arrow heads similar in design to those made during the contemporary Azilian period in France and Spain. As with Mas d'Azil there is evidence of the domestication of animals. Locally this Mesolithic culture is referred to as Castelnovian. In common with other Mesolithic cultures microliths are plentiful including finely crafted blades of just 10 or 20mm in length. The backed blades appear very similar to those found in the Azilian culture.

Also, in common with Azilian culture fish bones are very common and sea turtle shells also appear uniquely during the Mesolithic and not in any other of the layers. The Castelnovian culture so similar to the Azilian Culture reveals the tell-tale signs of a transition into the settled farming of the Neolithic Age.

In general, the Mesolithic for most of Europe marked a time of adapting to a new way of life forced on Europeans by the mass extinctions of mammoth and disappearance of the great reindeer herds. While in the far north as reindeer followed the melting ice caps northwards the old Paleolithic lifestyle continued largely unchanged. From the Magdalenian period onwards the rest of Europe began to settle down and build. Across Europe deforestation began by using mattocks and axes. Trees were felled mainly for construction, allowing grasses to appear over wide areas attracting, deer, horses, goats and aurochs. As we have seen some of these animals started to become domesticated thus paving the way for the great farming revolution that would gradually sweep over most of the planet, with relatively few hunter gatherer peoples remaining in various parts of the world to this day.

The forests still provided food for hunting, for animals like deer and boar, a tradition which remained important until the middle ages, and is of course still practiced today.

Mesolithic Europeans needed other sources of food to replace the mammoth and the reindeer. Increasingly fish became a readily replenishable supply of food, and new ways were found of catching them, including the net, the weir and using the canoe. The dugout canoe, another product from a felled a tree, hollowed out with a stone adze provided water transport across lakes, rivers and narrow stretches of sea.

Arrow heads become far more widespread across Europe than they had been in the Magdalenian as a result of the smaller game being more effectively hunted, with an easier portable supply of arrows compared to just a few large and cumbersome spears. Arrows had the further advantage of being a more precise weapon at distance compared to a large spear, and quicker to manufacture.

As fishing techniques improved, areas from North to South Europe close to the sea became specialized in fishing, and great kitchen middens from Portugal to Britain show evidence of the remains of thousands of meals obtained from the sea. Communities of fishermen and sailors sprang up around Europe on water fronts; sea, lake and river. Many of these brand new settlements developed further in the Neolithic to become small towns which survive as water front towns to this day.

In Denmark and Southern Sweden large accumulations of whale bones testify to the hunting and eating of whales, possibly by driving some of them into shallow waters with the help of canoes, rafts and nets. In Greece certain Mesolithic communities relied heavily on tuna fishing, which made up as much as 50% of the food remains found in the settlements. To this day certain communities in the Mediterranean still channel tuna with nets into confined spaces where they can be harpooned or gaffed aboard small boats.

Diversification of food sources extended to using plants as an important source of food for the first time in European history. Nut shell accumulations around Mesolithic settlements show that Europeans were also looking to trees and plants for year-round sustenance, instead of following the mammoth herds.

The felling of trees from the forests covering Eurasia provided a dual bounty. The trunks and principal branches provided timber for construction and the grassy clearings fed the domesticated livestock. These sturdy wooden buildings became more permanent, as did the settlements that they turned in to, the variety of food sources enabled Europeans to survive in one place for the whole year round. These widespread changes in behavior paved the way for the Neolithic which was about to arrive in Europe.

The age-old nomadic tradition of following herds of animals from North to South in the fall and in the opposite direction in the spring continued but in a slightly different form. Lowland winter grazing animals moved to higher land in the summer. In the Balkans and around the Alps this became part of the transhumance tradition in animal husbandry which continues to this day.

As the Mesolithic population of Europe increased, so did the competition for resources between established owners of land and neighbors and also with nomadic hunters bringing humans into conflict with other humans. For the first time in European history appears the beginning of a trend that was to continue unabated; more and more skeletons show the signs of interpersonal injury rather than injuries from large, dangerous animals. Weapons adapted for hunting small game were also well adapted to killing other humans. Having learnt the skill of killing large and dangerous animals efficiently, using coordinated hunters, the same skills were employed in killing fellow humans. The age of warfare, beginning with low-level conflicts, in the Mesolithic, had arrived.

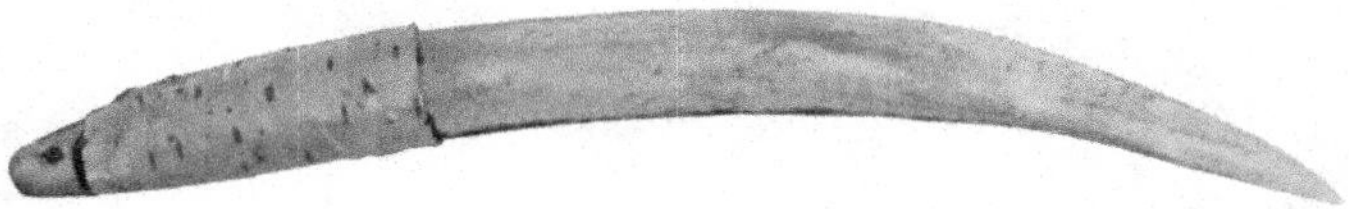

Illustration 78. Interpersonal conflict: a Mesolithic dagger

A totally new way of life was changing everything in Europe. Mesolithic communities became settled populations with local identities and customs. Well trodden paths between neighboring communities developed into rough but established roads. People developed specialized skills; the first tradesmen appeared with lifelong skills that enabled them to perform complex tasks requiring considerable learning. Specialized products were exchanged between communities enhancing and broadening trade across Europe which had hitherto been concentrated almost uniquely on stone tools. With the increased domestication of animals, together with the clearance of forests, farming began to spread around Europe. All these changes blossomed further around Europe in the Neolithic. Only the circumpolar nomads of the Arctic continued the old Neanderthal traditions of following the great herds.

LANGUAGE

The question of what language did the Ancient Europeans speak is a crucial but vexed one. The Linguistic Society of Paris in 1866 took it upon themselves to ban all present and future debates on the origins of language, a ban which has largely held until very recent times. Nevertheless, some researchers had looked into the question, but no consensus has been reached on the subject, indeed as we have seen in previous chapters it was thought up until quite recently that the Neanderthals weren't even capable of speech. Research into this crucial aspect of humanity had got off to a very bad start.

There are many theories on the origins of language which conveniently cover all the remotest possibilities. All bets are hedged on this subject. But it must be obvious to most readers of this book that by far the most likely origin of language is from the very earliest days of humanity, before even *Ardipithecus*. Even if one grunt for 'yes and two grunts for 'no' was the extent of their communication, it was still the basis for verbal communication, which over the intervening millions of years became slowly more sophisticated, dealing with not only physical things, but more abstract notions such as 'tomorrow' or 'love' or even the concept of 'thought'. This explanation is the basis of what is known as the 'Continuity Theory' of the evolution of language.

Given this slow development of language from the most distant origins of humanity, it probably isn't worth probing any further to try and establish some form of meaningful date at which point we can say 'language was invented here', beyond the invention of writing (for which we have a fairly clear idea: Sumer 5,100BP) in a later period which is outside the scope of this book. Before the invention of writing with no written records, we are in very difficult territory, and it is for this reason that discovery of language is one of the most perplexing questions that scientists have attempted to answer.

Who better than Charles Darwin to start the discussion?

> I cannot doubt that language owes its origin to the imitation and modification, aided by signs and gestures, of various natural sounds, the voices of other animals, and man's own instinctive cries. (Darwin, C 240)

Despite the challenges, by looking at all the available evidence we can make a number of meaningful inroads into the hitherto empty region of the origins of language; in part by building on what we have learnt in this book so far. To do this we can look at what we know from both ends of the spectrum. Thanks to the Ancient Greeks and Romans we know quite a lot about the spoken languages of Europe in the classical period.

At the other end of the spectrum as we have seen in a previous chapter 'Our Closest Relation' that even primates are capable of language. The later appearance of the FOXP2 gene, the development of Wernicke's and Brocke's areas provided the hardware for developing language including probably speech. *Ardipithecus* would have been capable of basic language skills, probably slightly more sophisticated than today's chimpanzees. Five million years later, Neanderthal with his highly developed brain would have been a skilled linguist, but what language did he speak?

Amidst the bewildering plethora of wild hypotheses on the origins of language one of them stands out, known as 'Tool Culture Resistance'. It has been found in chimpanzee, macaque and Capuchin monkey populations that without language, learnt skills can very easily be forgotten. As tool manufacture since the Olduwan technology has been progressively and smoothly developing and specifically not forgotten and re-learnt (akin to re-inventing the wheel), language has provided the means for retaining precious information over the generations and in the absence of writing has been the cultural memory of humanity. The importance of the spoken word as a way of transmitting information down through the generations has been observed in American Indians who before the arrival of modern Europeans had no writing relied on oral traditions to transmit their knowledge from one generation to the next.

> Oklahoma tribes classify and tell stories differently, but certain general patterns can be observed. Storytelling can encompass narratives that are viewed as truthful accounts of events in the ancient

> past. For instance, all Oklahoma tribes possess a unique narrative about the creation of the world. Storytelling also embraces stories that could be called folktales... Native communities possess rules and procedures for their telling. In some communities, it is believed that such stories should be told only during the winter. Certain behaviors are to be practiced by storytellers, such as spitting on the ground at the conclusion of a story or the use of traditional phrases or introduction or conclusion. Less-often-documented oral traditions also play an important role in Oklahoma Indian life. Historical information, such as family genealogy and cultural knowledge held within a tribal group, will most often be transmitted between generations through spoken narratives. Talk about tribal history and culture is pervasive in Indian communities... At the ceremonial grounds of the Northeastern and Southeastern tribes, specially appointed men deliver speeches that are important parts of larger rituals. Delivered in English or in Native languages, these speeches are forms of art that explain tribal history, culture, ritual, and proper behavior. Comparable speaking events take place among the Plains groups as well, for instance during powwows and peyote meetings. Like storytelling, such speaking reflects local cultural traditions and norms. (Jackson, J.B. 2)

With respect to oral traditions, the information imparted to children down the generations was not primarily intended as entertainment, a sort of poor man's television, it was vital for not only the survival of the growing child, but also for the future of the group. Animal behavior; which animals were most dangerous and at what times, how to make and mend weapons, where certain animals could be found at various times of the year. How to light a fire in wet weather? Which berries could be eaten and when, together with thousands of other pieces of vital information necessary to ensure survival. Any inaccuracies made during the telling and retelling of this precious information could have fatal consequences, so clarity of expression was important. Proper names must have been given to poisonous fruit and to edible fruit. A fallow deer must be properly distinguished from a belligerent aurochs. Precise words carried great importance. Models and pictures in caves helped the educational process. As we have seen Shaman were crucial in this process of transmitting precious information.

These vital oral traditions where the young would learn their family's history, hunting techniques and about the natural world were the embryonic origins of the Ancient Greek theatre, a form of formulaic story-telling, where a small number of people would inform an auditorium or theatre. In shamanic rituals the shaman wears a mask to act out sacred texts, just as all ancient Greek actors wore masks when presenting their pieces to their audience.

Language enabled the transmission of the vital processes of tool manufacture which have been with man from the earliest days. This in itself shouldn't be a surprise. Tool Culture Resistance Theory confirms that from Olduwan through to Magdalenian and beyond, the slow, unbroken progression of tool technology that we have seen in this book was managed by passing the necessary information on manufacture via language from one generation to the next in an unbroken line from *Ardipithecus* to Neanderthals and on to transitional early modern Europeans over millions of years.

We have conclusive evidence that Early Europeans had a language, but the difficult question is: what language?

Before attempting to answer this question, first of all, let's take a little background on the way languages develop.

Pidgins and Creoles

These are embryonic languages which have been studied around the world and have revealed surprising similarities in the process of their development despite being totally unrelated. Pidgins are rudimentary languages with rudimentary grammar and restricted vocabulary. In the most primitive form they consist of nouns, verbs and adjectives with few articles, auxiliary verbs, tenses or prepositions, the bare structural bones of communication. Often there is no fixed word order or inflection. So that 'Bird fly house' could mean that the bird flew into the house or the bird flew out of the house, or that the bird flew over the house. This is imprecise communication and needs improvement for the original meaning to become clear to the listener.

If pidgin is learnt by children who adopt it as their mother tongue then studies have found that improvements occur naturally, becoming fixed, with more complex grammar, phonology and syntax. This enhanced level of communication then becomes considered as a Creole language. Creole languages around the world despite being unrelated tend to develop the Subject-Verb-Object word order, suggesting that language reflects the way that our brains are hard-wired and we communicate more clearly when our sentences reflect the way that our minds process information.

As much as the S-V-O development is interesting in the way it develops it throws a bit of a spanner into the question of the origin of languages because it suggests convergent development. In other words that language structure is to a degree dependent on the brain's structure and that we will arrive at a similar language structure whatever our starting point around the world.

Maybe our only hope is in looking at basic nouns themselves, and chance upon some similarities across different languages.

Indo-European

Having seen that language had been around for millions of years, let us now trace our steps backwards from historical times.

Nearly all European languages spring from the same source, a prehistoric family of languages called Indo-European. Today there are an astonishing 445 of them including English, Spanish, Russian, Hindustani and Punjabi. Other less populous Indo-European languages include German, French, Punjabi and Italian. Today 46% of the planet speaks an Indo-European based language as its first language. The term Indo-European is slightly misleading, as it implies that the language has Indian and European roots, on an equal footing, with a possible emphasis on an Indian origin. In fact, Indo-European languages spread to Northern India relatively late in their existence, having originated a long time earlier in Europe. The south of India has languages that are considered to have separate origins from Indo-European and probably originated independently.

Curiously not all European languages are recognized as belonging to the Indo-European family, Basque and Hungarian have traditionally been considered to be non-Indo-European. Although this is by no means certain as we shall see later.

Ancient Greeks and ancient Romans (also Indo-European) were well aware that there were similarities between their languages even though their writing and alphabets were very different, indicating a common language origin long before the writing of Linear A, Europe's first writings appeared. Ancient Romans also noted with some surprise that their language had similar aspects to what they considered to be the barbaric languages of Celtic and Old German.

European travelers to India in the 16th century also noted similarities between European languages and Indian languages. In 1583, the English Jesuit missionary Thomas Stevens wrote a letter from Goa to his brother noting similarities between the ancient classics of Greek and Latin and the local Indo-Aryan language that he was learning.

So, we have a common source language that spreads from Spain to Russia and India and Germany to the Mediterranean including a great majority of intervening languages. But what people spread this one common source language so long before the earliest writing in the Mediterranean when there was a common culture spreading from Europe to Asia? This common source language for Indo-European is referred to as proto Indo-European or prosaically PIE language.

So now we know that at some point in prehistory, long before the ancient Greek and ancient Roman civilizations a culture had spread right across the vast expanses of Europe and into Western Asia. This culture carried with it a common language that had over time become regionalized so that the original language had evolved into a great number of localized languages, but still carrying discernable traces of its origins. The astute reader will probably already be guessing the answer to the riddle.

We know from the previous chapter on the Mesolithic, that as farming spread across Europe, so too did the tendency to settle down and create permanent settlements. From this point onwards, a host of regional cultures sprang up as people travelled less and focused on a life within a small radius of their own settlement. This trend continued through the Neolithic into Ancient Greek times, when the small settlements eventually developed into city states.

In other words, the pan-European proto-Indo-European language predates the Mesolithic. This fundamentally disproves the established view that PIE dates from the Neolithic. It is precisely during the Mesolithic and Neolithic when the Indo-European languages could not have spread over the continent. On the contrary it was during these two periods when the original Indo-European language became regionalized, so that by ancient Roman times each region had its own language, and only the very discerning, studious observers of people that some Ancient Romans were, were able to recognize that there were commonalities between Latin and, say, one of the Celtic languages.

Casting our minds back through the maps of European cultures which we have seen prior to the Mesolithic, the latest one that coincides with the region where the Indo-European languages were spoken is the Gravettian, that culture of superb creativity, by far the most advanced culture in the world at the time and more advanced than any had been anywhere before,. Of course, the PIE language may well have developed during the Aurignacian and earlier, but it must have been fully formed by the Gravettian at the very latest.

Taking a look at the maps of Indo-European Languages and the Gravettian-Aurignacian Cultures, we see that the Gravettian culture from about 30–24,000BP corresponds with the regions that spoke a language belonging to the Indo-European family. As the glaciers shown on the first map started to retreat Northwards Indo-European speakers followed in their wake, particularly up the Norwegian coast.

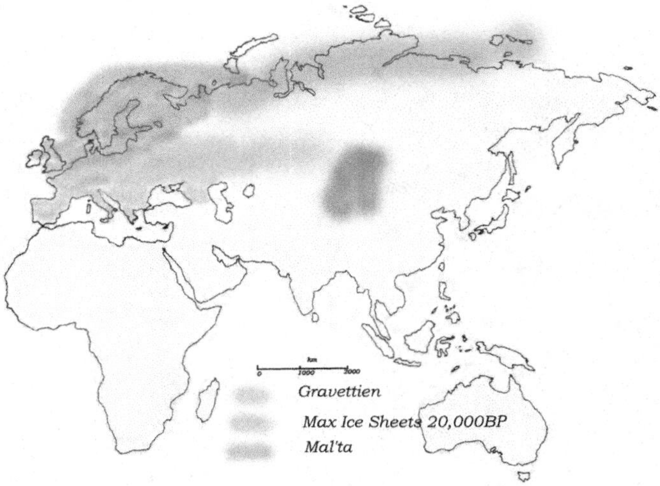

Illustration 79. Extent of the Mesolithic culture at the height of the last ice age

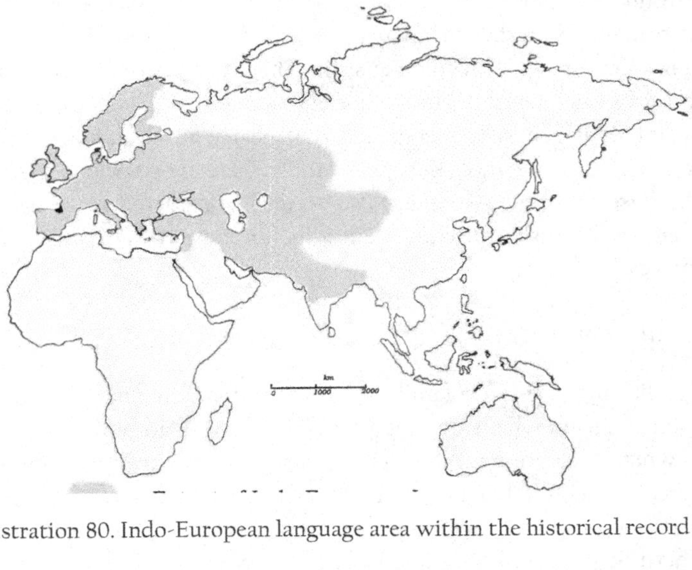

Illustration 80. Indo-European language area within the historical record

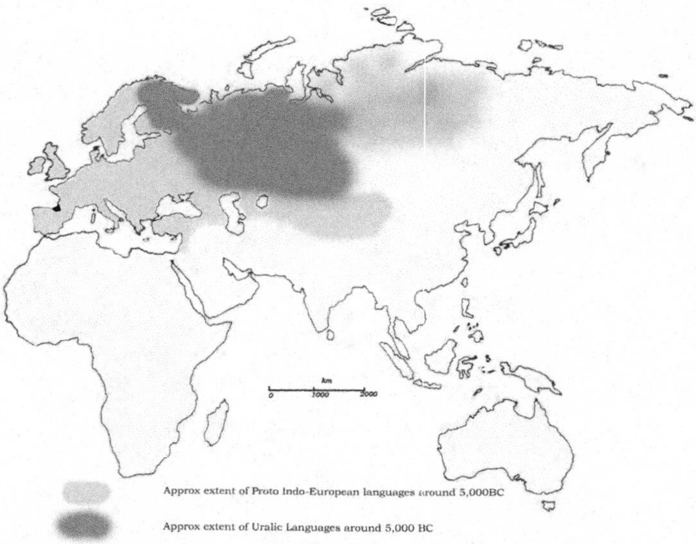

Illustration 81. Indo-European and Uralic languages at 5,000BC

Around 5,000BP peoples migrated from Western Asia to Iran/Northern India bringing with them a language derived from the Indo-European family of languages known as Vedic Sanskrit. This migration led to the extent of Indo-European languages shown in the second map.

While it is generally recognized that nearly all modern European languages belong to the Indo-European family there are some exceptions, such as the Basque language which is sometimes considered to be a linguistic anomaly and Finish and Hungarian which belong to the Uralic Family of languages.

Uralic Languages

Uralic languages are a family of languages including modern Hungarian, Finnish and Sami which are thought to have evolved around the Ural Mountains which separate central Asia from Europe. Today around 25 million people speak an Uralic language and it is considered to be one of the world's primary languages, occupying Finland, polar Norway, and great swathes of northern Siberia, with just one isolated outpost to the South; Hungary in central Europe.

There is considerable debate about whether there are links between the origins of Uralic and Indo-European languages. The first writers to associate the two families of languages were in the 1870s. Henry Sweet in the History of Languages in 1900 argued in favor of kinship between the two languages.

A number of phonetic similarities exist including 's' and 'i', 'u' and 'j', 'w' amongst others.

Many basic words are also similar or cognate in both families of languages: for example, Indo-European you is 'tu' Uralic 'tun'. Indo-European for he/she is 'so' Uralic is 'sa'. Indo-European for the verb to wet is 'wet' and Uralic it is 'weti'. Indo-European for fish is 'kalo-' and Uralic is 'kala'. And so on. There are very many similarities between Uralic and Indo-European.

The term for a family of languages encompassing Indo-European and Uralic family is Indo-Uralic, an unfortunate term which misleadingly excludes European.

So, if both Uralic and Indo-European emerged from the proto Indo-European when did that split occur? Given the very wide geographical range attributed to the Uralic family, it is highly unlikely that the split occurred after the Mesolithic. So, we need to look for a cultural split from the main European Western and Central European Cultures which occupied an area roughly corresponding to Eastern Europe and Western Asia. The obvious candidate is the Swiderian culture (see the chapter on the Mesolithic).

As we have seen the Swiderian took a different direction from the Azilian Culture around 11,000 BP. From this time onwards, it occupied the region around the East of the Baltic towards the Urals, and the influence spread eastwards. The areas occupied by Swiderian Culture and Uralic languages roughly coincide. We have already seen how the Swiderian culture spread up the Eastern Coast of the Baltic Sea as the glaciers retreated, eventually covering a large part of Finland, and Finnish happens to be an Uralic language.

As we have already seen Azilian like culture spread up through Denmark and followed the Norwegian coast northwards taking with it an Indo-European language up the Western Coast of the Baltic and following the reindeer herds as the Great Scandinavian Ice Cap retreated northwards. Meanwhile the Swiderian culture spread up the eastern coast of the Baltic Sea. So, the Baltic became a dividing line between both cultures and languages. As the Scandinavian ice cap slowly withdrew northwards, and the northernmost part of Scandinavia became ice free thousands of years after the Last Glacial Maximum the nomadic hunters from the west of the Baltic encountered those from the east of the Baltic, each with their separate cultures and languages. Thus, the cultural/national border between Sweden and Norway on the west (Indo-European) and Finland to the east (Uralic speaking) came into being.

As for the Southern Uralic enclave, the pre-historic origins of Hungary or the Magyars are slightly vague. But the understanding is that the Magyars originated from the Southern part of the Urals at least as early as 4,000BP, and had probably been there for several thousand years already. The Urals were part of the Uralic language heartland, hence the name. The history of the period leading up to the fall of the Western Roman Empire in the 5th century AD was one of great movements of peoples from Western Asia heading towards the prosperous Roman Empire. As part of these great mass movements some of the Magyars migrated West of the Urals occupying areas between the Urals and the Volga, some also moved to occupy regions around the Don.

As the Byzantine Empire sought to defend its border north of the Black Sea against invasions from the north and as part of its century's long wars with the Bulgars there were further great movements of peoples including the ever belligerent Pechenegs. This seemingly caused the Magyars to move to more secure lands from the 8th century AD, skirting the Pechenegs and the Bulgars to the North, they crossed the Carpathians and settled in modern Hungary, causing them to become isolated from the rest of the Uralic speaking world.

This cultural evolution in Eastern Europe enables us to identify the moment when Uralic and Indo-European languages separated; roughly in the period leading up to 11,000BP, around the time of the development of the Swiderian culture.

Indo-European Language Family

The building block at the heart of the proto-Indo-European language family is the morpheme. This is the smallest basic unit of a word to which grammatical links with the rest of the phrase are added. For example, the word 'small' in English can be added to, to become 'smallest', or 'run' can become 'runner'. But in PIE because the inflexion to indicate grammatical relationships the morpheme is rarely found by itself, but more usually together with the suffix, thus creating the stem. Then in a further level of accretion a desinence would be added to form the full word. This building block nature to words is still splendidly visible in German where words can be very long indeed as extra meanings are added before the full word is completed.

Also, Indo-European languages use the ablaut principal, which changes a vowel in a word according to the tense for example 'sing', 'sang' and 'sung'.

The ablaut although not used systematically in all modern Indo-European languages is a tell-tale inheritance from the Indo-European origin. The inherent vowel in most PIE morphemes is 'e'. But this will change upon context to become a short 'o', long 'o', long 'e' etcetera.

PIE nouns are declined in 8 or 9 cases, similar to German and Latin. Also, like German there are three genders: masculine, feminine and neuter.

PIE pronouns are complicated. But PIE verbs obey similar rules to nouns using the ablaut system, but beyond that obey a bewildering set of rules such as having a voice which is either an active voice or a mediopassive voice.

Anyone interested in studying the details of proto-Indo-European can't fail to be impressed by its eye-watering complexity, which allows an insight into the reasoning ability of European ancestors 30,000 years ago. Proto-Indo-European speakers were not simple minded by any stretch of the imagination, but were sophisticated communicators with a wide range of precise linguistic constructs at their daily disposal to pass on their thoughts. Possibly even more impressive was the educational system which allowed this complex language to become pan-European so long ago, at least 24,000 years ago.

Hans Krahe in 1964 published his study of Old European Hydronyms which postulated that the oldest pan European cultures named European rivers according to a similar system. Theorizing that despite the evolutions of languages since pre-history the origins of river names has been preserved. This naming scheme used by ancient European peoples spanned from Scandinavia to Southern Italy and from the British Isles to Eastern Europe. Krahe noted that the majority of river names in Europe stem from words that no longer exist in modern languages. Further, he states that individual river names derive from the proto-Indo-european for water itself. Conforming to the morpheme principal that we've already looked at, he identified 11 different suffixes used in river names. More recent localized changes occurred to complicate the picture, so in Moorish Spain, Arab prefixes were added to pre-existing ancient river names, such as Guadiana (Guadi being Arab for river and Anas being old Celtic for muddy). The River Anas having been recorded by the geographer Ptolemy.

One example for the Proto-Indo-European for river is Isar, which provides 20 or so river names from Spain through Belguim and Britain to the Czech Republic, including such rivers as Aire, Isar, Isere, Yser, Iseran, Isieres, etc.

Other river root names are 'Al/Alm' and 'Sal/Salm' which equally cover Europe from north to south and west to east. As we have seen throughout this book for the last several hundred thousand years in Europe and Western

Asia, prehistoric settlements have systematically been discovered in close proximity to rivers. Rivers never lost their importance to our ancestors.

So, even though different languages adapted and became more regional during the Neolithic the old river names remained broadly the same, carrying with them through the millennia, the DNA of the very earliest of proto-Indo-European through to the present day.

On the basis of the Tool Culture Resistance theory described at the start of this chapter and the continuity of tool technology improvements we can be reasonably certain that the origins of Proto-Indo-European go back to classic Neanderthal times with their great brains and language processing genes and that over tens of thousands of years the Indo-European language, or as it should more properly be termed the ancient European language slowly evolved.

Leaving Our Past Behind

In this book we have seen how humans and their ancestors have evolved from being an insignificant tree-dwelling member of the great apes family in tropical Africa, occupying a small environmental niche in tropical Africa's ecosystem, to become the most dominant living being on the planet, being responsible for exterminating many other species and changing by domestication many others.

All species have the ability to adapt, it is how they all evolved from single cell organisms, and this adaptation is part of evolution. In evolution there are three broad activities. Speciation where a new species is created, anagenesis where there is adaptation within a species and extinction where a species ceases to exist. This book has seen all three processes interplaying.

Indeed, it is the mistaken identification of various stages of human evolution which has been considered to be speciation, but in actual fact has been anagenesis which has been one of the main causes for taking the understanding of our pre-history down various blind alleys. Speciation is the process of creating new species and that has been applied for example to Neanderthals which were considered to be a separate species, hence the scientific binomial *H. neanderthalis*. However, in fact Neanderthal was a case of anagenesis, as he has successfully interbred with other human sub-species.

One of the most important natural events in the history of human evolution, not only for Europeans but for our species as a whole, is the last Ice Age. Charles Darwin developed the theory of Natural Selection as one of the key processes in evolution. He wrote in *On the Origin of Species*:

> If during the long course of ages and under varying conditions of life, organic beings vary at all in the several parts of their organization, and I think this cannot be disputed; if there be, owing to the high

> geometrical powers of increase of each species, at some age, season, or year, a severe struggle for life, and this certainly cannot be disputed; then, considering the infinite complexity of the relations of all organic beings to each other and to their conditions of existence, causing an infinite diversity in structure, constitution, and habits, to be advantageous to them, I think it would be a most extraordinary fact if no variation ever had occurred useful to each being's own welfare, in the same way as so many variations have occurred useful to man. But if variations useful to any organic being do occur, assuredly individuals thus characterized will have the best chance of being preserved in the struggle for life; and from the strong principle of inheritance they will tend to produce offspring similarly characterized. This principle of preservation, I have called, for the sake of brevity, Natural Selection.'

(Darwin C. 62)

The last Ice Age was a period in time when what Darwin referred to as the 'conditions of existence' were almost constantly changing. At least 20 great cyclical shifts during the Ice Age changed the environment so greatly in Europe that for each one species of trees appeared or disappeared and so did species of mammals. Only one mammal of note persisted throughout and that was European man. Whereas all other species were so dependent on their environment that when it changed as it did so many times in the Ice Age they disappeared in search of an environment which they were designed for, or perished. The Ice Age in Europe had brought about through the process of Natural Selection a being that was inherently flexible, capable of adaptation in the most extreme of conditions, manipulating and exploiting his surroundings to bridge the gap between unsupportable environmental conditions and what his body could tolerate. He did this through thought and the use of tools to make things that would improve his condition. He used his unique ability for complex communication to pass these new survival tactics on to his immediate relations and contacts and so the successful survival tactics were disseminated throughout the population. This is not a slow process of slight genetic changes occurring over thousands of generations, but changes which occur at the speed of verbal communication and walking between neighboring communities.

Ice Age man became an expert at problem solving, another unique talent which allowed him to observe a situation, weigh up its impact on him, and whether it should be thought of in the future as a hindrance or an asset. If it was a hindrance, then what could he do to alter it to his own advantage or nullify its negative impact on him? Solutions were found to problems. This process of problem solving is exemplified in the continued improvement of tools but it is seen in all human activities throughout the Ice Age.

Ice Age Man's brain was honed through the process of Natural Selection to become a tool of incredible power, it needed to be. Those individuals who could not find a way of adapting to the changing environment either by learning the appropriate survival skills or by inventing them in the first place died. For all the various changes that occurred to the bodies of Ice Age Europeans during the Ice Age the most important one was the development and organization of the brain. He used this immensely powerful tool for each new environmental challenge which occurred, and when survival wasn't the all-consuming activity, he used his brain for other activities such as artistic expression, religion, conversation, and decoration of tools, ornamentation, exploration and so many other non-essential activities which entertained and occupied him. The less time and energy that he could afford to divert to pure survival the more he could divert to non-survival activities. Thus, arts and leisure were invented to occupy the vast thinking apparatus that was his brain.

Technological developments from *Ardipithecus*' time, millions of years ago, to the start of the Neanderthal era were mind-numbingly slow. But when change started to occur during the Ice Age it did so on steroids. Technologies that would previously have endured millions of years now lasted just a couple of thousand before being replaced by something superior. By this yardstick, European man's ability to develop had improved a thousand-fold.

This amazing process of changing is now part of our daily lives, whether it be a new generation of smart phone, or a great leap forward in medical science, computing technology or so many of the other changes which affect our modern lives and which to us have become routine.

Whereas the process of natural selection required that a body profit from a random change in its make-up to improve its survival chances, humans have overcome this basic evolutionary process. We use our brains to find a solution to the problem. We have stepped outside the rules that apply to the rest of the animal kingdom and we learnt to do that effectively during the Last Ice Age. The rules of survival that govern the rest of the animal world are not the same rules that govern our lives.

When Mesolithic man began to control the natural world around him, he started what was probably an involuntary process to sever his links of mutual dependence on the nature that surrounded him. We have looked in detail at Shamanism in an earlier chapter and how Ice Age Europeans belonged to nature. But as Mesolithic man started to use nature for his particular needs that relationship began to change, and as it did so, his belief system started to change also. Shamanism, which had for so long been a way of life, was less well adapted. From the Mesolithic onwards in Europe outside of the Polar North, Europeans used nature at their convenience; they had become masters of the world around them. The welfare of European animals became subject to his discretion, became property. Man no longer an integrated part of the animal kingdom according to Shamanic beliefs, he managed the animal kingdom. From this point onwards in settled Europe shamanism began to be a religion with less relevance to daily lives. The uncontrollable processes of the weather, rising and setting of the sun, the onset of winter, became the most important factors in his daily lives. Thus, the sun, the moon and other astral bodies became the new focus of man's religious beliefs, a process that would reach fruition in early historical times. The ghosts of old animalistic traditions would be still be seen throughout Europe, so that for example Ancient Egyptian Gods would combine a celestial aspect with also an animalistic representation. Just to take one example, the Ancient Egyptian Sun god Ra, the creator of all life. As the creator of all life he was the God of the Sun. He was also represented as a zoomorphological figure with a falcon's head. The ancient Greeks too held on to a few animalistic traditions. pan, the lecherous minor God with a flute, had the back end of a goat. Zeus appeared as a bull, etcetera.

Even in Christianity a very distant echo of our pre-historic animalistic past endures with the association of each of the four evangelists with an animal. So, St Luke is represented as a winged bull, St Mark as a lion etcetera.

By the time Europeans had reached the Mesolithic period the die was cast for the future, a future in which we belong to this day. Many of the basic parts of everyday life were in use up until the Industrial Revolution. From being an insignificant little creature taking refuge in some trees in tropical Africa, we have come to be masters of the world around us. From being a part of the natural world, we have become the masters of it. But are we using this new-found great responsibility intelligently?

The Great Journey

When I first started thinking about this book in the 1990s I wanted to call it 'The Great Journey'. It seemed to me appropriate not just as a 6-million-year journey from apes to ourselves, the dominant animal on the planet, but also as journey in book form to follow as closely as possible in the footsteps of our ancestors from that far distant time, to the present.

But I realized that I wanted to focus particularly on Europeans, and an attempt to write an equivalent of this book for all the continents was far too ambitious for one book, and more importantly too ambitious for me.

Some people may feel understandably frustrated that the story doesn't carry on through the Neolithic and into the Copper and Bronze Ages and thus bring people into a period of recorded history where writings have left the thoughts of peoples who died nearly 3,000 years ago. But ancient history (Neolithic to the Bronze Age) is a dense, detailed subject and has been covered by people who possess considerably more knowledge than me. I hope that by leaving the reader at the end of the Mesolithic I have left him or her with enough enthusiasm to pursue his or her curiosity with the help of one of the very many works already available.

I have attempted to achieve a number of objectives in writing this book, some of which came to me during the process of writing and others were with me from the outset. From the beginning I was aware that the majority of theories on pre-history didn't always pass what is sometimes referred to as the sanity test. They didn't stack up, were often self-contradictory and from the outset I felt alarms ringing when I read widely accepted versions of pre-history. Without necessarily having preconceived ideas, I spent years reading into the background and research that had been made, and cringing at some of the conclusions that had been made from the empirical evidence.

My first task was to see whether I could find explanations that were a better fit for the available evidence on all the crucial questions, and from these isolated conclusions, seeing whether I could join up the dots to make a coherent explanation.

Today we see humanity as a parallel existence to nature. We observe it from the comfort of our living rooms. We wonder how animals survive the winter outside, and we interfere with the course of nature when we see an animal suffering. But this is very much the approach of an outsider. Our ancestors belonged to nature; they weren't distanced from it as we are now.

The main religions in Europe today, our lodestones, have disconnected themselves from nature, just as the majority of people have also. We use the world around us for our own ends, and occasionally make a gesture towards nature, a salmon ladder, or a saucer of milk for the local hedgehog. But having for the most part transformed the natural world to suit our purposes these are tiny gestures. The natural world has become a resource and when we are at our best we have are stewards of it, but more often the story is about exploitation.

The Great Extinction at the end of the Paleolithic with its huge consequences not just for the exterminated animals but for Europeans should serve as a lesson. Some still deny that humans were the determining force in the Great Extinctions of this period; undoubtedly the thought that our ancestors were responsible for this Great Extinction is an uncomfortable thought. But it should serve as a warning for us today. Today dozens of species are going extinct every single day. Scientists consider that although extinctions in nature occur naturally, they are now occurring at between 1,000 and 10,000 the average long-term rate. The Great Extinctions of the Mesolithic pushed ancient Europeans into farming which was the beginning of taming the natural world to serve our needs. Given our domination as a species, this new way of living with nature had a finite life-time and we are coming to the end of that process now.

As our population rises we expect the natural world to make yet more sacrifices to sustain us. In the pursuit of chasing ever growing GDP and ever rising populations, we are developing pesticides to increase the productivity of crops at the expense of insects. Certain animals are considered to be the enemies of farmers and are hunted to close to extinction. Certain religions consider that human life is sacrosanct and that everything else can be sacrificed in order to save a single human life, without putting into the balance the damage done to the natural world and the long-term consequences for the planet.

If already in the Paleolithic the population of Europeans was sufficient to extinguish all those magnificent European mammals like the rhino and the mammoth, the population of Europe today is squeezing the last drops of servitude out of the natural world, and at what cost?

It may go against the grain to consider that with our smart phones, ability to travel in space and our LED TVs could in any way make us less intelligent than our ancestors. But maybe in the most important aspect of all, our place on this planet, they had more understanding than we had.

One of the great lessons of this book, I feel, is that we depend for our existence on the animals with which we share the planet. No amount of plastic-wrapped meat in the supermarket can disprove this fact. We ignore the lessons of our distant ancestors at our gravest peril.

Appendix A. Analytic Methods and Philosophy

In order to properly understand our prehistory, we are very limited in hard evidence with which we can fill in all the missing parts of the story from the last common ancestor with the chimpanzees onwards. If, as is often the case, one only examines a very small-time segment in a limited geographical space, then providing an explanation for the evidence can be relatively easy. It is when the whole pre-history is considered that many inconsistencies appear which render at least some of the explanations invalid.

Because many of the theories for our pre-history were developed in such a piecemeal fashion and accreted over the years, the study of paleoanthropology has become a hotchpotch of various theories some of which are demonstrably untrue but nevertheless due to the length of time that they have been generally accepted, have achieved respect through venerable age.

In classical times processes of analysis and deduction were extensively considered by Aristotle. He postulated two approaches. The first that begins with our initial beliefs and the things that we intuitively recognize and from there we attempt to explain natural laws. Secondly, empirical analysis begins with perception and proceeds by induction and generalization to an explanation which can be tested by experience and improved when found wanting. Since Aristotle's day the scientific method of inquiry has evolved slightly but is based in principal on the 2nd method.

The scientific method of explaining an observed phenomenon begins with first principles. A first principle is a basic self-evident proposition or assumption, an indivisible fact, i.e., it doesn't depend on other facts in order to be stated or deduced. By combining first principles in a logical method, deductions can be made. So, the famous syllogism 'Socrates is a man. All men are mortal. Therefore, Socrates is mortal', is a correct deduction.

The scientific method requires that deductions be consistent with other related deductions in a system. When two related deductions are incompatible with one another, then an error of deduction has been made somewhere, and at least one of the two deductions must be reconsidered. However, when all related deductions in a system are mutually compatible, then that system is understood and the component deductions are considered to be correct.

The philosopher Descartes went a stage further in seeking out the truth. He questioned everything in a method which became known as Cartesian Doubt. By continually asking 'why?' and drilling down into a subject he eventually arrived at an indivisible truth which he termed 'a priori truths' in other words we are back at first principles again, but using Cartesian doubt we have a method of finding them. One of his most famous a priori truths was 'cogito ego sum' or 'I think therefore I am'. Descartes' approach was a good one, even though he may not have applied it as rigorously as he might. For example, cogito ego sum implies that if 'I am no longer thinking that I am dead or non-existent'. However, I may be under general anesthetic, when conscious and unconscious thought are suspended. But his approach is a good one if applied rigorously as it helps us to find the first principles which we can use as building blocks on which we can try to make further deductions.

In the 21st century we are extremely fortunate in being able to look at subjects with the benefit of standing on the shoulders of scientific giants. Scientists have developed theories from first principles which have been subject to acute examination, by testing against observable phenomenon and proved to be true. So, if we understand the theories in the various sciences we have a prodigious tool kit at our disposal with which we can explore new areas of human knowledge.

However, the current understanding of our distant pre-history is one which is rife with self-contradictions, and theories unsupported by all the available evidence, indeed it is a subject with many experts presenting mutually contradictory theories. It is thus a prime candidate for Cartesian Doubt and many widely accepted assumptions in the subject do not survive rigorous enquiry. A clean start is sorely needed, starting once more from first principles and building an understanding from there.

The very fact that so many theories about our pre-history are mutually incompatible demonstrates that the subject has until now been poorly understood. To take just one example; the conflict between the 'multi-regional' and the 'single origin' theory of evolution. The two are mutually incompatible, one of them at least must be wrong.

Then we have demonstrably false assumptions or falsisms: *Homo sapiens* and *H. neanderthalis*. Both 'species' belong to the genus Homo, and both are considered as separate species. The definition of species is that they cannot inter breed successfully. How then to explain the combination of sapiens and Neanderthal DNA in a large portion of the world's population? Despite this obvious falsism, these two binomials are used systematically in nearly all the standard textbooks on human evolution over the last 500,000 years.

Then again, the Out of Africa II theory states that the world's population all stems from a group of Africans who crossed into Europe and Asia 70,000 years ago. Meanwhile the mitochondrial Eve theory states that the youngest common female ancestor 'mitochondrial eve' existed between 170 and 100,000 years ago. These two statements are inconsistent with overwhelming observable facts. For, if true, then all the female descendants of Mitochondrial Eve must have been condensed down into that group who left Africa 70,000 years ago, and that every other individual human female born around the world before those two dates has no surviving descendants. Furthermore, we know that many of us contain substantial amounts of Neanderthal DNA, and classic Neanderthal DNA originated 500,000 years or so ago which means there is an unbroken line between 500,000 years ago in Europe and modern populations, which therefore categorically disproves the theory that all our ancestors arrived from Africa 70,000 years ago.

Another frequent mistake is to look at the style of certain stone tools in association with an unidentified fossilized bone and based on the style of tool manufacture identify the fossil.

This is the equivalent of the following syllogism:

[Man Type A makes tool type X

Man Type B makes tool type Y

Therefore, all tools of Type X are made by Man Type A]

which is clearly not necessarily true. Man Type Y may also make Tool Type A.

One can say that the style of stone tool suggests a certain type of individual, but without more precise evidence, one must stop there and not leap to an unjustified conclusion, the evidence is not strong enough for that. Nevertheless, jumping to unjustified conclusions in this way has resulted on very many occasions in this example. 'It is not a Mousterian tool; therefore it is not a Neanderthal bone. '

All these examples aren't minor mistakes on the fringes of the subject, but lie at the heart of paleoanthropology today. The examples given above (there are plenty of others that could be mentioned) are very often taken as the building blocks of the subject or the first principles on which other theories are based. Cartesian Doubt is required for any serious enquiry into this subject, in order to obtain a history which bears some basis in fact.

When one throws away the standard text books in a subject, where on earth should one start from fresh?

There has been a huge amount of work carried out by archaeologists in the field around the world, painstakingly searching for the smallest of items which could in some way relate to human ancestors and by applying sound scientific analysis have established reliable facts. Many hundreds of thousands of man-years of effort have been expended over the past 150 years, and latterly the soil horizon contexts have also been carefully scrutinized to help in the dating of the finds. In the last 20 years or so enormous scientific progress has been made in dating artifacts. In many cases, the usual practice developed in physics of calculating the error for each date is also provided, so that we can be confident in the time range if not the absolute date; for example 50,000BP +/- 2,500 years. Meaning that the calculation of the date is certain to be between 52,500 and 47,500BP, but is likely to be around the 50,000 mark. In those fossils which have been reliably dated, we have some first principles on which we can work.

DNA analysis is a thorny issue, as it has the potential of providing precious information about a subject, but because it is a young science, because of the potential of contamination, because of the lack of reliable references, because of various unknowable assumptions such as rate of mutation at a particular moment in time, it has provided false answers in the past. On multiple occasions DNA results have contradicted themselves. Considerable caution must be exercised when looking at the results of DNA analysis, and if the DNA analysis contradicts a host of other evidence, then doubt must be applied to the DNA evidence. In cases where DNA evidence backs up other demonstrable evidence then the probability of it being reliable is significantly increased.

Using the dating of archaeological finds can provide us with some precious, reliable information about our past, but it is not enough to tell the whole story. This is where deduction from first principles can provide more answers. So, for example:

- [Cave bears inhabited caves throughout Europe during the Paleolithic.
- Neanderthals inhabited caves throughout Europe during the Paleolithic.

- Therefore, it is highly likely that cave bears and Neanderthals competed for caves.]

There isn't much direct evidence of that conflict, although there is plenty of evidence of Neanderthals using cave bear bones and plenty of evidence of both using the same caves at different times. In balance it seems reasonable that cave bears and humans, while both species co-existed in Europe, competed for the same caves. But this is not a first principle. In terms of reliability, it is likely without being certain. If some evidence came to light that suggests that it is a false conclusion then we must demote it from being a likelihood to a possibility.

Explained in this way, the logic above may seem to be stating the obvious, but Paleoanthropology is full of conclusions built on other unreliable conclusions, which is then shown to be in direct conflict with yet other conclusions. Thus, the whole area of study is characterized by considerable discord.

When as many first principles of the subject are known as possible and then as many secondary facts which are likely have been derived then we can start to formulate theories to explain our prehistory. But the subject has been researched in the opposite direction, with theories arriving early on in the last century and then other theories being based on these. This explains why there are dozens of explanations given why the Neanderthals apparently suddenly went extinct.

It is very likely that in the years to come, new established facts will be discovered which may prove some of the theories in this book to be inaccurate, in which case they should be revised. Sometimes when things get in a real mess, it's best to start afresh, and that is what I have done with this book.

Appendix B. The Out of Africa II Theory

For many years a crucial stage of human evolution has been explained by the controversial Out of Africa II Theory. This theory evolved at a time when paleoanthropology was in its early days, and theories were developed based partly on long-standing prejudices and partly on scant facts. Discoveries over the last 20 years or so, far from validating the theory have undermined it. Nevertheless, the theory has taken hold, developed an impetus of its own and remains taught in schools and universities to this day. I mention it in Appendix form (as to ignore it would be to ignore the elephant in the room), because it rightly doesn't belong in the body of this pre-history, and list some of the evidence which renders the Theory an irritating red herring in human pre-history.

Firstly, I should make clear that this Appendix is not concerned with the *H. erectus* emigration from Africa, referred to commonly as Out of Africa I, which is perfectly valid and is dealt with in detail in the chapter on *H. erectus*.

The Out of Africa II theory postulates that some African *Homo sapiens* migrated out of Africa via Egypt. They then split, the Northern group migrating up the Eastern Mediterranean, through modern Turkey and then into Europe. The southern group followed the Arabian coast colonized all India then on into South East Asia.

These two groups of individuals managed to somehow cause the annihilation of the many millions of humans who had been occupying these continents for over 1.5 million years and in virtually no time at all had fully replaced them. Many Out of Africa II proponents go as far as to say, based on interpretation of DNA evidence that all humans alive today originate from a small band of AMH who left Africa around 70,000 BP.

Deducing from the observable facts that Out of Africa II is factual fails the basic test of a formal logic system. In a formal logic system with a set of propositions which are consistent with one another, it is probable that some of the statements can be deduced one from the other. The proposition that all Europeans and Asians originated from a small group of African migrants who left Africa 70,000 years ago needs to be consistent with a very large number of other verifiable facts in order to be taken seriously. This book is full of observed facts which cannot be explained by the Out of Africa II theory, any one of which would render the theory invalid.

One of the most glaring issues was the method by which this small group of African migrants managed to kill off millions of Neanderthals and Peking man, *H. erectus* etcetera so totally and so effectively. Lending the theory far more gravitas than it deserved many scientists have proposed a very wide range of explanations varying in their absurdity, many of which contradict one another; for example, Neanderthal wasn't capable of speech because he lacked a hyoid bone and so wasn't as efficient in coordinating his resistance to the African immigrants. Once a fossil Neanderthal hyoid bone was found this theory was replaced by another and so on.

Linked and sometimes confused with this claim is the debate over mitochondrial Eve. The definition of mitochondrial Eve is the person who is the matrilineal most recent common ancestor of all people living today. Otherwise expressed as the one woman who in a direct unbroken maternal line is the maternal ancestor of everyone on the planet today. Calculations on the time when mitochondrial Eve existed vary between 250,000 years ago and 100,000 years ago. The basis of this concept is the transmission of mitochondrial DNA from mother to offspring which changes very little from mother to child. Those changes that do occur are mutations. After examining differences in mutations in mitochondrial DNA from around the globe, and choosing an approximate mutation rate it can be established the point at which all the DNA was the same in one-person, Mitochondrial Eve.

A similar calculation can be made on male inheritance using the changes to the Y-chromosome, which leads to the calculation of Y-chromosomal Adam, who it is estimated lived between 200 and 300,000 years ago.

In both the calculations of mitochondrial Eve and Y-chromosomal Adam there is a great diversity in the calculated age depending on who has performed the calculation.

We do not even know where mitochondrial Eve or Y-chromosomal Adam lived.

The mtDNA haplogroup argument in favor of Out of Africa II is based on the L3 haplogroup which is supposed to have originated in either Africa or Asia. Estimates of its origin date from a variety of possible dates either 104–80,000BP or from 70–60,000BP. L3 represents the most common matrilineal haplogroup of all people outside of Africa and some people inside Africa too, today. It is particularly common within Africa in North East Africa around Egypt. L3 spawned two clades (i.e., subgroups belonging to the L3 haplogroup) M and N which are carried by most people outside of Africa today.

According to Maca-Maeyer in 2001, "L3 is more related to Eurasian haplogroups than to the most divergent African clusters L1 and L2. L3 is the haplogroup from which all modern humans outside Africa derive." For the rest of Africa apart from North East Africa, the dominant haplogroup L1 and L2 are dominant

This then is the main evidence used to back up the Out of Africa II Theory. But we have already seen at various points in this book that Neanderthals migrated into Africa with traces of them being found North of the Atlas Mountains, and that Ancient Egyptians carry Neanderthal inherited characteristics, Ancient Egypt being in the North East of Africa. If the L3 carrying individuals were so incredibly successful that they managed to cause the demise of millions of perfectly cold adapted Neanderthals in the middle of the Ice Age as well as many million other indigenous peoples who had occupied their regions for over 1 million years, why on earth didn't they do a little better in Africa where they supposedly originated and make some incursions into their continent of origin? The answer is straightforward, L3 was a Eurasian haplogroup which as we have seen caused some migration out of Eurasia into the region of Egypt and possibly a little beyond where they butted up against the L1 and L2 people who were far better adapted to life in the tropics and got no further.

So, the very evidence used as a backstop to justify the Out of Africa II theory is best used to counter it. Quite simply L3 peoples, who originated in Eurasia from Neanderthal ancestors having already occupied Europe and Asia, as we have seen, propagated throughout the rest of Asia and finally migrated across Berengeia into the Americas, and across the narrow straits into Australasia. Some moved south from the Levant where there is plenty of evidence of Neanderthals having occupied the Nile valley to become with some local mingling of genes to become eventually the people we know as Ancient Egyptians. Whereas haplogroups L1 and L2 occupied the rest of Africa and remained for a long time technologically isolated from the rest of Eurasia.

It should be noted that this is simply a more logical interpretation of the evidence used to justify the Out of Africa II Theory and happens to dovetail with the pre-history explained in this book, the latter being based on a plethora of other evidence cited previously in this book.

The Out of Africa II theory is pure nonsense.

Appendix C. Chronology of the Ice Age

	Last Ice Age		Weichselian (in Europe) 115,000 - 11,700 BP
Date (la BP)	Phase	Period	Comments
Early Glacial			
115,000-60,000			
115-107	stadial	Herning	Sharp drop in temperatures, leaving steppes
107-104	interstadial	Amersfoort	Starts with subarctic, then boreal forest
104-101.5	interstadial	Brorup	slight cooling expansion of grasslands
101.5-87	?	?	
87-82.5	stadial	Rederstall	Steppe
82.5-76	interstadial	Odderade	Starts with subarctic, then temperate forest
76-60	stadial	Schalkholtz	Sterile sand deposits
High Glacial			
60,000 - 12,500			
60-56	interstadial	Oerel	Treeless tundra with sedge grass
56-54	stadial	Ebersdorf	Treeless, grassless tundra, sand deposits
54-51	interstadial	Glinde	Treeless tundra
51-43	interstadial	Moershoofd	Treeless tundra with sedge grass
43-41	interstadial	Hengelo	Sedge and dwarf birch
41-36	stadial	Huneberg	subarctic conditions, 7C drop in temperatures
36-33	interstadial	Denekamp	Tundra landscape with cold resistant shrubs
33-32	interstadial	Maisieres	Temperate forest dominated by birch, oak and hasel
29-27	interstadial	Tursac	Temperate forest
26-24	stadial	Brandenburg	Ice sheet advances to North Germany
24-22	stadial	Frankfurt	
21-20	interstadial	Lascaux	
20-17	stadial	Pommeranian	
17-15	stadial	Mecklenburg	

Late Glacial			
14,500-11,700			
14.5-13.8	interstadial	Meiendorf	Dwarf birches
13.8-13.7	Stadial	Oldest Dryas	Grassy steppe, with arctic flowering plants
13.7-13.6	interstadial	Bolling Oscillation	Birch forest
13.6-13.4	Stadial	Older Dryas	Reduced tree pollens
13.4-12.7	Interstadial	Allerod Oscillation	Birch forest
12.7-11.7	Stadial	Younger Dryas	Grassy steppe, 6C drop in temperature, dry

The above table contains dates which are approximate; not all authorities agree on the exact dates. Phases such as the Older Dryas aren't currently detectable throughout Europe. This may be because they are relatively localized events. Different parts of Europe see different climactic variations, with stadials and interstadials given different names. The above list is based mainly on observations carried out in Germany and valid mainly for Northern Europe.

Bibliography

Choi, Charles Q. "Deceptive Chimp Hides Ammo." *Livescience.* May 17, 2012.

Coon, C.S. *The Races of Europe*. USA: The Macmillan Company. 1939

Darwin, Charles. *The Descent of Man*. John Murray London. February 24, 1871.

Darwin, Charles. *On the Origin of Species*. John Murray, London November 24, 1859.

Endo, B. "Analysis of the Stress around the orbit due to masseter and temporalis muscles." *Journal of the Anthropological Society of Nippon*. 78. 1970.

Fiske-Harrison, Alexander 'Talking With Apes', *Financial Times*, Weekend, 24–25 November 2001.

Fouts, Roger, "My Best Friend is a Chimp." *Psychology Today* : July 1, 2000.

Gamble, C. "Gibraltar and the Neanderthals 1848–1998." *Journal of Human Evolution*. London. 1999.Gleick James. *Chaos: Making a New Science*. New York. Viking Press. October 29, 1987.

Jackson, Jason Baird. *Oral Tradition, American Indian*. Oklahoma Historical Society. https://www.okhistory.org/publications/enc/entry.php?entry=OR002 Oklahoma 2010.

Merriam-Webster. *Merriam-Webster Dictionary*: https://www.merriam-webster.com/dictionary/subspecies

Ojibwa. Native American Netroots. https://nativeamericannetroots.net/diary/1377 Sept 11, 2012.

Partridge, Dennis N. *Blackfeet Tribe, How They Lived*. https://www.accessgenealogy.com/native/blackfeet-tribe-how-they-lived.htm 2017.

Ruggles, C & Cotte, M. *Heritage Sites of Astronomy and Archaeoastronomy in the context of the Unesco World Heritage Convention*. ICOMOS. June 2010.

Segerdahl, P., Fields, W., Savage-Rumbaugh, S. *Kanzi's Primal Language*. Palgrave Macmillan UK, 2005.

Waal, Frans de. *Chimpanzee Politics*. Baltimore, Maryland : The John Hopkins University Press, 1998.

Yirka, Bob. *Neanderthals manufactured Chatelperronian amid cultural diffusion with humans, study finds*. https://phys.org/news/2012-10-neanderthals-chtelperronian-cultural-diffusion-humans.html Max Planck Society, 2012.

Index

C

D

I

J

K

L

M

S

T

Printed in the United States
By Bookmasters